a day with the Lord

VOLUME 3
ORDINARY TIME:
WEEKS 1-20

Rev. John A. Crowley

Our Sunday Visitor Publishing Division
Our Sunday Visitor, Inc.
Huntington, Indiana 46750

Our Sunday Visitor Publishing Division
Our Sunday Visitor, Inc.
200 Noll Plaza
Huntington, Indiana 46750

International Standard Book Number: 0-87973-473-6
Library of Congress Catalog Card Number: 90-60645

PRINTED IN THE UNITED STATES OF AMERICA

Cover design by James E. McIlrath

473

To
Mary, Mother of Priests

Preface

After returning from missionary work in Central America, I was assigned to St. John Vianney College Seminary in Miami in 1967. Seminary work was to be my assignment for the next sixteen years. Five of these years were spent at the minor seminary in Miami, and eleven of them were spent at the major seminary of St. Vincent de Paul at Boynton Beach.

During my tenure in the seminary, I taught Spanish, English, and Latin American Studies. Being director of St. Vincent de Paul Seminary Library also fell to my lot.

Seminary professors do not have to preach every day; they take their turn, and a good week or more might intervene before they mount the pulpit again. Not until my assignment to a parish church in West Palm Beach did I realize what a challenge preaching every day on the daily Gospel really was.

The Second Vatican Council stressed the importance of proclaiming the word of God, and urged that it be done every day. I did just that, and found myself delving into my files, Scripture commentaries, and the spiritual classics in order to give the people a good solid talk for the day.

At first, I simply threw these little homilies away. Later I realized that perhaps other priests and ministers might profit from all the work I poured into this homily preparation. The thought also occurred to me that perhaps the laity could use these homilies as a meditative help and guide for their daily reflection on the Gospel message for each day. With that in mind I began to save them and put them into computer files in 1985.

These sermons are a product of years of reading and reflection. The plan I adopted was to both make this work a versatile tool in the hands of the homilist and a good meditative aid to the average lay person.

From the Gospel situation and milieu, I strove to weave the Gospel into our everyday life situation, draw a practical spiritual and moral lesson from it, and apply it to modern life. There are many sermon-illustration stories to help make the Gospel applicable to modern-day life.

These talks are structured into major and minor divisions. They are placed accordingly under both Roman and Arabic numerals. This is principally for the benefit of the homilist, who at any time can eliminate some of the points of the homily, add his own, and still maintain a unified and coherent talk. It has the built-in advantage of being able to be used in its entirety or to be modified by the homilist at will.

Each homily is accompanied by a series of petitions which are in harmony with the theme of the Gospel of that day. The homilists pick out one point from the Gospel and develop that point, so that the lesson taken from the Gospel is maintained throughout the talk.

Included in this work will be an extensive subject and biblical index (to be published as a separate volume). It will serve to put a given subject into the Gospel *Sitz in Leben* or milieu and enable the homilist to work out from a scriptural setting.

Hopefully, those who use this work might find it a real asset, a positive meditative aid, and a supple tool, especially in the area of the daily homily.

Rev. John A. Crowley
February 25, 1990
St. John of the Cross Parish, Vero Beach, Fla.

ORDINARY TIME:
WEEKS 1-20 OF THE YEAR

Monday of the First Week: Mk. 1:14-20

I. Today is the first weekday of Ordinary Time of the liturgical year, and St. Mark's Gospel has been selected by the Liturgical Commission to run for the first nine weeks of Ordinary Time.

II. St. Mark was not one of the twelve Apostles; he was a disciple of St. Peter and a cousin of Barnabas. He knew St. Paul, since he accompanied him and Barnabas on their first missionary journey. For reasons unknown, Paul would not take Mark with him on his second missionary journey. This was the occasion of Paul's rupture with Barnabas. Mark is subsequently seen with Paul in Rome. Paul later referred to Mark as his fellow worker, so their obvious incompatibility to work with each other had been overcome.

III. St. Mark's Gospel is an account of the life and teachings of Our Lord Jesus Christ which he learned from the prince of the Apostles, St. Peter. Mark's Gospel, then, can be called the Gospel of Mark as seen through the eyes of Peter.

1) He is the author of the second Gospel, which he wrote in Rome between A.D. 64 and 67 (*Jerome Biblical Commentary*). He was the first Evangelist to write a Gospel narrative. The *Roman Martyrology* lists St. Mark as having been put to death during the reign of the emperor Nero, who ruled A.D. 54-68.

2) He is depicted in art as a winged lion because he opens his Gospel narrative with John the Baptist in the desert boldly and courageously proclaiming his message of repentance.

3) Because St. Mark makes little effort to show any connection between the Old Testament and the Gospel message, it is obvious that his message is directed to the Gentiles.

IV. The thrust of St. Mark's Gospel is to prove that Jesus Christ is the Son of God and the Messiah.

1) To prove his point, he has God the Father proclaiming Jesus as His only begotten Son. Mark does this in his account of Jesus' baptism in the Jordan and again in his narration of the transfiguration.

2) His Gospel has been called the Gospel of Miracles. In his effort to prove that Jesus is the Messiah, he gives many accounts of the "signs" or miracles of Jesus.

3) In Mark's Gospel, even the demons identify Jesus as the Messiah as Jesus is casting them out of the possessed: "What have you to do with me, Jesus, Son of the Most High God?" (Mk. 5:7).

4) Mark has a Gentile, a Roman centurion standing near the cross, declare Jesus to be the Son of God (Mk. 15:39).

V. St. Mark stresses that Jesus' work was centered on his passion, death, and resurrection. He teaches that we too must participate in the mystery of the passion and death of Our Lord Jesus Christ.

VI. Today's Gospel narrative is taken from the first chapter, where he has Jesus beginning His public ministry preaching the need of repentance and conversion. Jesus preaches that the kingdom of God is at hand and that the requisite for being a part of it is sincere repentance, with conversion and belief in the good news of the Gospel.

VII. In today's pericope, St. Mark also nàrrates the call of four of the Apostles: Simon Peter, his brother Andrew, James, and his brother John.

1) These Apostles enthusiastically followed Jesus because they hoped to profit from His popularity and perhaps become important people in this "kingdom" Jesus was talking about. Their conversion and commitment to Jesus was far from perfect. They were merely in the incipient stages of faith.

2) We are all called to follow Jesus and intimately share in His kingdom, but the question of true conversion and commitment to Jesus is with many merely in an incipient state of faith. It is a conversion that has made too many compromises with the world in which we live. So many Christians remain on the fringes of Christ's kingdom.

3) Many people are "supermarket" Christians who pick and choose what they like and put the harder messages of the Gospel on the back burner. So often it takes the hard knocks of life to bring us to grips with the challenging message of the Gospel.

4) The Apostles too had to go through the school of hard knocks to finally come to know, love, and be really committed to Our Lord Jesus Christ. This was the case with St. Francis, St. Augustine, St. Vincent de Paul, Charles de Foucauld, etc. It was the case with Dorothy Day, Fulton Oursler, Charles Colson, and many others.

5) In his *Confession*, St. Patrick, reflecting on his youth, reveals how he was captured and sold into slavery by Irish raiders. He writes: "I was barely sixteen, and I knew not the true God . . . for I

had turned away from God and kept not His commandments. . . .
Now after I came to Ireland, daily I herded flocks, and often during
the day I prayed. The love of God and the fear of Him increased
more and more, and my faith grew. . . . There the Lord opened up the
understanding of my disbelief, so that at length I might recall my
sins, and that I might be converted with all my heart to the Lord my
God" (Quasten, *Ancient Christian Writers*). The providence of God
used the servitude of Patrick to bring about a total conversion and
commitment to Him, so that God might bring about the conversion
of a nation to Christianity. So too will God use the hard knocks of
life to bring many people to conversion.

****

1) That the Lord impart to us a deeper and more enlightened
faith.

2) Through the intercession of St. Mark, that we come to love
sacred Scripture.

3) That we more frequently reflect on the Gospel so that it might
take deeper root in us and bring about a deeper commitment to Our
Lord Jesus Christ.

4) That those who are searching for meaning in their lives might
find it through the word of God in sacred Scripture.

5) The Holy Spirit is a Consoler; during times of difficulty and
trial, that we remember to have recourse to the Bible for light and
consolation.

6) For an increase in vocations to the priesthood and the
religious life.

7) For peace in the world and for respect for the dignity of all
human life.

Tuesday of the First Week: Mk. 1:21-28

I. In the early days of the public ministry of Jesus, before there
was such hostility toward Him, Jesus frequently entered the
synagogues to teach the people.

1) The synagogue and the Temple were not the same. There was
only one Temple in Israel, and it was the center of Jewish worship
and sacrifice. It was located in the capital city of Jerusalem on the
hill where David told his son, Solomon, to build it.

11

2) The Temple in Jerusalem was the only building in which animals were offered in sacrifice. The Temple then was principally a place of worship and sacrifice, whereas the synagogues were basically places of instruction and catechesis. There was only one Temple, but there were many synagogues throughout Israel and the Diaspora.

3) Jewish law required that a synagogue be erected in places where there were ten or more Jewish families (Barclay, *The Gospel of Mark*). Hence we can envision a great number of synagogues in Jesus' day.

II. The synagogues did not have permanent preachers or teachers. When the people met at the local synagogue for a service, it was up to the ruler of the synagogue to call upon any competent person to give an address or talk (Barclay, *ibid.*).

1) There was no professional rabbi attached to the synagogue. Perhaps on account of the small number of families, it would have been unaffordable to maintain a professional rabbi.

2) As Jesus' popularity grew as a teacher, the demand for Him to speak in the local synagogues also grew. Jesus availed Himself of the opportunity to use the synagogues to preach His Gospel. When Jesus incurred the displeasure of the Pharisees, word went out from the Sanhedrin to bar Him from speaking in the synagogues.

III. In what way did Jesus' teaching differ so much from the teaching of the scribes and Pharisees? Jesus taught on His own authority. No scribe ever gave a decision on his own; he would always quote an authority. Even in dealing with demons, Jesus drove them out of possessed people on His own personal authority.

1) In Our Lord's day, the Jewish people believed that demons were very numerous and that they caused physical illnesses as well as blindness, deafness, and paralysis.

2) A Jewish or pagan exorcist would use elaborate incantations to cast out devils. At a single command from Jesus, the devils would leave the possessed. When Jesus expelled demons, He did not need to invoke help from His Heavenly Father.

3) The devils would even acknowledge the greatness of Jesus in recognizing His identity by using such titles as "Holy One of God," "Son of God," and "Son of the Most High God" (Lk. 8:28).

IV. The Church teaches that there are three sources of temptation to sin: the devil, the world, and our own passions. Of these three, the devil is the principal source of evil in the world. He is a master psychologist; he has much experience on working on the weaknesses of human beings whom he has seen passing through the corridors of time down the centuries.

1) Although Jesus broke the power of Satan, He did not annihilate it. The devil does have plenty of access to tempt us, but Jesus has given us adequate means to overcome those temptations. Thus we can gain merit before God, prove our love for Him, and earn a closer relationship with God each time we remain faithful in resisting temptations. When St. Catherine of Siena complained bitterly to Our Lord about His not being near her when she was undergoing a very strong temptation, Our Lord replied, "Daughter I was there all the time watching you gain the victory."

2) The devil was permitted by God to afflict Job physically and emotionally to get him to sin. Job's reward was tremendous for remaining faithful.

3) Our principal weapon against the devil is prayer, constant and persistent prayer. Through prayer, we become alerted to the presence of the devil and even his temptations lose their power.

4) Let us never deceive ourselves; the devil and his demons constitute a formidable force, roaming the world fanatically to bring about the condemnation of souls. St. Peter put it well when he wrote in his first epistle: "Your adversary the devil prowls about like a roaring lion, seeking some one to devour. Resist him, firm in your faith. . ." (1 Pt. 5:8-9).

****

1) That we all pray frequently, so as to be alerted to the presence of the devil and temptation, and that we may respond generously to God's grace to be able to overcome them.

2) That those who are frequently overcome by temptations arising from their own passions not give up but resort more firmly to prayer.

3) For all those who are tempted to quit or abandon their commitments in life.

4) That the spirit of loving sacrifice reign in our Christian

marriages, and that all couples having difficulties pray and strive to solve their differences and heal their grievances.

5) That the Lord diminish the power of Satan in the world.

6) For an increase in devotion to the Blessed Virgin Mary, who crushed the head of the serpent.

Wednesday of the First Week: Mk. 1:29-39

I. Mark's Gospel has been called the "Gospel of the Miracles of the Lord" because of the space he devotes to Jesus' miracles, especially His miracles of casting out devils from the possessed and of curing the sick, the lame, the blind, the deaf, and the paralyzed. In short, Mark brings out Jesus' power over both spiritual and physical evil. Jesus, the Messiah, is the healer of the whole person, both body and soul. He manifests His absolute dominion over the prince of evil — the devil.

II. The compassion of Jesus is evident in His responsiveness to the plight of Peter's mother-in-law. He performed this miracle without the presence of a large audience. He had no need to impress people. The truth was evident in Him. He was merely fulfilling the signs that Isaiah had predicted of the Messiah.

1) Jesus was probably tired from a day of preaching and teaching and sought rest away from the crowd. Peter more than likely suggested Jesus spend some time at his house, which was close by.

2) No matter how tired He was, Jesus would always respond to someone in need. No sooner had He entered Peter's house than He found someone in need — Peter's mother-in-law.

3) Throughout the pages of the Gospels, we see Jesus constantly reaching out with His understanding and compassion, making the sufferings of others His very own, and responding to their cries for help and healing.

III. No sooner had Peter's mother-in-law been healed than she began to attend to the needs of those who had entered the house.

1) Jesus heals us so that we might better serve others. He Himself said that "the Son of man . . . came not to be served but to serve" (Mk 10:45). We have been placed on this earth to make our contribution: to serve God and our brothers and sisters.

2) When Jesus touches us to heal us from spiritual, emotional, or

physical debilities, He does so that we, like Him, might better serve and thus help to spread God's kingdom on this earth.

IV. When we scan the pages of history, the men and women who are remembered and revered are those who spent themselves in serving others. Shortly after the turn of the century, a poll was taken in France to determine who of all French men and women was the most outstanding citizen. One might think, perhaps, of Napoleon, of Jean Jacques Rousseau, Cardinal Richelieu, or one of their more famous kings. The uncontested choice of the French people was Louis Pasteur, the celebrated French chemist and bacteriologist, who spent his entire life studying ways to heal people and prevent diseases (Gold Label Preaching).

1) As Jesus indicated, the places of honor in the kingdom of heaven will be reserved for those men and women who humbled themselves and served their brothers and sisters who were in need.

2) Christlike service requires that the well-being of others be considered even before our own. "Greater love has no man than this, that a man lay down his life for his friends" (Jn. 15:13).

3) When the Jews were being slaughtered in Europe by Hitler, Raoul Wallenberg, the Swedish diplomat and committed Christian, offered his services to use his political influence to save Jewish people from the gas chambers. He used his own money, risked his own life and intervened personally to save many Jews, getting them out to safety in other countries. He was last seen in a Siberian concentration camp.

4) In Christianity, there is little room for spectators, or for men and women to stand by with arms folded. The Holy Spirit moves us to mobilize our efforts to be compassionate and help others. Just reflecting on the environment in which we live and scanning over the scene there, we will soon see many ways to help others and make the warmth and compassion of Christ present to them.

****

1) That we express our gratitude to Almighty God frequently for His goodness toward us, especially in giving us Our Lord and Savior, Jesus Christ.

2) That we respond with compassion to others in need, especially to suffering and hurting members of our own families.

3) For all those who work with the sick and elderly, that they may be blessed with patience and continue to serve with compassion and understanding.

4) For an increase in vocations to the priesthood and religious life.

5) That we always be generous in almsgiving.

6) That the Lord bless us with that beautiful attitude and disposition of Christ: that we seek to serve rather than be served.

Thursday of The First Week: Mk. 1:40-45

I. In Old Testament and New Testament times up into the Middle Ages, there was no disease more dreaded than leprosy. The person who contracted it was for all practical purposes considered dead, for society had nothing more to do with victims of leprosy. They were generally sent off to distant or remote places, and they were allowed no contact with healthy people.

II. There were different kinds of leprosy. In one kind the skin would exhibit eruptions and develop into nodules which would ulcerate and give off a foul and repulsive odor. Another type would attack the nerves, causing the person to lose sensation and even muscular movement. This would develop into paralysis and loss of one's extremities (McKenzie, *Dictionary of the Bible*). Invariably death would ensue, and for many of these poor creatures it would come as a liberation.

1. The average course of the disease was nine years. For many, it ended in mental decay, coma, and finally death. The leper became utterly repulsive to himself and to others (W. Barclay, *The Gospel of Mark*).

2. Lepers were declared unclean and were barred from entering into the temple to participate in any service. Mosaic Law also mandated that a leper was to wear his/her hair disheveled, his/her clothes torn, and was to shield the upper lip and cry "unclean, unclean!" when healthy people approached. They had to live outside of the city, town, or village (Lev. 13).

3) Leprosy would be analogous to AIDS today; there was no cure; its victims were condemned to certain death. Many nurses, doctors, funeral directors, and rescue workers do not want to deal with AIDS victims for fear of contracting the dreaded disease.

4) If anyone was fortunate enough to be cured of leprosy, he/she was to show him-/herself to the priests, who also served as doctors in Old Testament times. After examination and a long ceremony of purification, the leper would be declared clean. (Lev. 14).

III. For the vast majority of lepers, theirs was a living death, and real death was their only escape. For many it couldn't come soon enough. In answer to John's disciples who came to Him to ask if He was really the Messiah, Jesus gave as a proof the healing of lepers: "Go and tell John what you hear and see: the blind receive their sight and the lame walk, lepers are cleansed. . ." (Mt. 11:4-5).

1) In today's Gospel, the leper saw hope in approaching Jesus. He knew it was against the law to approach a non-leper. According to the Mosaic Law anyone who touched a leper was automatically unclean and would be barred from participating in the Temple services until he/she underwent the rite of purification.

2) The leper was desperate. Jesus' fame had reached the isolated lepers. This leper no doubt wanted to get back with his family and friends. He knew in his heart that Jesus could restore him to health, so he resolved to approach Jesus. He knew that Jesus could do it, so he said, "If you will, you can make me clean." Moved with compassion, Jesus stretched out His hand and touched him. The leper felt the instantaneous cure.

IV. The compassion of Jesus could not refuse this man of faith. Compassion is a daughter of the virtue of charity. The word comes from the Latin "cum" plus "passio," and means to suffer with or empathize with a person.

1) We cannot work miracles, and most probably we will never meet a leper, but we can be compassionate toward others in need. Our compassion must not end with emotional sighs; it must push us to respond by doing what we can to alleviate another's plight.

2) A young girl walked into a jewelry store and told the proprietor that she wanted to buy a birthday present for her older sister. After looking over the display case, she decided on a string of pearls. Not realizing they cost fifty dollars, the little girl handed the man a fifty-cent piece' "I want to spend every bit of this for my sister," she explained, "because it is her birthday. She is my mother now. Our mother died last week." Passing the necklace to the little girl, the man said, "Keep your money, sweetheart, and wish your big

sister a happy birthday from me too" (*Nova et Vetera*). That is compassion put into action. That is Christianity.

****

1) That the Lord heal us of the consequences of the leprosy of sin in our lives.

2) That the Lord fill us with a real and deep hatred of sin, especially mortal sin.

3) That we never procrastinate in the matter of grave sin, but get to the sacrament of reconciliation as soon as possible.

4) That the Lord fill us with a sensitivity and delicate compassion toward the afflicted.

5) That we strive to reduce our compassion to action whenever it is possible for us to do so.

6) That we be generous in almsgiving.

7) For peace in the world and an end to terrorism.

Friday of the First Week: Mk. 2:1-12

I. As soon as the people learned that Jesus had returned to Capernaum, they crowded in and around the house in which he was staying. Generally the houses had flat tile roofs which were accessible by an outside stairway, and people used to go up there in the cool evenings to relax. The tiles were not hard to remove and replace.

II. In Mark's Gospel this is the first confrontation Jesus has with the scribes, the official interpreters of the Law. In the book of Exodus we read, "I the LORD your God am a jealous God, visiting the iniquity of the fathers upon the children to the third and fourth generation of those who hate me, but showing steadfast love to thousands of those who love me and keep my commandments" (Ex. 20:5-6). From this the Jewish people believed that physical afflictions and diseases were directly linked to one's personal sins.

1) The paralytic, therefore, in the eyes of the Jews and especially in the minds of the scribes, was paralyzed because of some sin he had committed, and in justice God had meted this chastisement out on him.

2) Any cure he might receive — whether it be by removing the cause, which was thought to be the paralytic's personal sins, or by

healing the man's physical disability — would require divine power. Any miraculous cure would indicate Jesus had divine power.

III. Jesus knew well the censorious minds of the scribes and the Pharisees, so He decided to challenge them in an open confrontation before the crowds. He addresses Himself to the paralyzed man saying, "My son, your sins are forgiven." Straightaway the scribes thought to themselves, "Why does this man speak thus? It is blasphemy! Who can forgive sins but God alone?"

1) To support a miracle unseen by human eyes, namely, the forgiveness of sins, Jesus substantiates His claim to have forgiven the man's sins by following up with a miracle which could be seen by human eyes. Jesus says to the scribes, "That you may know that the Son of Man has authority on earth to forgive sins" — He turns to the paralytic — "I say to you, rise, take up your pallet and go home."

2) The scribes and Pharisees remained dumbfounded, but bitter and hostile toward Jesus because He clearly manifested divine power by forgiving and healing on His own authority. The simple folk, on the other hand, all gave praise to God saying, "We never saw anything like this!"

3) The scribes labeled Jesus a blasphemer because He dared to forgive sin, a thing that only God could do. This same charge they would level at Jesus at His trial before the high priest Caiaphas on Good Friday morning to bring about His condemnation and death, for blasphemy was punishable by death in Jewish law.

IV. The paralytic has two requisites for healing: faith and contrition. Without these Jesus would not forgive, nor would he grant physical healing.

1) Not only did the paralytic have faith, but so did the four stretcher-bearers. Such was their confidence in Jesus, that they would get what they set out for, that they ascended to the roof, removed one of the tiles and lowered the man down right in front of Jesus to get His attention.

2) That action spoke for itself. It said in so many words, "Lord, we have taken this man to You because we believe that You can and will heal him." The paralytic had the same optimism and faith. Also couched in this is the confession of the paralytic to being a sinner, because being a Jew, he believed that his affliction was due to his sins. He implicitly was asking for forgiveness. Jesus responded to his

19

faith and contrition by forgiving his sins and healing his physical infirmity.

3) Jesus would later clearly indicate that physical afflictions were not necessarily caused by one's sins. Modern medical practice believes that physical healing is related to the spiritual dispositions and interior sentiments of one's soul.

4) Today's Gospel clearly indicates that before we ask for any physical healings we must be deeply sorry for our sins, seeking healing of them before seeking any physical or emotional cures.

****

1) St. Augustine observed that there were many kinds of alms the giving of which helps us to obtain pardon of our sins, but that none is greater than forgiving from the heart a sin that someone else committed against us; that the Lord give us the grace to sincerely forgive those who have offended us.

2) That we may generously volunteer as mediators between people when they need us to serve as bridges in helping to resolve their differences.

3) That husbands and wives especially forgive each other and not harbor suspicions and grudges.

4) That we strive to eliminate all hostility and grudges that we may feel toward others.

5) That world leaders honestly strive to heal their differences and help establish peace in the world.

6) That family members forgive one another and not harbor grudges.

Saturday of the First Week: Mk. 2:13-17

I. In this pericope dealing with the call of Levi to apostleship, St. Mark is referring to St. Matthew, for Matthew was the only publican, or tax collector, among the twelve Apostles. Somewhere further on in Jesus' ministry, Levi received the name of Matthew. Perhaps Jesus Himself conferred this name on him; this was certainly the case with Simon, whose name Jesus changed to Peter. Saul, a confirmed member of the Pharisee party who set out to persecute the Jewish converts to Christianity, became known as Paul after his conversion to Christ. He became the great apostle to the Gentiles.

II. Matthew had his tax-collecting booth set up in Capernaum, a frontier town, a town through which many travelers passed who would be accessible to the tax collectors. The Jews hated the tax collectors, or publicans as they were called, because the majority of them were extortioners and cheats who had the backing of the Roman government behind them. Anything over and above the government's share was theirs. Many of them became wealthy men. They were referred to as sinners and unclean. They were barred from the Temple, were treated as traitors, and were shunned and despised by the people. The love of money, no doubt, drew many men into the ranks of publicans. The only friends they had were other publicans, whom they didn't trust, or the "friends" their money could buy.

III. When Jesus accepted the invitation of Matthew to dine at his house, the scribes and Pharisees had a golden opportunity to condemn Jesus' "scandalous" behavior, because He was deliberately dining in the home of a sinner. According to their interpretation of the Mosaic Law, Jesus contracted ritualistic impurity and thus became legally defiled. This would bar Jesus from the Temple until He would undergo the purification rite to become legally clean.

1) The scribes complained to the disciples of Jesus, asking why Jesus was eating with those "sinners." Jesus overheard the complaint and immediately responded: "Those who are well have no need of a physician, but those who are sick; I came not to call the righteous, but sinners."

2) The scribes and Pharisees once again were cut to the quick by Jesus' answer. Jesus spoke with authority, as one having the right to break the Mosaic Law (or better, the scribes' interpretation of that law) for a higher good, namely, a work of mercy: to forgive a man's sins and offer him a new lifestyle.

3) Matthew was a man who was now open to God's mercy and grace. The scribes and Pharisees were proud and smug. They were the ones who were to determine how the law was to be kept. As a result of their conceited blindness, they closed their hearts to the invitation of Christ, which included accepting Him as Messiah, and to His message — the Gospel. They were excluding themselves from the very kingdom of God which Jesus was establishing.

IV. There is a similarity here between the parable of the proud Pharisee and the humble publican (Lk. 18:10-14) and the call of

Matthew to intimacy with Jesus as an Apostle (*Nova Daily Homilies*). The proud Pharisee stood up in front of the temple telling the Lord how good he was, while the humble publican kept beating his breast confessing his sins and his sorrow. The latter was justified; whereas the Pharisee was rejected.

V. Since the Mosaic Law forbade Jews to mix with sinners, in calling Matthew to be a member of His Apostles Jesus was calling a "reject" into intimacy. The main thrust of Jesus' mission was to reach out to sinners. Jesus would respond to those in need regardless of society's laws or customs, which might go contrary to an individual's need.

1) The scribes and Pharisees felt no need of forgiveness; they were self-righteous. They didn't need Jesus, and so they cut themselves off from the Source of life itself.

2) We are all sinners in need of forgiveness. We accept Jesus and we ask His forgiveness; otherwise we will never enjoy intimacy with Him. Humility is the beginning of the spiritual life; on it depends our growth and intimacy with God. Let us always express our need for Jesus and our dependency on Him.

3) As Jesus accepted society's rejects, let us be open to accept back into our friendship those who have offended us and who have expressed their sincere sorrow for it.

****

1) That we recognize that we are sinners and have need of God's forgiveness.

2) That we sincerely forgive those who have offended us.

3) That we show our friendship and warmth to those who have hurt us and who are truly contrite.

4) That members of families bury their grievances and grudges, reaching out to one another.

5) That husbands and wives forgive and accept each other in their efforts to make their marriages successful.

6) For an increase in vocations to the priesthood and the religious life.

Monday of the Second Week: Mk. 2:18-22
I. When we allow our minds to become fixed in familiar ways,

we are not likely to permit new truths or new ways of doing things to readily establish themselves there.

1) When our bodies are not conditioned through exercise and dietary discipline, they are not likely to hold up under new demands made on them, for they lose buoyancy and resiliency.

2) Older people generally dislike anything with which they are not familiar. Adjusting for them is difficult. Time dries up their flexibility and adaptability.

II. Jesus understood that His Gospel was new, that His message would be hard to accept for those who were hardened by pride — those who kept their minds and hearts closed to anything that was new, anything that didn't fit into their regular channels of thinking. Such was the case with the scribes and elders — the intelligentsia of Jewish society. On the other hand, the simple folk found Jesus' message refreshing and quite acceptable.

1) Jesus was inaugurating messianic times. It would involve a new message which would sometimes clash with the prescriptions of the Mosaic Law with regard to such things as fasting, Sabbath observances, ritualistic cleansings. Jesus' message called for minds open to the truth and ready to make the necessary changes His Gospel called for.

2) Jesus uses the startling example of new wine (His Gospel) needing new wineskins (minds and hearts open to the truth). Throughout antiquity, wine was kept in animal skins. New wine had to be kept in new animal skins because of the fermentation. Fermentation would cause the mass to expand, and this called for skins which would have the needed elasticity. The old wineskins had lost their resiliency and would split if undue expansion was demanded of them, as would be the case if new wine was poured into them.

III. Jesus was unacceptable to the old guard, the elders, scribes and Pharisees. To them, Christ's ideas were much like new wine; they were too expansive, too daring, too revolutionary. Besides, He was saying these things on His own authority. In no way would they allow the perpetrator of new doctrine to gain sway over the people. Jesus' Gospel was bursting the limits of the Mosaic Law, challenging the people to a new way of life highlighted by charity in action.

1) Though we grow old with time, the grace of God will always

give us that necessary suppleness to see more and more of the new in the Gospel of Our Lord Jesus Christ, and it will constantly challenge us to change more and more for the better in the work of our sanctification.

2) Jesus went as far as to say that His Gospel would occasion division in families, causing father to go against son, mother against daughter, for with Jesus there could be no middle ground: one would be either for Him or against Him, would either accept Him or reject Him.

IV. Openness and understanding are gifts of God. Jesus longed for the Jews, God's chosen people, to open their minds and hearts to His message. This is God's desire for us as well, for all peoples.

1) The wineskins symbolize our minds and hearts, our attitudes. Much of what Jesus preached is difficult to carry out, especially His doctrine of forgiving one's enemies, or His doctrine on the beatitudes, which would involve patience in bearing with persecution and sufferings, turning the other cheek.

2) Very often rigidity of mind and heart is due to personal prejudice, pride, and self-love. We see a classic example of this in the racial clashes of the 1960s disrupting Martin Luther King's marches. Many whites would not accept blacks as equals.

3) Closed minds are often a reflection of egotistical self-centeredness: my view, right or wrong. Charity demands that we at least be open to dialogue in order to learn why people act and think differently from us.

****

1) That God give us a sincere openness which will enable us to broaden our understanding of truth.

2) That we cultivate a love for truth and openness toward other people, listening to them and trying to appreciate where they are coming from.

3) No one has a monopoly on truth except God Himself; that we may form a deeper knowledge of God and of ourselves.

4) That there may be greater understanding and tolerance of the different races.

5) For racial equality and peace in South Africa.

6) That we all accept the challenge of the Holy Spirit to work positively on our own sanctification.

7) That leaders of nations be honest, open, and frank in their discussions for peace and justice throughout the world.

Tuesday of the Second Week: Mk. 2:23-28

I. In today's Gospel narrative, Our Lord Jesus Christ considers the essential purpose of the Third Commandment and its sabbath observances.

1) All of God's laws have been given to us for our spiritual and bodily well-being, and they all collaborate to promote the end and purpose of all divine law — charity.

2) God's laws will never frustrate the exigencies of human need and compassion. They are designed to help and protect us. Laws are for people and not people for laws.

II. The whole purpose of the sabbath rest is to free and dispose a person to better worship God together with his/her brothers and sisters as members of the community.

1) One day of the week is set aside for God's people to come together to worship Him as a family of God's children. The ordinary work and business routine of the week is to be stopped, so that one may better focus his/her attention on God and the things of God.

2) The Sabbath day is God's day, and it is basically a spiritual and a family day.

III. The scribes and Pharisees had circled the Sabbath around with numerous rules and regulations; all work was absolutely forbidden.

1) The rabbis considered the breaking of the sabbath law very serious, but they made its observance next to impossible by their interpretation of it, and by the additional regulations they tacked on to it.

2) They had made it forbidden to prepare food or even to light a fire on the sabbath day. Walking beyond a certain distance was also prohibited on the Sabbath.

IV. When the Pharisees saw Jesus' disciples plucking and shelling corn to satisfy their hunger on the Sabbath, they became indignant, for such activity was expressly forbidden.

1) Jesus confounds them by citing the example of David, how he

25

entered into the sanctuary of the temple and took the showbread. Twelve loaves of bread were placed on a table before the Holy of Holies as an offering to God. Each loaf represented one of the twelve tribes of Israel. These loaves could only be eaten by the priests, but David took them to satisfy his hunger and that of his men, a thing which was strictly forbidden.

2) David had a balanced view and overall perspective of the law. He did not act out of contempt for the law, but out of human need.

V. The pendulum has swung to the other extreme today. We can ask ourselves the obvious question: what has happened to the Third Commandment? It mandates that God's day be kept holy.

1) Sunday is rapidly becoming desacralized and is much like any other day of the week. Shopping malls bustle with commerce. People spend a good part of their day shopping. Construction goes on. Unfortunately, Sunday has become a "business as usual" day.

2) This is clearly a violation of the Sabbath, which makes exception only for necessary work and business. The focus of the modern world's Sabbath is not on God.

VI. It is up to you and me and all Christians to break this syndrome and not collaborate with it. The business world always adjusts to its clientele, and we are that clientele.

1) Sundays, if properly used, can give more meaning to the rest-of-the-week's work. The whole week's work should be offered to God in the Sunday sacrifice of the Mass.

2) Sunday is a day when attention should be paid to the family, when time is set aside for the family to be together, whether it be on an outing together, a day at the beach or the park, or whatever. It is a day for promoting family union, development, and growth.

3) The Sunday dinner should be special in honor of the Sabbath. Sunday honors the focal point of our faith — the resurrection of Our Lord Jesus Christ from the dead.

4) In short, the Sabbath is God's day and a family day. Let us work to keep it that way.

****

1) That we reflect more often on the true meaning of the Sabbath and the rich day it should be for oneself and for one's family.

2) That we avoid all unnecessary work and shopping on Sundays.

3) That we strive to build up stronger family ties and unity on the Lord's day.

4) That we spend a little more time at prayer and spiritual reading on the Sabbath.

5) That all Christians collaborate to restore dignity to the Lord's day.

6) That God bless our Christian marriages with greater stability and family unity.

Wednesday of the Second Week: Mk. 3:1-6

I. Another conflict story on the Sabbath is presented in today's Gospel. The focus is not so much on the cure itself but on why Jesus performs this miracle on the Sabbath. Healing in rabbinical law was classified as work. According to the Pharisees' interpretation, medical attention could not be given on the Sabbath unless the person's life was endangered.

II. In the synagogue, at the time, was a deputation from the Sanhedrin (the ruling authority and ultimate judge in Israel). They were scrutinizing Jesus' every action. The most they would permit on the Sabbath was to allow medical attention to be given just to the point of preventing the person from getting worse. A strict Orthodox Jew in our Lord's day would not even defend his own life on the Sabbath if it were threatened (W. Barclay, *The Gospel of Mark*).

1) This, of course, is difficult for us to understand. It all puts in question the true meaning of the Sabbath. The word "Sabbath" comes from the Hebrew word *Shabbat*, meaning rest. In the story of creation, the sacred author tells us God "rested" on the seventh day. The Book of Exodus states, "Six days you shall do your work, but on the seventh day you shall rest; in ploughing time or in harvest you shall rest" (Ex. 23:12;34:21).

2) The Sabbath is then set aside for physical rest, so as to more readily be able to praise and worship God.

It was meant to be a joyous day, a day when penances were relaxed. It was a day for re-creating life, a day set aside for the Creator of life. It is believed that St. Paul changed the Sabbath from Saturday to Sunday (*Catholic Encyclopedia*).

III. "The Sabbath was made for man, not man for the Sabbath" (Mk. 2:27). The Commandment to keep holy the Sabbath is of

27

Divine Law. All laws are to work in a harmonious whole to bring about the total purpose of the law: charity — love and reverence of God and of our brothers and sisters in the world.

1) When the Sabbath interferes with the alleviation of human suffering, it ceases to prohibit one from doing that work of mercy.

2) The scribes and Pharisees just could not bring themselves to accept this. For them the law was to be served as an end in itself.

IV. Jesus challenges this blindness of the scribes and Pharisees: "Is it lawful on the sabbath to do good or to do harm, to save life or to kill?" They, embarrassed, remained silent. He said to the man with the shriveled hand, "Stretch out your hand." The man's hand was instantly restored. Defeated and chagrined, the scribes and Pharisees went out to plot with the Herodians (supporters of Herod Antipas, who had ordered the death of John the Baptist) on a way to do away with Jesus.

1) The religion of the scribes and Pharisees was a blind observance of rules and rituals that they in large part concocted. They closed their eyes to the logical reasoning of Jesus even in the face of a miracle.

2) Like the Pharisees, those who are enslaved to rules, regulations, and ritual subordinate the good of people to rules. Their priorities are awry. They feel more compelled to observe a regulation before helping a person who sorely needs help.

3) We must ask ourselves, are we willing to change our established ways and our customary routine in order to help someone who needs our help? Even though this might mean upsetting our schedule for the day, charity and true religion demand that we do this.

4) Is charity the true foundation of our religion and the guiding norm of our actions? If it isn't, our religion is false and mechanical. For Jesus, a compassionate response to the cry of someone in need is more important than participating in liturgies or performing pious devotions.

****

1) That God bless us with simplicity in our religious practices and that we always consider the practice of charity the highest expression of religion.

2) That those who are blinded by rules and regulations be enlightened to see that charity must be the end and object of all law.

3) That people in authority carry out their duties with compassion.

4) For all the sick, crippled and infirm.

5) That those working with the elderly and senile treat them with loving kindness and consideration.

6) That we always examine our motives for doing what we do, so that God may really be glorified in what we do.

7) That the Lord bestow His wisdom and prudence upon us, so that we may perform our duties well.

Thursday of the Second Week: Mk. 3:7-12

I. The demons recognize Jesus for the person He really is — the Messiah and the Son of God. Seeing all that Jesus was doing, the demons knew He fit the description of the Messiah. The proud scribes and Pharisees refused to see. They had their own preconceived idea of what the Messiah would be like, and Jesus didn't fit into it.

II. Evil sees Jesus for who He is; evil sees Jesus as God's power come into the world to destroy all that would snatch men and women from the grip and power of demons and evil as such.

III. We might ask ourselves a question: Why did Jesus sternly bid the demons not to reveal His identity to the people? The reason is probably due to the popular notion prevalent at that time about the Messiah. The Jewish people had the idea that the Messiah would be a strong military leader who would overthrow the Roman occupation forces to make Israel a world power, with its citizens enjoying a high standard of living. Once the people discovered who the Messiah was, they would immediately make Him king of Israel.

IV. The popular notion of Messiahship was completely opposite to the role Jesus was fulfilling. He thought of Messiahship in terms of redemptive love and service, of suffering service and redemption. A king — yes, Jesus was that, but not an earthly king. A liberator from servitude and oppression — yes, Jesus was that. The servitude and oppression He came to free us from immediately, however, was the servitude and oppression of sin which was destined to bring about our eternal condemnation.

V. The people thought of the Messiah in terms of Jewish nationalism and political liberation. This was obviously alien to Jesus' thinking. Jesus had to prepare the people for a change in their thinking to make it easier for them to accept His type of Messiahship; therefore He forbade those who really knew Him, namely the demons, to shout out His real identity — the Son of God. Jesus' ordering the demons to be silent about His identity has come to be called the Messianic secret, and St. Mark especially develops this theme. It would ultimately take His passion and death to make Jesus' Messiahship known and accepted.

VI. Educating the people as to His real identity would be a difficult task. Jesus had to deal with two types of blindness: the blindness and hardness of heart of the scribes and Pharisees, which would make Jesus unacceptable no matter what marvels He would work; and the blindness of the ordinary people, which was the blindness of ignorance. The latter could be overcome by educating people slowly to accept Him, for what He would teach along with the signs and miracles that would accompany His Gospel.

1) The people feared the scribes and Pharisees because they were the rulers and influential leaders of the nation. They held the threat of excommunication over disloyal heads. They set about prejudicing the people against Jesus.

2) Pride and fear are obstacles to truth. Fear prevents the light from dispelling the darkness that holds one in bondage.

3) Pride shackles one to the ignorance and darkness and enslaves one to it. In the search for truth, fear is an easier obstacle to overcome than pride. Fortitude and courage are those virtues that mobilize against fear. Humility and simplicity are the virtues that kill pride.

VII. Pride is the root of all sin. It was the sin of Lucifer and the fallen angels. It was at the root of the sin of our first parents. In popular terms it is called self-love, and we all inherit it. We must constantly struggle against it, for it keeps us shackled to earth and prevents our minds and hearts from soaring heavenward. Humility is the basis of the spiritual life. Without it we simply cannot build a spiritual edifice. Without humility we will never attain to a deep and lively faith. God is disposed to bestow a deep and lively faith on the humble. Humility disposes us to come to a deeper knowledge of God and a closer relationship with Him. We can never pray enough for the virtue of humility.

****

1) That the Lord give us an appreciation and a love of humility.
2) That we always hunger for a deeper knowledge and love of God.
3) That the Lord increase our faith.
4) That the Lord fill us with a lively confidence in our prayers.
5) For all those who fail to recognize Our Lord Jesus Christ as Messiah and Lord.
6) For all missionaries and catechists, that they may have a successful apostolate instructing people in the faith.
7) For the success of the ecumenical movement, that all Christians may be truly one.

Friday of the Second Week: Mk. 3:13-19

I. St. Mark tells us that Jesus went up a mountain before selecting His future Apostles. He went to the mountain to pray, to consult with His Heavenly Father about the men He was to select.

1) In sacred Scripture, mountains are setting for solemn events. Moses went up to Mt. Sinai, where he prayed and fasted for forty days before receiving the Ten Commandments from the Lord.
2) On Mount Carmel, Elijah put down the false prophets of Baal who were deceiving the Israelites. On Mount Horeb, Elijah communed with God and was told what God wanted him to do.
3) Jesus often went up a mountain to pray. So often in the Bible, going up a mountain meant being in close communion with God and having the necessary solitude to commune with Him.
4) Jesus took Peter, James, and John up Mt. Tabor and there revealed His divinity to them by being transfigured before their very eyes.

II. God will always use human instruments to do His work. Jesus now decides to select His Apostles — the leaders and pillars of His Church. Just as Israel was founded on the twelve tribes which emanated from the twelve sons of Jacob, so too Jesus selects twelve Apostles, reminiscent of the leaders of the twelve tribes of Israel, to

31

be the foundation stones of His Church. First Mark lists Simon Peter, who was to be the leader, and Judas, the traitor, is listed last.

III. The twelve Apostles are quite different in talent and in personality.

1) Simon the Zealot and Matthew would represent two extremes in the Jewish nation. A tax collector like Levi-Matthew was considered a traitor because he collaborated with the Romans, the conquerors of Israel.

2) Simon the Zealot was an exponent of Jewish nationalism and would be diametrically opposed to anyone who collaborated with the hated Romans.

3) Thomas was a pragmatic realist; Peter was spontaneous, forward, and forceful. John was inclined to be more of a thinker and more mystical than the rest.

IV. *E pluribus unum.* "From many, one." Their differences and talents were all drawn upon to work for Jesus. Their unity would spring from their love for and loyalty to Jesus.

V. Jesus picked ordinary people who had no special gifts or qualifications. Jesus selected them not so much for what they were at the time of their call to apostleship, but for what they could and would become through the action of God's grace operating within their souls.

VI. Jesus had these twelve Apostles spend time with Him to get to know Him and who He was. He trained them by His constant teaching and preaching. He would send them out ahead of Him to prepare the people to receive Him. They too were spreading the good news about Jesus, the Messiah who had come to save Israel.

VII. A much similar thing happens to us. We too are called by Christ through our own baptism and confirmation to go out to bear witness to Him and spread the good news about the Messiah come to save us.

1) Like the Apostles, we must frequently spend time alone with Jesus, meditating on His word to get a deeper knowledge and appreciation of Our Lord.

2) This means being alone with Our Lord, especially before the Blessed Sacrament, learning to enjoy His company and communing with Him in silent adoration.

3) The majority of the world's population is non-Christian.

Christianity has been around for nearly 2,000 years. It isn't that the message of Christ hasn't reached the whole world; rather, the witness of Christians bearing the message of the Gospel was and still is unconvincing. Too few Christians are bearing convincing witness to the Gospel.

4) There is no more convincing message than the Gospel of Our Lord Jesus Christ, but those who propagate it must really live it. If the Gospel were truly lived throughout the centuries, the whole world would be Christian today.

****

1) That we frequently express our gratitude to Almighty God for having called us through baptism into Christ to be members of His Body the Church.

2) For an increase in vocations to the priesthood and religious life.

3) That God strengthen all priests, brothers, and sisters in their sublime vocation, that they feel a sense of joy, privilege, and accomplishment in the work of their sublime calling.

4) That parents inspire and encourage vocations to the priesthood and religious life among their own children.

5) For all the sick and deceased priests and religious of the diocese.

6) That the Lord give us a prudent and tactful zeal for souls.

7) That we truly strive to live the Gospel message in our daily lives so that we might better serve as lights to those who are searching.

Saturday of the Second Week: Mk. 3:20-21

I. Simeon foretold that Jesus would be a sign of contradiction. He simply did not fit into the pattern the Jewish authorities expected of the Messiah. Jesus' life objective was to do the will of His Father, cost what it may. Whether His message would be acceptable or not, whether it would win Him friends or cost Him friends, neighbors, or even relatives mattered little to Jesus. The salvation of souls was the purpose and reason for His coming to earth, and the only way to show men and women the road to salvation was to preach His Gospel, whatever the cost might be.

II. Jesus was already on a collision course with the scribes and Pharisees, the leaders of the people. He had been curing on the Sabbath, forgiving sins, and speaking on His own authority. All of these things were bringing down the wrath of the religious leaders on Jesus. His relatives and friends were getting worried, not only for Him but for themselves, for the powerful pressure of the scribes and Pharisees might descend upon them also for not silencing Jesus.

III. St. John tells us that Jesus' relatives did not believe in Him (Jn. 7:5). To save their own skins and Jesus also, they came to take Him away because they thought He was out of His mind. In all His years at Nazareth, Jesus had never spoken or acted like this. Where did He get all this? He had never attended the rabbinical schools; He was too poor to go to any of them. Their conclusion then was that He had lost His mind or was hallucinating. In any event, Jesus had to be stopped, and that is what these relatives of Jesus set out to do. Jesus obviously ignored their suggestions and did not accede to their desires.

1) To his friends and relatives, Jesus appeared to be a blind man leading the blind. His followers were unlettered fishermen. How could they stand up to the scribes and Pharisees?

2) In the family's minds this band of fishermen should be back working their nets, supporting their families, and not going around the countryside with a madman.

IV. It is difficult when strangers reject us. It is much harder when members of our families, relatives, or friends reject us, and frequently it is because what we do or say does not fit into their way of thinking or behaving. Jesus warned His disciples, "A man's foes will be those of his own household" (Mt. 10:36).

1) On another occasion, Jesus said, "Do not think that I have come to bring peace upon the earth; I have not come to bring peace, but a sword" (Mt. 10:34) What Jesus meant by this was that unless His word was accepted, it would not bring peace but division. Jesus would have no fence-sitters. He would either be accepted or rejected.

2) Differences would invade families: "For I have come to set a man against his father, and a daughter against her mother, and a daughter-in-law against her mother-in-law" (Mt. 10:35). Implementing the Gospel could and often did bring about family divisions.

V. It is difficult to be a real follower of Christ: His route is the narrow way; yet it is the only way to eternal happiness. It has been said that it is hard to live a good Catholic life, but it gives an easy and a happy death to those who live it.

1) To be sure, living out the Gospel message will not make one popular, nor will it win one many friends. On the contrary, it may well be the reason for the loss of so-called friends.

2) So many people cave in to human respect: the "what-will-people-think" attitude if they behave the way the Church teaches. In order to cultivate such friends, they make concessions, and thus never really grow in their relationship with God.

3) Young people readily cave in to peer pressure, and for this reason they get hooked on drugs. In many cases, it is also the reason they indulge in illicit sexual conduct.

4) To follow Christ means that we have to pay a price and a heavy one, but the Lord will give us the grace and strength to do the right thing even in the face of heavy pressure. He is not slow to reward His faithful ones with His divine visitations and gifts.

****

1) That the Lord give us the courage and strength to live out our faith in our daily lives.

2) That the Lord give us the light to know and carry out His will.

3) In times of doubt, that we look to the magisterium of the Church, especially to the Holy Father, for light and guidance.

4) That Christians realize how much more important it is to please God before pleasing men and women.

5) That we learn to count it gain when our friends "drop" us for carrying out God's law and remain faithful to the teachings of His Church.

6) That those in authority carry out their office faithfully and not give in to bribes or the bad example of their peers and colleagues.

Monday of the Third Week: Mk. 3:22-30

I. The Pharisees were attributing the good works of Jesus to Satan. Such a charge was in itself blasphemy. To say that evil can do good is to say that black is white and night is day. To say that Jesus'

35

miracles were the work of the power of the devil and not of God is to say that the goodness of God was the evil of Satan.

1) When Peter saw Jesus work a miracle, he said, "Depart from me, for I am a sinful man, O Lord" (Lk. 5:8). Peter recognized goodness in itself, and his reaction was humble repentance.

2) In the parable on the proud Pharisee and the humble publican, the publican saw the evil of his own sins and didn't even dare to raise his head toward the altar; rather, he kept striking his breast, acknowledging his guilt. The Pharisee, on the other hand, stood up front telling God how good he was, and proceeded to narrate a litany of good works, but he failed to see his own sins. The publican was forgiven; the Pharisee was not.

3) The Pharisees see Jesus cure diseases and heal those suffering from various afflictions. They see him cast out devils; yet they fail to recognize the goodness present, and they proceed to attribute these great works of Jesus to Satan and call them evil.

II. Such hardness of heart is a sin against the Holy Spirit. When a person repeatedly rejects God's graces and continues inclining him-/herself toward evil, soon he/she will become impervious to the prompting of the Holy Spirit and will be unable to recognize his/her own sinfulness. Such a person will fail to see the need of repentance. As a result, he/she cannot be repentant, and because of this lack of contrition, such a person cannot be forgiven. Such is a sin against the Holy Spirit and is consequently self-condemnatory. When a person sees good as evil and evil as good, how can he/she really repent?

III. Today the Holy Father is saying that many people have lost their sense of sin. They are victims of a constant, though subtle, diabolical bombardment from many areas of the culture in which they live and work but especially from the communications media. Such bombardment has the effect of blunting consciences. For the media, "sin" is a taboo word.

1) How many people see abortion as good. How many young people regard chastity as weird or outdated. Many feel that it cramps their style and is an affront to personal freedom.

2) The movie industry dresses up evil in such a way as to make it look attractive and indeed the "in thing." Television soaps demean marriage. In so many of them adultery is acceptable and expected to fill the emotional needs of an unfulfilled spouse.

IV. We hear so little of the prevalent but scarcely spoken-of seven capital sins: pride, covetousness, lust, anger, gluttony, envy, and sloth. These sins are very much in existence today, and men and women are their perpetrators; yet so many people fail to recognize them as the evils they are.

1) Sins of pride are excused in the necessary effort to get ahead in the world. Other people might get trampled on in the effort, but that is all casually disposed of in the need to achieve one's goal.

2) Lust is rationalized under the heading of psychosexual development. Envy is smothered under one's right to challenge and be competitive. Covetousness has its outlet in law suits these days. People sue one another for the flimsiest of reasons. At the base of many law suits is pure greed.

3) Gluttony is not limited to food and drink. It also includes excesses in tobacco, alcohol, and, needless to say, drugs. Gluttony is justified under one's need to unwind and enjoy oneself.

4) We live in an age of rationalization and irresponsibility. Nevertheless, the Lord will hold us responsible for our actions; the Ten Commandments are as binding today as they were for ages past. As Shakespeare observed, a rose is a rose by any other name; the same can be said of sin today. One may resort to euphemisms, but sin is still sin, the detestable evil that drives God out of our hearts and souls.

****

1) That God give us the light to recognize evil as such and not seek to rationalize it in the name of psychology or because of the vast number of people doing it.

2) That we may be more sensitive and responsive to the movements of grace in our hearts and souls.

3) That we use our influence as individual citizens to work against public evil and injustice such as abortion, pornography, racial and social injustice.

4) That parents correct their children when they see them doing wrong and offer them guidance and direction.

5) That we strive to improve our prayer lives so as to be more open and responsive to God's grace in our daily lives.

6) For all children who are victims of broken homes.

Tuesday of the Third Week: Mk. 3:31-35

I. When we pray the Lord's Prayer, we say, "Thy will be done on earth as it is in heaven." God establishes His kingdom in our hearts and souls and will reign there if we do His will. Conformity to God's will builds a deep relationship with God. Jesus said as much when He said in today's Gospel, "Whoever does the will of God is my brother, and sister, and mother." Baptism makes us formal members of God's household, His sons and daughters properly speaking. Obedience makes this relationship vital and intimate. It makes God proud of us.

II. What Our Lord Jesus Christ is saying in today's Gospel is that true kinship with God and with one another is based on obedience to God's will more than the ties of blood relationship. In God's eyes, ties based on blood are not the highest bonds.

1) Jesus has stated that He came to set father against son and mother against daughter, father-in-law against son-in-law, mother-in-law against daughter-in-law (cf. Lk. 12:53). Doing God's will by living out the Gospel message in one's daily life will cause division even within families.

2) Those who choose to do the will of human beings in preference to the will of God will at best enjoy an inferior relationship with God or none at all.

3) Natural family relationships can indeed be very close. Often such relationships make one willing to transgress God's commandments in order to keep on the good side or in the good graces of another family member. Such a member may urge one to do him/her a favor which would involve offending God.

III. St. Thomas More was definitely a family man who loved and was dedicated to his wife and children. When he was condemned to the tower of London for refusing to sign the oath of allegiance to King Henry VIII, his wife and children would visit him when the prison authorities permitted it. His wife Alice and daughter Margaret pleaded with him to sign the document recognizing Henry VIII as the head of the Church in England. They naturally wanted him free and home with them to continue enjoying the life they knew and loved. Thomas asked them how long more he might live with them. They answered perhaps twenty or even thirty more years. "And what are twenty or thirty years here on earth in comparison to eternity?" He would not offend God by watering down or rationalizing his convictions. He preferred martyrdom in spite of the cost of separation from his family.

IV. "My food is to do the will of him who sent Me" (Jn. 4:34). Carrying out His Father's will was not an easy task for Jesus. He even spent three hours in the garden of Gethsemane pleading with his Heavenly Father to take the cup of suffering from Him.

1) More than sacrifices or ceremonial observances, God wants an obedient heart. This was the repeated message of the prophets.

2) In the Letter to the Hebrews we read, " 'Thou hast neither desired nor taken pleasure in sacrifices .. and sin offerings'. . . then he added, 'Lo, I have come to do thy will' " (Heb. 10:8-9).

V. Doing the Will of God will always cost us and purify us; for this reason the Church has so many martyrs.

1) It may well be said that Al Smith could have won the presidential election of 1928 if he would have changed his religion.

2) Many a good Catholic immigrant who came to New York or Philadelphia at the turn of the century had to forego opportunities for getting a job or advancing in one because he/she was Catholic and would not deny it for monetary gain. As a result, many suffered physical hardships and privations. Many lived in dire poverty.

3) In spite of all, true freedom accompanied by joy and peace of conscience is the reward of striving to do God's will. Doing the will of God has a direct effect on our relationship with Him; it literally makes us one with Him, as Jesus said, "Whoever does the will of God is my brother, and sister, and mother." In all things, Jesus sought to do His Father's will. God truly reigns in the obedient soul, and in it He finds His consolation and joy.

4) "God will always bring joy out of sorrow when we accept His will" (W. Ciszek, S.J., *He Leadeth Me*).

****

1) That we faithfully carry out God's commandments and the precepts of His Church.

2) That we always strive to know God's will and carry it out in our daily lives.

3) That we keep our priorities straight and seek first to please God rather than human beings who pressure us to do otherwise.

4) That children may see in their parents God's legitimate authority lovingly placed over them, knowing that when they obey their parents they please God.

5) That young people may not bow to peer pressure, especially in the areas of drug taking and illicit sex.

6) That the young reverence and respect the elderly as a manifestation of God's will.

7) That the world might see the wisdom of the Ten Commandments and the true freedom they bring to the soul.

8) For peace and harmony in our Christian marriages and homes.

Wednesday of the Third Week: Mk. 4:1-20

I. Knowledge means enlightenment. It serves as a foundation for wisdom. Knowledge is the first level of learning. The second level of learning is understanding, that is, knowing how one bit of knowledge relates to another bit of knowledge. Discovering relationships between seemingly unrelated bits of knowledge is the highest order of understanding. The third level of learning is wisdom. Wisdom empowers the mind to perceive the immediate and ultimate meaning of what is known and understood.

II. Knowledge enters the mind in word packages. Words, then, become the basic vehicle for transmitting knowledge to the human mind. Our Lord compares words to seeds. The Sower is God, the seed is His word, and we are the ground on which He scatters that seed. The parable of the sower and the seed is analogous to the three levels of knowledge of which the human mind is capable.

1) Relating knowledge to seeds, Jesus tells us of the threefold receptivity of the ground. The seed has the power to communicate the life that is contained in it, but the ground must receive it. So too the word of God has the power to communicate the knowledge and divine life contained within it.

2) The ground is compared to the human mind. Jesus is describing the different ways the mind, like the ground, receives His word. In one case the word is received but not understood. In another case the word is received, understood, but is not related to oneself. Still in another case, the word is received, understood, and is related

40

to oneself, but is not reduced to practice. It really doesn't do much for that person. Finally, the word is received, understood well, and is related to oneself; it is then put into action and produces a great harvest.

III. In Jewish mentality, words were packed with meaning. The Hebrew language had a vocabulary far less extensive than that of the Greeks or the Romans. For the Jews, a Hebrew word almost existed in its own right. Although they used Hebrew words sparingly, each word was charged with energy. The parable of the sower and the seed, therefore, had deep significance for the Jewish people. Our Lord capitalized on this in His analogy, a comparison of the word of God to a seed, loaded with the power to germinate and grow.

IV. As with the seed, the fate of the word of God depends upon the hearer. As in the case of the seed falling on the footpath where the birds gobbled it up immediately, there are some people who just refuse to listen to God's word; consequently it becomes impossible for the word to do anything for them. Like the proud but blind scribes and Pharisees, they seal their own fate and make their salvation impossible.

1) The rocky ground refers to superficial and shallow Christians who receive the word with initial enthusiasm, thus allowing the word to germinate and begin to grow, but then fail to nurture it with reflective meditation and prayer, so what begins well fails to sink into their minds. These people are slaves to the next attractive thing that enters their minds: they run after whatever is new and flashy, but they soon tire of that also. They are totally lacking in discipline.

2) The seed that fell among thorns applies to those Christians who receive the message of the Gospel, understand it reasonably well, relate it to themselves, but fail to put it into action. They are not sufficiently motivated to give God's word priority in their lives. They mean well, but God's word keeps getting bumped; that is, their resolutions and good intentions constantly get postponed for other interests or attractions, which may be all good in themselves but obviously much less important than their relationship with God. The speed of modern life, their work schedule, pursuit of wealth — all keep crowding the time needed for reflection and meditation on God's word. These are the thorns that choke out the word of God.

3) Finally there is the good ground, the wise and prudent listeners, the clever and thrifty businessmen and businesswomen of God who take in the word of God, reflect on it, apply to themselves, and put it into practice. They produce an abundant harvest.

****

1) That we may be always eager to hear the word of God.

2) That we learn how to relate God's word to our own lives and convert it to practice.

3) That we become wise and prudent businessmen and businesswomen in the things of God.

4) That we realize that by reason of our baptism we are missionaries, and that we carry the word of God into the marketplace, especially through the testimony of our example.

5) That the Holy Spirit may give us the wisdom and patience to receive the word of God, relate to ourselves, and put it into action.

6) That the Lord enkindle in the hearts of all Christians a love for sacred Scripture and a desire to read and reflect on it frequently.

Thursday of the Third Week: Mk. 4:21-25

I. Jesus said to Philip, "He who has seen me has seen the Father" (Jn. 14:9). By familiarizing ourselves with Our Lord Jesus Christ in the Gospels, we get a very good idea of what God is like in Himself.

II. Jesus is the embodiment of truth. He Himself said, "I am the way, and the truth, and the life" (Jn. 14:6). To see and know the truth is to see and know Our Lord. To St. Augustine, the Old Testament made no real sense without using Jesus Christ as the criterion for its comprehension.

III. Truth has the quality of making us free. "You will know the truth," said Our Lord, "and the truth will make you free" (Jn. 8:32). Truth, then, liberates us from darkness and frees us from fear.

1) Embracing Our Lord Jesus Christ and living out His Gospel message free us from captivity by our own passions and prejudices, ridding us of the haunting apprehensions we might have in regard to the future. Obstructions that blind us to the truth are servitude to our passions and attachments to sin.

2) St. Paul zeros in on licentiousness as being a huge obstacle to truth. To the Ephesians, he writes, "You must no longer live as the

Gentiles do, in the futility of their minds; they are darkened in their understanding, alienated from the life of God because of the ignorance that is in them, due to their hardness of heart; they have become callous and have given themselves up to licentiousness, greedy to practice every kind of uncleanness" (Eph. 4:17-19).

3) In his letter to the Romans, St. Paul attributes people's ignorance about God and knowledge of divine things as being due in large measure to sexual promiscuity. "They exchanged the truth about God for a lie and worshiped and served the creature rather than the Creator. . . . For this reason God gave them up to dishonorable passions" (Rom. 1:25-26).

IV. Truth is light, and the light must not remain hidden. Our Lord asks, "Is a lamp brought in to be put under a bushel, or under a bed, and not on a stand" in a place where it can diffuse its light?

1) Isaac Newton, the famous English mathematician-physicist, defined light as matter transformed into pure energy. The sun gives off tremendous light because of the stupendous amount of energy it expends. It is steadily consuming itself.

2) To give off the light of Christianity, we must expend ourselves transforming the message of the Gospel into the bright and moving power of our good example.

3) By living the chaste lives that Christ asks of us, we open our minds up to a knowledge of divine truths. We are lifted above earthly attractions, and we come to cultivate a savor and relish for divine things.

V. Our faith is a light that should never be placed under the bushel basket of shame or fear. Many people fail to put the dictates of their faith into practice because they fear persecution or even the criticism of their peers.

1) By bearing witness to our faith we become light-bearers in the dark world of secularism. So many people need the encouragement and support of seeing others living up to their faith.

2) Our Lord tells us in today's Gospel: "The measure you give will be the measure you get, and still more will be given you." If we are willing to bear witness to the truths of our faith and translate them into practice in our daily lives by our good example and good works, in spite of criticism leveled against us, we become so many lampstands that tower up to give off yet more light to those in

darkness. God will then deepen and strengthen our faith to make it the cause of real joy for us by allowing us to bask in its consoling wisdom. At the same time, our good example will be a channel of encouragement and support to our weaker brothers and sisters.

****

1) That we may be ever grateful for the gift of faith and never hide it or be ashamed of it.

2) That we have the courage to do the right thing even in the face of opposition and peer pressure.

3) That we always hunger for a greater love of God.

4) That we redouble our efforts to grow in our faith.

5) That by seeing our light and example, others may be drawn to Christ.

6) That God pardon our sins of sloth and indifference in the pursuit of Christian perfection.

7) For peace in the world and the conversion of the Soviet Union.

Friday of the Third Week: Mk. 4:26-34

I. Nature can teach us lessons about God which so many of us fail to even notice, let alone allow to affect our lives. The mysteries of life and growth are in the hands of God. The farmer can prepare the ground for planting, but in the final analysis he cannot make the seed germinate and grow up to maturity. In this sense, he is helpless.

II. The farmer may work during the day, but he must sleep during the night in order to be able to continue his work the following day. This is not the case with Mother Nature. She will encourage the plant to grow day and night, and it patiently inches its way along with assistance from the heat of the day's sun and the moisture of the spring and summer rains.

1) A man can help a plant grow by eliminating obstacles like weeds and insects, but by and large he cannot make it grow one centimeter. This is completely out of his hands.

2) He can encourage growth by creating favorable conditions that are necessary for its growth, but he must patiently wait for nature to do the job that God ordained it to do.

III. Nature is essentially God's work, and it will plod on with or without us.

1) So too the kingdom of God on earth is essentially God's work, and it will go on according to the divine plan with or without our help; but like Mother Nature, we can help the growth of God's kingdom on earth by our prayers, our example, and our apostolic work.

2) Just as a plant in its growth to maturity can split rocks and roads, so too does God's kingdom plod on to fulfill the divine plan regardless of the resistance of men and the machinations of the devil.

3) Like nature itself God is patient in awaiting the growth of His kingdom on earth. Like the farmer who helps nature to bring about the growth of his crops, the Lord expects us to be good stewards and do the best we can to extend His kingdom on earth.

IV. There is also the lesson here aimed at families. No matter how well-born or well-reared a child may be, his/her growth toward a spiritually mature member of God's kingdom is largely independent of his/her parents.

1) True, parents play a vital role, providing the environment in which their children will grow and develop. Like the farmer preparing his soil for planting, he carefully sows the seeds and fertilizes the ground. Later on, he weeds and sprays his crops as they struggle to be mature plants, so too the good and solicitous parent provides the environment conducive to the physical, moral, and spiritual growth of his/her child.

2) Parents can instruct, counsel, and protect their children from evil influences, but in the end the hope for a good mature product will depend on the free choice of the child him-/herself.

3) Many saintly parents have had to suffer a great deal because their children turned out to be anything but what they desired them to be.

4) Many parents have struggled to put their children through Catholic schools only to see them turn out to be shiftless and irresponsible adults who have ceased to practice their faith.

V. The lesson of the Gospel is that, like the farmer, you and I do indeed play a part in the extension of God's kingdom here on this earth, but in the end we must totally depend on God for the harvest. This, of course, should not diminish our zeal for souls, for as members of Christ's Mystical Body, we are His coworkers in His vineyard, and we are our brothers' and sisters' keepers. Charity urges us to be zealous for the salvation of others. St. James assures us: "Whoever brings back a sinner from the error of his way will save his soul from death and will cover a multitude of sins" (Jas. 5:20).

****

1) That we learn to depend upon God for everything and go to Him as our Father frequently.

2) That we never give up our hope in being instrumental in saving the soul of a relative or friend who no longer practices the faith.

3) For parents, that they be tirelessly dedicated to their children even after they have grown, and that they persevere in their prayers for the salvation of their children, especially for those who have abandoned the practice of their faith.

4) For an increase in vocations to the priesthood and religious life.

5) For the success of the ecumenical movement, that all Christians may soon be one flock under the one shepherd.

6) That the Lord fill us with a lively zeal for souls.

Saturday of the Third Week: Mk. 4:35-41

I. The Sea of Galilee is famous for its sudden and terrifying storms. Although it is only thirteen miles long and eight miles wide, it is situated some 696 feet below sea level. To the west of the lake there are high hills with deep gulches and ravines which catch the strong west winds and channel them down the side of these hills. The winds are compressed as they blow through these ravines and gulches, causing them to hit the water with a tremendous force capable of churning up large waves which can capsize fishing vessels and rather large boats (Barclay). Within a very short time and with little warning, a dangerous storm could suddenly arise.

II. Such a storm did arise when Our Lord was asleep on the Apostles' fishing vessel while all of them were aboard. They were in danger of sinking. There was little hope of preventing the vessel from going down. They simply had no recourse except to prevail on Jesus to do something, so they decided to waken Him and ask Him to act. Jesus rose from the cushion and bade the storm to be still. A calm came over the sea immediately.

1) With Jesus present, any storm, however violent, can be calmed. There will be many difficult storms in the course of our lives in which the waters of apprehension, anxiety, and worry will seem to inundate us to the point of despair. By that time we will, like the beleaguered Apostles, cry out to the Lord to do something to alleviate our plight.

2) With Our Lord Jesus Christ present in our hearts and souls, peace and tranquillity can and will prevail if we call upon Him with faith and confidence.

III. We see something of this in children. Even though a danger or threat hovers over them, as long as one of their parents is present, they feel security and are consequently at peace.

IV. Tom Dooley worked in Vietnam and Laos as a volunteer doctor, eventually dying in Asia. He felt threats in the interior jungles of Indochina, especially after he learned he had terminal cancer. On one occasion, he wrote from the hospital, "Inside and outside the winds blow . . . there are times when the storm around me doesn't matter. A wider storm of peace gathers in my heart. What seems unfathomable, I fathom. What is unutterable I utter, because I can pray. I can communicate. How do people endure anything on earth if they cannot have God?"

V. The root of peace, security, and joy comes unquestionably through the possession of Our Lord Jesus in the soul. This possession comes through persevering prayer and sorrow for sin, together with the generosity of forgiving those who have offended us and serving those in need. It comes, in other words, through a sincere conversion, turning toward God, our brothers, and our sisters in charity.

1) We will possess Him more when we spend ourselves for others, for it is precisely in this giving that we receive the hidden treasure of great price.

2) As a young priest, St. Vincent de Paul suffered tremendously from stormy attacks of doubt regarding the faith. It cost him dearly. At one point he couldn't bring himself to recite the Apostles' Creed for fear of the strong doubts that would arise in his mind. One day while visiting the hospital for the poor in Paris, the Hôtel-Dieu, he was moved to make a vow dedicating his life to serving the poor. Immediately the dark clouds of doubt that had pursued him lifted. His heart was filled with a deep faith and love for God and neighbor,

and never again did he ever suffer another doubt about the faith. From then on he always was at peace, and he found abundant joy in serving God in the poor.

VI. Even though a tempest of trials and problems may assail us, God is always present, even when it feels as though He is miles away. Out of these trials, patiently born, God enhances our faith and increases our merit.

1) St. Catherine of Siena complained to Our Lord for abandoning her when she was sorely tempted to sin. When the trial passed, the Lord appeared to her, as He frequently did with her, and she asked, "Lord, where were You when I was so fiercely tempted?" "Daughter, I was there at your side watching you gain so much merit," He replied (Bl. Raymond of Capua, *Life of St. Catherine*).

2) As we advance in virtue and increase our merits, which are gained through overcoming temptations and patiently bearing trials and sufferings of one kind or another, our relationship with God grows more intimate, and the Holy Spirit infuses more of His gifts and fruits into us.

****

1) That we strive for an ever richer possession of Our Lord Jesus Christ in our hearts and souls.

2) That we frequently take refuge before the Blessed Sacrament to confide our anxieties to Jesus in confident prayer.

3) That we have recourse to sacred Scripture for light during times of distress and difficulty.

4) That Our Lord may impart to us and to our families His abiding peace.

5) That the Lord enrich and deepen our faith, enabling us to support with equanimity all trials that come our way.

6) That young people find in the Blessed Virgin Mary the comfort and support that they are looking for.

7) For peace in the world and an end to terrorism.

Monday of the Fourth Week: Mk. 5:1-20

I. Many modern Christians tend to see the devil as a sort of comic-opera figure. In the secularistic and sophisticated world of today, many people feel half ashamed of believing in the reality of devils.

II. To confront this tendency, Pope Paul VI spoke on the subject of the devil on November 15, 1973. He stated quite clearly: "It is not a question of one devil but of many . . . but the principal one is Satan, which means adversary, enemy, and with him there are many fallen creatures — fallen because of their rebellion and damnation. . . . The devil is the enemy number one, the tempter par excellence."

III. Our Lord called Satan "the father of lies." There is no truth in him. Since he is the father of lies, his all-consuming ambition is to destroy truth. He cannot stand truth, and for this reason he tries to weaken respect and reverence for the magisterium of the Church.

IV. Who are these devils, these masters of deceit and workers of evil in the world? They are basically the fallen angels. Angels are made in the image and likeness of God, and before they could behold the beauty and magnificence of God in the Beatific Vision they had to pass a test of love and fidelity. We know very little about this saga of the angels except that all of them did not remain faithful to God. Many of them chose to align themselves with Lucifer (Satan), the prince of the fallen angels, in an attempt to make themselves equal to God. From the moment of that great sin, God created hell and thrust all of these unfaithful angels down into it forever with no chance for redemption.

V. After the fall of the angels, God created man and gave to man the opportunity to gain what the angels had lost. In their ravenous envy, these fallen angels go about seeking ways to destroy our opportunity of achieving the goal that was once theirs. They seek to bring about our final condemnation to hell.

1) Such is their bitterness toward us that St. Peter tells us that they prowl around like roaring lions, seeking someone to devour (1 Pet. 5:8).

2) They are the most miserable of beings because they cannot experience any love whatsoever. They are envious of those who experience love and peace, and they strive to sow the seeds of disquietude, suspicion, distrust, and hate. They endeavor to sadden us, for in sadness we are much more open to temptations against faith, chastity, and loyalty to Our Lord Jesus Christ.

VI. In today's Gospel, St. Mark narrates the instance where Our

Lord ordered the devil to confess his name. The response was, "My name is Legion; for we are many." A legion in the Roman army was composed of six thousand soldiers. There were, therefore, many devils occupying the possessed man's body.

VII. St. John records Our Lord referring to the devil as the ruler of this world and His adversary at least three times (Jn 12:31, 14:30, 16:11).

1) St. Paul calls him "the god of this world" (2 Cor. 4:4). He warns us of the struggle in the dark that we must wage, not against only one devil but against many of them.

2) In his letter to the Ephesians, St. Paul calls the devils "spiritual hosts of wickedness" (Eph. 6:12). Our Lord Jesus Christ defines the devil as "a murderer from the beginning" and "the father of lies" (Jn. 8:44).

VIII. Pope Paul VI called him "the treacherous and cunning enchanter, who finds his way into us by way of our senses, the imagination, lust, or in disorderly social contacts in the give and take of life to tempt us."

1) The devil is not the only source or cause of evil in the world. The other sources of evil are our own fleshy and unruly appetites together with the lure of the world in which we live — that constant source of seduction for us by reason of its wealth, comforts, and pleasures.

2) It is true that those who do not watch over themselves with a certain strictness are exposing themselves to these forces of evil that strive to bring them down.

3) Pope Paul VI in his talk on the devil in 1973 said: "The Christian must be militant; he must be vigilant and strong (1 Pet. 5:8), and he must sometimes have recourse to special ascetical exercises to stave off certain diabolical attacks. Jesus teaches this, indicating 'prayer and fasting' as the remedy (Mk. 9:29)."

****

1) That we may be aware that God has given us guardian angels to alert us to the presence of the devil and other evils, and that we frequently pray to them.

2) That we pray from time to time to our guardian angels to sharpen our sensitivity to the presence of evil.

50

3) That Catholics, especially the young, do not fall victim to the secular world which denies the existence of the devil.

4) That we pray frequently as Our Lord urged us, so that we do not fall into temptation.

5) That young people may resist the temptation to take drugs or indulge in promiscuous sex.

6) For an end to terrorism in the world.

7) That we may quickly have recourse to the Blessed Virgin Mary in the times of temptation to protect us from the wiles of the devil.

Tuesday of the Fourth Week: Mk. 5:21-43

I. Faith, earnestness, and persistence underscore the dispositions of both the woman suffering from the hemorrhage and Jairus, the ruler of the synagogue. Both receive the reward of their faith and perseverance.

II. The case of Jairus was more heroic. Jesus was now an enemy to the scribes and Pharisees, and these were held to be the official interpreters of Judaism. To be allied with Jesus was to run the risk of incurring the displeasure of the scribes and Pharisees, and possibly even of being excommunicated, which meant being barred from the temple and the synagogues.

1) Jairus was putting his position as the ruler of the synagogue on the line. He knew his dealings with Jesus could easily have brought the wrath of the scribes and Pharisees down upon Him and that he might be removed as ruler of the synagogue.

2) Jairus must have heard Jesus speak and heal in one of the synagogues, for he was convinced that Jesus could and would heal his daughter. Moreover, Jairus's love for his daughter drives him to Jesus to seek healing for her.

III. It was a supreme act of humility for Jairus to come to Jesus personally and then to throw himself at the feet of Jesus, thus rendering him homage. Any prejudice that Jairus may have had about Jesus because of the Pharisees' position had now gone by the board.

1) When the messengers came to Jairus as he was imploring Jesus, they said, "Your daughter is dead. Why trouble the Teacher any further?" Jesus interjected, "Do not fear, only believe." Jairus

did so, and Jesus went to his house and raised Jairus's daughter from the dead.

2) The despair of the flute players and mourners is placed in sharp contrast to the calm confidence that Jesus exudes. The darkest crisis in life, when met with Our Lord Jesus Christ, can only be met with hope, optimism, and calm, for Our Lord's words to the man and woman of faith are the same as they were for Jairus. For those who possess Jesus, despair is impossible.

IV. In the eyes of the Jewish hierarchy, Jairus made a fool of himself by throwing himself at Jesus' feet, but the ruler of the synagogue cared little for what others were thinking of him. He was determined to implore Jesus for all he was worth.

1) Very often when we make fools of ourselves for the sake of Jesus Christ, the worldly-wise are confounded. By the same token, if we want something strong enough, we soon forget the opinions of others and what they will think of us.

2) To fall victim to human respect or peer pressure is cowardice. It may please human beings, but it will get us nowhere with God. Jairus obviously parted company with his peers, the scribes and Pharisees, in his views about Jesus. What they thought didn't faze him, nor stop him, and he was rewarded for this.

V. The woman who suffered from the hemorrhages had spent her money on doctors and medicine to no avail. Like Jairus, she was desperate, and Jesus was her answer. Such was her faith that she believed that by merely touching His clothing she would get well.

1) Sensing power going out of Him in curing the woman, Jesus turns and asks that the person who touched Him identify herself. Jesus kept looking into the crowd. Realizing that Jesus was looking for her, she, fearful and trembling, came forward and threw herself at His feet, confessing what had happened to her. The crowd recognized the great faith of the woman who bore such confidence in Jesus, believing, as it were, that the mere touching of His garments would suffice to heal her. Jesus publicly praises her faith.

2) Today's Gospel gives us two examples of what faith, persistence, and determination can and will accomplish. Undoubtedly both Jairus and the woman suffering from the hemorrhage went away singing the praises of Jesus and worked for the extension of the Lord's kingdom here on earth.

3) In our own prayers for healing, be it for emotional, physical, psychological, or spiritual healing, may our faith, our determination, and our persistence be strong, and may our motive for seeking healing be that we may better be able to serve God in the extension of His kingdom on earth in our brothers and sisters in the world.

****

1) When we pray for certain favors, that our prayers may always be graced with confidence, determination, and persistence.

2) That we may realize that God at times will try our faith but will reward our perseverance.

3) That we try to be mindful of the needs of others, especially the infirm and the elderly.

4) While waiting for God's response to our prayers for healing, that we may offer up our spiritual, emotional, and physical suffering to God our Father in union with Jesus Christ crucified.

5) For all the sick and elderly of our parish, that they may feel the comfort of their faith by a more palpable sense of the Lord's presence in their hearts.

6) That through the intercession of our Blessed Lady God may increase our faith.

Wednesday of the Fourth Week: Mk. 6:1-6

I. Familiarity breeds contempt, the adage goes. How true it is that the closer we live to a person the less likely we are to see his/her greatness.

II. Jesus' public ministry was no more than three years. The other thirty years were mostly spent in Nazareth as a growing boy and a young carpenter with no academic background. To speak with the authority of a rabbi would at least demand the background and the training of a rabbinical school. Jesus had no such training, and His friends and neighbors knew this.

1) To see Jesus get up in the synagogue that He attended as a youth to comment on the Scriptures as a skilled rabbi was bad enough, but to speak on His own authority with such certitude was too much for them to take. The educated scribes would never do this.

2) These people refused to allow the facts to speak for themselves. Jesus had already worked many miracles in other parts

of Israel, and He worked these on His own authority. In their synagogue, Jesus was speaking clearly, logically, and profoundly on the Scriptures.

3) With their attitude and in their estimation, no matter what Jesus said or marvels He worked, their comment would be, "Isn't this the carpenter?" "Where and how did he come by this knowledge?" "Just who does he think he is?"

III. The Gospel states, "He could do no mighty work there, except that he laid his hands upon a few sick people and healed them. And he marveled because of their unbelief."

1) The people of Nazareth refused to accept this "workingman." Miracles require faith and belief. Jesus then said in summing up, "A prophet is not without honor, except in his own country, and among his own kin, and in his own house."

2) How quickly these people forgot their own history and how God chose humble, insignificant people to do His great deeds, people like David, Gideon, Deborah, Judith, Amos, etc.

IV. Prejudices often blind us or only permit us to see what we want to see, and thus we do not arrive at truth. Ignorance is often closer to the truth than prejudice, because an ignorant person is often more open to see the truth when its light shines on his/her mind. The prejudiced person has pulled the blind down on the window of his/her mind so as to block the light of truth from entering.

1) Prejudice lies in the will of a person and not in his/her mind. It is a situation wherein the person doesn't want to know the truth for fear of the consequences involved in knowing it or the changes that he/she will have to make to adjust to it.

2) Prejudice causes a person to discriminate according to his/her preconceptions. It produces hostilities and brings about a great deal of human suffering. Mahatma Gandhi was interested in the Bible in his student days. He seriously thought about becoming a Christian, because Christianity offered a solution to the caste system that was dividing India. One Sunday he set out to see a minister and to ask for instructions in Christianity. When he entered the church he liked, the ushers refused him a seat, suggesting that he go and worship with his own people. Gandhi left and never went back. "If Christians have their own caste system also," he said to himself, "I might as well remain a Hindu" (Nova).

3) A prejudiced person cannot grow intellectually or spiritually. Prejudice stifles growth because it chokes off the light of truth.

V. We must always try to lift the clouds of prejudices from our minds. It should be a periodic subject of our reflective and meditative prayer, plumbing the depths of our psyche and examining our past to see why we feel the way we do about other people, other races, changes in the Church, or any areas where we have mental blocks, to see if we are too locked into ourselves or are lacking in understanding of them.

VI. The sermons of the greatest Speaker in the world, Our Lord Jesus Christ, fell flat on the ears of many of His listeners because they were not open to truth.

1) The same thing can happen to any speaker; if he/she is not liked, his/her message will fall flat. The same holds for priests and ministers giving sermons. What they say in their sermons may well have merit and value, but the prejudices of the listeners can shut out that good message.

2) Because of the harm prejudices do to us, we must strive to cut them out of our lives, and constantly to work against their creeping into our minds and hearts. They simply prevent us from growing, both in our relationship with God and with our brothers and sisters in the world.

****

1) That we strive to be objective and honest in all our dealings with others.

2) That we may be open to the truth in the many ways and the many disguises in which it may come to us.

3) For a true, honest, and warm dialogue among Christian sects, that all of them strive for unity so that there may be but one flock under the one shepherd, as the Lord desires.

4) That we strive to be open and forgiving toward those to whom we are ill-disposed.

5) That we truly forgive those who have wronged or slighted us.

6) For the success of missionaries working among non-Christians.

7) For an end to unjust racial and sexual discrimination.

Thursday of the Fourth Week: Mk. 6:7-13

I. In the East, hospitality was considered a sacred duty. When a stranger entered a village, it was the duty of the villagers to offer food and lodging to him. Furthermore, a guest was to be protected from danger even at the cost of the life of a member of the host's family. In return, the guest was bound to commit no offense against anyone in the village. Moreover, if the host and the guest were at odds with each other, the acceptance of hospitality involved their mutual reconciliation.

II. Such was the mentality of the Jews toward hospitality that Jesus instructed His disciples that if hospitality was refused to the point that both the homes and the ears of the Jews were closed to them, the disciples were to shake the dust off their feet in testimony against them; the disciples would have fulfilled their responsibility of communicating the good news to them. Shaking the dust off their feet would indicate that they would no longer have such a responsibility toward them.

III. The message they were hearing was one of supreme importance and was to have top priority. Time was not to be lost, for there were many people to be reached. The disciples were not to bog themselves down with provisions. The people were to provide them, since what they were receiving far outweighed any material remuneration; the bearers of such news should at least have their physical needs taken care of.

1) When St. Dominic set out to preach against the Albigensian heresy, he found out that his endeavors were gaining little fruit because the people admired and tended to follow the ascetical heroes of the Albigenses.

2) Understanding that they were neither impressed nor attracted by this Catholic priest who, like so many others, traveled with horses and retinues, stayed in the best inns, and had servants, Dominic changed his tactics. He set out with three Cistercian priests and began an itinerant missionary style along the lines of today's Gospel, going his way with a minimum of physical provisions. He continued his work for ten years with tremendous success. Out of this group of itinerant priests, Dominic founded his famous Order of Preachers and stemmed the tide of the Albigensian heresy.

3) The Apostles were to travel light, and they were to undertake

their mission with a spirit of detachment and a complete dependence on and confidence in the providence of God.

IV. The Apostles were instructed to preach repentance, the same message that Jesus preached at the beginning of His public ministry. Repentance is the one essential condition necessary for God to open to us the treasury of His graces.

1) For St. Paul, repentance is the foundation and the first principle of the doctrine of Our Lord Jesus Christ (cf. Heb. 6:1). It is requisite to any relationship with God. Like baptism, it opens up the soul to the action of the Holy Spirit.

2) A truly contrite person is repentant because he/she has felt keenly that sin is what caused the crucifixion and death of Our Lord and has been the cause of driving God out of his/her life.

V. Thomas Merton wrote, "The lives of the saints who have been truly close to God have taught us that the saints are the ones who more than all others felt in themselves the evil of sin and the need of pardon."

1) In the Roman Synod on Penance and Reconciliation in 1983, it was stated that many people in today's world have lost the notion of sin, failing to recognize it as such, and consequently they see little need of penance or repentance.

2) As long as a person closes his/her eyes to the reality of sin he/she cannot be converted. It is the Holy Spirit who illumines one's conscience so that he/she may recognize sin as such, and thus be moved to repentance and be liberated from all that clouds his/her eyes to sin. More joy is given to God by a sinner who truly repents his/her sins, for it means that a son or daughter is finding his/her way home, welcoming God back into his/her soul.

VI. Sin makes our souls uninhabitable to God where He longs to dwell and communicate with us.

1) St. Paul tells us that we are temples of the Holy Spirit (2 Cor. 6:16). Sin, however, drives God out of the temple of our souls.

2) Sin is to the soul what cancer is to the body. Its object is ultimately to kill the supernatural life of our souls which we received in baptism.

3) If hospitality was such an ingrained duty in Old Testament times, how much more should it be in New Testament times, especially since the guest of our souls is none other than the Triune

God Who wishes to dwell there. Because of this, how much more should we strive to make our souls more hospitable and attractive to the Divine Guest to dwell there. Let us do everything in our power to keep sin out of our lives.

****

1) We are all in need of repentance, a metanoia or continual turning toward God; that we frequently tell God in prayer that we are truly sorry for having offended Him.

2) That we be conscious of our need to make reparation in the form of the corporal works of mercy.

3) That we be generous in almsgiving.

4) That we appreciate the value of the sacrament of penance and use it frequently.

5) That those who have lost the sense of sin may be illumined in mind and heart so as to turn to God with contrite hearts.

6) That we all receive the last sacraments of the Church consciously and fruitfully before death.

Friday of the Fourth Week: Mk. 6:14-29

I. When Herod Antipas heard of Jesus, the first thought that flashed in his mind was that this was none other than John the Baptist come back from the dead to haunt him.

II. It is a popular belief among the Jews that before the coming of the Messiah, Elijah would come again to be His herald and forerunner. Even to this day, when the Passover is celebrated an empty chair is place at table and called the Elijah chair (W. Barclay).

III. John the Baptist was courageous and feared no man when God's cause was in question. He rebuked Herod Antipas for marrying his brother's wife, Herodias; for this John was thrown into prison. Yet with all his indignation, Herod still respected and revered John. That, however, was not the case with Herodias. Humiliated by John's rebuke, she was determined to silence him forever.

IV. Herodias got her opportunity at Herod's birthday banquet. She arranged for her daughter, Salome, to dance before the guests. Herod was so moved by her performance that he swore to give whatever the girl asked for even though it might be half of his kingdom.

1) Such an offer for a thing as transient and superficial as a dancing performance only goes to show the caliber of Herod Antipas. To place such value as half of his kingdom on a dancing performance demonstrates a mind that was indeed shallow and an emotional instability that would allow him to be carried away.

2) Taking counsel with her mother, Herodias, Salome, at her mother's request, asked for the head of John the Baptist.

V. Herod was caught in a bind from which he was not man enough to extricate himself honorably. He worshiped the opinion and esteem of his peers. In short, he was a victim of human respect and would bend principles to avoid the criticism of his peers.

1) Deep down, Herod liked John and respected him, because he knew that John had the qualities he admired but didn't have himself. John was a leader; Herod Antipas was not, for he lacked the courage of his convictions.

2) This is that contradiction that goes on in all of us, the two-way tension of which St. Paul wrote: "For I do not do the good I want, but the evil I do not want is what I do" (Rom. 7:19). We are all attracted to both good and evil, but we must have the courage to make the good prevail.

VI. Herod made a reckless promise, and when the consequence of it came home to him, the embarrassment of it was too much for him to change. Evil would prevail over the good that he knew in his heart and soul he was meant to do.

1) How often we too are caught in the throes of human respect and give way to it because we lack the courage to do the right thing. How much more at peace would our consciences have been had we but been strong enough to have born the price of a little self-effacement.

2) Herodias thought she might free her conscience of this "nuisance" John the Baptist by eliminating him, silencing the one who was not afraid to rebuke her publicly.

3) So, too, many people strive to quell their consciences and harden them by repeated sin, thinking that their conscience will finally stop annoying them, not realizing, of course, that an account must be given to Almighty God somewhere down the road.

VII. John the Baptist lived the truth and died for it. All of us who live the Gospel will inevitably, like John the Baptist, prick the consciences of those who are living loose lives. The most effective evangelization is striving to live the Gospel message in our daily lives. As Mark Twain put it, "There are few things as hard to put up with as the annoyance of good example."

****

1) That God give us the courage to always do the right thing.

2) That God give us the strength not to buckle under peer pressure or bow to human respect.

3) That people holding positions of authority may be faithful to their commitments and not give way to bribes.

4) That the members of our law enforcement community not give in to bribes in the discharge of their duties.

5) That parents have the courage to correct, discipline, and direct their children.

6) That teachers may be an inspiration and an example to their students.

Saturday of the Fourth Week: Mk. 6:30-34

I. So frequently in the Gospels we see Jesus going off to spend time alone with His Heavenly Father. In today's Gospel, Jesus takes His Apostles to a remote, quiet place to pray.

II. No apostolate, however organized, will be effective unless its workers are solidly grounded in prayer. The higher a tree grows, the deeper it must penetrate its root system into the ground. A tree grows upward before it extends an elaborate horizontal branch system. We must anchor ourselves to God in prayer before we can safely move out into an active apostolate.

1) In the apostolate, there must be a balance between prayer and apostolic work. We simply must be plugged into God before we can hope to be successful in bringing His message to the marketplace. By the same token, the more involved we become in apostolic activity, the more firmly rooted we must be in our relationship with God in prayer. Mother Teresa insists that her sisters devote two hours to mental prayer every day.

2) In the '70s we saw the consequences of those who became overly active in inner-city apostolates to the neglect of their prayer

lives. Many of them lost their religious vocations and left to get married.

III. If Our Lord Jesus Christ found it necessary to be apart, alone with His Heavenly Father, how much more should we learn to do the same thing: to go off to a quiet place devoid of all noise and distractions so as to better converse with God and learn also to listen to Him with the ears of our souls. The Lord will not compete with unnecessary noise and distractions.

IV. When Martha complained to Jesus about her sister just sitting at His feet while she busied herself preparing the meal, Jesus responded that Mary had chosen the better part. The Church has always recognized the primacy of contemplatives who dedicate their lives to solitude and prayer over those dedicated to the active ministry.

1) At the canonization ceremony for St. Thérèse of the Child Jesus, Pope Pius XI said that even though she never left her monastery, she was responsible for winning as many souls for God as the great St. Francis Xavier.

2) Arnold Toynbee, the British historian, said that two outstanding people of the nineteenth century were St. Thérèse of the Child Jesus and St. Bernadette of Lourdes, because of the influence they exerted on society for good.

3) St. Francis of Assisi found it a most difficult decision to make whether to have his order completely dedicated to a prayer life as contemplatives or to the active apostolate. After discussing this with St. Clare, he decided to mix the contemplative life with the active apostolate.

4) St. Thomas Aquinas maintained that a balance between the active and contemplative life is the ideal for which to strive.

V. Mahatma Gandhi led a very active life, yet he was a man of eminent prayer. "Ever since my childhood," he said, "prayer has been my solace and strength." In all his disappointments, during periods of utmost darkness, he confessed that it was prayer that saved him and saw him through difficulties and crisis.

VI. Prayer, however, that does not culminate in good works cannot be authentic prayer. We go to prayer for strength, direction, and light. The fruit of a good prayer life does not terminate in oneself. The rhythm of our spiritual lives should alternate meeting with God in solitude and the activity of serving our brothers and sisters in the world in which we live. This is how our service to others becomes a continuation of our formal prayer with God.

1) St. John Vianney said God built us like a cross, the vertical part of us stretches up to adore God in prayer, and the horizontal part of us reaches out to help our brothers and sisters in the world about us.

2) Martha and Mary must be part of all of us: while there must be that fervent contemplative prayer of Mary, it must flow out into the activity of the loving service for Christ in our brothers and sisters.

****

1) That we cultivate a love for solitude, so as to more readily commune with God and prepare ourselves to work in the world.

2) In all serious undertakings, that we always go to God in prayer for light and direction.

3) In the time of crisis, that we learn to have recourse to prayerful reflection on the Gospels.

4) That drug addicts have recourse to frequent prayer and meditative reflection on the Scriptures as their source of strength to stay clear of drugs' influence in their lives.

5) That we strive to prioritize our day, so as to always save some time for God and ourselves to be alone with Him in quiet, meditative prayer.

Monday of the Fifth Week: Mk. 6:53-56

I. Do we all need miracles to believe? Émile Zola, the French novelist of the nineteenth century, was at Lourdes one day. He said even if he saw a miracle, he still would not accept or believe in Christianity. It happened that while he was near the grotto at Lourdes, he witnessed a first-rate miracle of healing happening before his very eyes; nevertheless, he still refused to believe.

II. Because of an illness he was not able to accept, Giovanni Battista Tomasi decided to go to Lourdes to commit suicide as a gesture of rebellion against God in front of the grotto where Our Lady appeared to St. Bernadette Soubirous. When he placed himself in front of the grotto, the Blessed Virgin Mary obtained for him such an interior illumination that he immediately became aware of the value of sufferings and abandoned his plan to commit suicide. He was stricken with repentance.

1) Giovanni Battista Tomasi was so moved that he decided to work among the sick and crippled to help them in their faith by getting them to go to Lourdes.

2) He founded an association which transports poor afflicted people to Lourdes. Today membership in this association numbers in the thousands.

III. To many people throughout history miracles were the only way they would have accepted Jesus Christ as their Lord and God and Savior.

1) St. Augustine said, "I should not be a Christian but for the miracles."

2) St. Paul the Apostle changed from an enemy of Christ to His most zealous Apostle through the miracle of his conversion and conversation with the Risen Christ while on his way to Damascus to bring back to Jerusalem for prosecution those Jews who converted to Christianity.

3) Many people were brought to the faith because of the miracles witnessed at Lourdes. The Lord still uses miracles to bring about conversions to the faith.

IV. Today's Gospel portrays Our Lord as a miracle worker. Anyone who was brought to Him was cured by simply touching His garments.

1) One of the signs of the authenticity of the Messiah and of the establishment of God's kingdom on earth was given by Isaiah: "Then the eyes of the blind shall be opened, and the ears of the deaf unstopped; then shall the lame man leap like a hart, and the tongue of the dumb sing for joy" (Is. 35:5-6).

2) When John the Baptist was in prison, he sent his disciples to Jesus to find out if Jesus really was the Messiah, since the style of Jesus' ministry and apostolate was quite different from John's. Jesus' approach of meekness and gentleness puzzled John and his disciples. When John's disciples asked Jesus if He was "he who is to come," meaning the Messiah, Jesus does not give them a "yes" or "no" answer. He simply cites the prophesy of Isaiah concerning the Messiah: "Go and tell John what you have seen and heard: the blind receive their sight, the lame walk, lepers are cleansed, and the deaf

hear, the dead are raised up, and the poor have the good news preached to them" (Lk. 7:22). These were the very signs and miracles that Jesus was working, all of which point to faith in Jesus but never compel one to believe in Him. Jesus is merely saying to John's disciples, "Consider the evidence."

3) Miracles are for many people like beacons which lead them to the port where the Light itself has its origin. This is abundantly evident, especially in the shrines dedicated to the Blessed Virgin Mary. Many of them are loaded with the testimony of gratitude to Almighty God for these miracles by the abundance of crutches and articles which identify their infirmities left as a testimony to miraculous cures obtained at these shrines.

V. In one of the churches in Paris, people beheld Our Lord present visibly in the sacred host in the form of a little child. Many people witnessed this. Someone ran to King St. Louis' private chapel, where he was assisting at Mass, to inform him of the miracle. The saintly king responded, "Our Lord is present here in this chapel as truly as He is there. Such miracles are for the benefit of unbelievers. Let those go to see it who do not believe. For me, faith is enough. I prefer to believe in Our Lord's real presence simply because He has said that He would remain present in the Eucharist."

****

1) That God bestow upon us the gift of a deep faith.

2) That we pray with a lively confidence and persistence to our Heavenly Father, always prevailing on His goodness and generosity.

3) That we also be mindful that the Lord wants us to ask for our needs but at the same time to give Him what He wants — our love, our devotion, and our fidelity.

4) For all the sick and the incapacitated, that they may see the apostolic value in their suffering united with Jesus Christ crucified.

5) For an increase in devotion to the Blessed Virgin Mary.

6) That we try to visit Our Lord Jesus Christ more often, truly present in the tabernacle.

Tuesday of the Fifth Week: Mk. 7:1-13

I. Isaiah describes true religion as breaking unjust fetters, letting the oppressed go free, breaking every yoke, sharing your bread with

64

the hungry, giving shelter to the homeless, clothing the naked, and not turning your back on your neighbor (Is. 58:6).

1) What a difference there is between Isaiah's idea of religion and that of the scribes and Pharisees. The scribes' and Pharisees' interpretation of religion was fidelity to the external observances of numerous rules and regulations.

2) For the scribes and Pharisees, a man might be full of hate, envy, and bitterness, but if he observed the regulations prescribed regarding ritualistic washings, he was to be commended and considered a good man.

II. Isaiah accused the people of his day of honoring God with their lips only, while their hearts were far from Him. For the scribes and Pharisees, religion was legalism; that is, observance of external rules and regulations.

1) Originally, for the Jewish people, the Law consisted of the Ten Commandments and the ordinances of the Pentateuch, the first five books of the Bible, whose authorship was ascribed to Moses. These two sources were the guiding principles from which Jewish morality, behavior, and worship were deduced.

2) Some four or five centuries before the coming of Christ, the scribes, a class of legal "experts," came on the scene, and throughout the centuries they continued to expand and add numerous rules and regulations to the moral system handed on to them by Moses.

3) The scribes became the guardians of the "traditions of the elders." Their interpretations of the Pentateuch as it related to moral behavior became a series of regulations known as the "Oral Law."

4) It was quite a while after Jesus' death (c. A.D. 200) that these oral traditions and interpretations were finally written down and came to be called the Mishnah. The Mishnah is part of the Talmud, a collection of Jewish rabbinical literature. The Talmud is the basis of religious authority for traditional Judaism today.

III. To the scribes and Pharisees, the rules and regulations of the Oral Law were the essence of religion. To observe these was the primary way to please God. To fail to keep them was evil.

1) The scribes succeeded in producing a legalistic religion: the attendance to external observance of these rules was taken to be more desirable than the pure intention of pleasing God and serving one's neighbor, which is the fundamental end of the whole law.

2) Our Lord Jesus Christ frequently condemned this externalistic attitude and pharisaical mode of behavior. Very often those who meticulously kept these regulations had their hearts full of envy, hate, and bitterness; yet they would pass themselves off as justified because they kept the external appearances of observing the law.

3) In short, this sort of thing bred hypocrisy, which is nothing more than dishonesty and deceit, which does nothing but drive honest people away from formal religion. Jesus reserved His bitterest criticisms for the scribes and Pharisees for fomenting and nurturing this sort of religion.

IV. In today's Gospel, Jesus thoroughly and roundly condemns such hypocrisy and dishonesty. Our exterior actions must reflect the sincerity of our hearts. The virtues of religion and simplicity demand this honesty.

1) How often do we do things or observe external regulations just to be seen by or to win the applause of others?

2) Do we perform acts of charity to win approval or praise? Or do we do them out of a sincere desire to please God and a genuine concern for our neighbor?

3) For any of our actions to be pleasing to God, they must flow from a sincere heart. Sincerity is the first requirement of the virtue of religion; without it, religion is hypocrisy. May the Lord free us from all hypocrisy and bestow upon us all the genuine virtue of religion which is so acceptable and pleasing to Almighty God.

****

1) That God give us the gift of simplicity, prudence, and sincerity in all of our dealings with others.

2) That the Lord bestow upon us the gift of the virtue of religion.

3) That husbands and wives love each other out of sincere and generous motives, having each other's true good at heart, namely, their sanctification and salvation.

4) That in all our work and recreation, we strive to please and glorify God, making them a continuation of our prayer.

5) That the foundation of all our devotions and religious observances be true love of God and of our brothers and sisters in the world.

6) That we may always be honest and responsible in our dealings with others.

Wednesday of the Fifth Week: Mk. 7:14-23

I. Jesus is telling the scribes, Pharisees, and assembled listeners that it is not what goes into the mouth that makes a person unclean. Rather, it is what springs from the heart that makes a person unclean.

II. In one sweeping statement Jesus abolishes the Jewish dietary laws regarding animals listed in the book of Leviticus as being unclean.

1) The full implication of this would only be realized when the young Church would have to deal with whether or not the Gentile converts would have to observe the Jewish dietary regulations.

2) What God has created is all clean. It is not the handling or consumption of these things that make people unclean. Rather, it is the evil actions that spring from and are consented to in a person's heart that make such a one unclean.

III. Jesus makes it clear that the essence of religion must be in the human heart, in true and sincere conversion to God, and in the reverence, respect, and kindness shown to one's neighbor.

1) This must be the basic condition also for genuine worship of God in religious ceremonies. Our Lord would later say, "If you are offering your gift at the altar . . . first be reconciled to your brother. . ." (Mt. 5:23).

2) Jesus is saying in effect that all religion must be essentially an honest expression of sincere love of God and neighbor. The institution of the Eucharist would be an outward sign of union with God and with one's brothers and sisters who would accept and believe in Our Lord Jesus Christ as Redeemer and Son of God.

IV. When we look at the Old Testament, we see it as being a prolonged contest between God and the Jewish people over their faithfulness or insincerity, their fidelity to Yahweh or their lack of it. When we examine the parables of Our Lord, nearly every one of them deals with sincerity or the lack of it. At the bottom of the practice of religion must be sincerity and fidelity. These are the building stones of religion.

V. In His sweeping statement, Jesus declares the whole body of Jewish regulations regarding clean and unclean as irrelevant to religion.

1) Jesus goes right to the heart for the source of uncleanness. The

heart is where all evil actions are formulated and the font from which they flow.

2) Evil designs — fornication, adultery, theft, murder, envy, slander, deceit, pride, etc. — do not issue from outside the person but from the inner recesses of the mind and heart.

3) Temptations can and do arise outside a person, but as such they are indifferent until knowing and willing consent is given to them. Such consent can only come from the human will. As Shakespeare wrote, " 'Tis one thing to be tempted . . . / Another thing to fall."

4) For this reason Our Lord cautions us to pray always without ceasing lest we fall victim to the many temptations that arise from the devil, the world, and our own passions. The ultimate cause of sin, however, must be ourselves, for those evil thoughts, words, and deeds we knowing and willingly consented to.

5) In the final analysis, it is basically from the interior free will of the person that evils must flow, and it is only there that true conversion and a real turning to God can take place. True religion, then, must flow from the heart.

VI. Sincerity comes from the Latin *sine*, meaning "without," and *cera*, meaning "wax." In the Greco-Roman world, businessmen sometimes would have damaged works of art repaired with wax, and touched up to be sold as if undamaged.

1) When it was proved that a given work was "sincere," that is, without wax, its value was accepted as genuine and authentic. Hence to be sincere was to be "without wax," that is, genuine and authentic.

2) When it comes down to it, the underlying theme of the Bible might be said to be sincerity or its counterpart hypocrisy or insincerity. To be sincere and true to the Gospel's message is the Christian's basic goal and challenge.

3) Grantland Rice, the famous syndicated sports writer, wrote, "When the One Great Scorer comes to write against your name, He marks — not that you won or lost — but how you played the game." How sincerely you played the game, that is.

****

1) That we may be men and women of prayer, aware of the fact that we are weak and subject to temptations.

2) That God deliver us from hypocrisy and all forms of duplicity.

3) That we develop a warm relationship with our guardian angels and beg them to alert us to the presence of evil and/or of the devil.

4) That we have frequent recourse to the sacrament of confession as a means of growing in God's grace and of withstanding temptations.

5) That sincerity be at the bottom of our acts of religion.

6) That God fill us with the desire to commune with Him each day.

7) That we have immediate recourse to the Blessed Virgin Mary for help in the time of temptation.

Thursday of the Fifth Week: Mk. 7:24-30

I. The scene of today's Gospel finds Jesus in Gentile territory. Tyre and Sidon were cities of Phoenicia. Today they would be part of Lebanon. Tyre lay some forty miles northwest of Capernaum. It served as a great seaport city from early times.

1) Jesus is confronted by a Gentile woman whose petition He finally granted after she confidently persisted.

2) Through this miracle, Jesus shows that He is Savior not only of the Jews, but also of the Gentiles. His Gospel is for all mankind.

II. The woman had been following Jesus and crying out so much that the Apostles asked the Lord to send her away because she was an embarrassment to them (Mt. 15:23).

1) Jesus engages her in conversation, letting her know that He was sent to the House of Israel and that it was not right to throw bread meant for the children to the dogs.

2) The word "dog" was often used by the Jews as an expression of contempt for the Gentiles. In that day, the Jewish people felt that salvation was meant exclusively for them, because they were of the bloodline of Abraham, Isaac, and Jacob.

III. Could Jesus be guilty of insulting this woman? Did He really call her a dog? Jesus did not use the usual word for street dog. He used the affectionate term that applied to house or lap dogs, "kunaria" (*A Catholic Commentary on Holy Scripture*). The woman manifested her alertness and capitalized on the tender diminutive employed by Jesus for the word "dog." She responded quickly, much to the admiration of Jesus, Who saw in her quick and intelligent reply a deep faith, "Yes, Lord; yet even the dogs under the table eat the children's crumbs."

IV. The woman recognized what Jesus meant by its not being right to take the children's food and give it to the family pet. She realized that the Messiah was to come first to the Jewish people. She also felt, however, that the pups — that is, the Gentiles — also have a right to the food of the kingdom, and that the Messiah was not to be the exclusive property of the Jews.

V. Jesus was heartened and gladdened by the woman's response, since it showed a uniquely strong faith.

1) This Gentile woman's faith stands in stark contrast to the insipid legalism of the scribes and Pharisees.

2) She symbolically represents a Gentile world which was ready to hear the message of Jesus and to receive His Bread of life which the Jews refused to accept or believe.

VI. The Syro-Phoenician woman's persistence and faith wring words of praise from Jesus. He responds by healing her daughter. The woman's faith is further heightened by the fact that her daughter was not present for Jesus to lay His hands on her to heal her. The woman believed, like the centurion, that it was not necessary for Jesus to actually go to where the sick lay, that it was sufficient for Him just to say the word.

1) This Gentile woman had, to a remarkable degree, the true qualities of prayer of petition: humility, for she recognized her place; faith, as she believed unswervingly in Jesus; and persistence, since she would keep at Jesus until He responded to her petition.

2) These qualities should accompany our prayers also. How many people have "given up" because they either felt God was not listening to them or because they have not received an immediate response and therefore think that God will not grant their petition.

3) As is evidenced in today's Gospel, God will try our sincerity, our faith, and our confidence. He has told us, "Whatever you ask in prayer, believe that you receive it, and you will" (Mk. 11:24).

4) It is a law of nature that we patiently persist in developing our talents; otherwise they will not be brought to any degree of perfection, nor generate the fruit they should. That we persist is the will of God, and this is especially manifest and evident in regard to prayer.

****

1) That the Lord give us a strong and vibrant faith in prayer.

2) That we realize the importance of humility in our lives and in our prayers by acknowledging that we are sinners in need of God's help and protection, and that we preface all our petitions with an act of contrition for our sins.

3) That we persevere and persist in our prayers, knowing that if it is a good thing that we are asking for, the Lord will grant it.

4) That we may be quick to render thanks to Almighty God for favors received.

5) That we go frequently to Mary to implore her intercession.

6) For all those who are people experiencing doubts in their faith or who have lost their faith.

Friday of the Fifth Week: Mk. 7:31-37

I. Jesus, still in Gentile territory, works yet another miracle: giving hearing to a deaf man and also curing the man's speech impediment. We notice that Jesus takes the man aside and goes through a ritual which the Church uses in the ceremony of baptism. When he baptizes, the priest touches the ears of the infant, as it were to open them to be receptive in hearing the word of God.

1) Jesus' gestures, putting His fingers into the man's ears and touching his tongue, are "sacramental": they are signs that symbolize what actually happens. "*Ephphata*, be opened," and the man's hearing was restored, his tongue loosed so that he could speak freely.

2) Some Scripture scholars think that Jesus' actions — taking the deaf-mute aside, spitting, touching the man's ears and tongue — were all done to arouse the faith in the man which would be needed for Jesus to work the miracle (*A Catholic Commentary on Holy Scripture*). Such miracles Jesus already did by a mere word, but in this case He labored ostensibly to arouse a stronger faith in this man.

3) The response of the crowd was immediate: "He has done all things well; he even makes the deaf hear and the dumb speak." This is a clear allusion to Isaiah's description of the Messianic age, wherein the deaf would hear and the dumb speak (Is. 35:5-6).

II. Not only are the deaf man's ears open to listen to the word of God, but his tongue is loosed to respond to God's goodness by praising Him and in carrying the good news to others.

1) So much in today's Gospel relates to what takes place in baptism, showing us that we are not only to be hearers of the word of God but we must become its proclaimers.

2) Baptism not only makes us members of God's kingdom, because it literally plugs us into the life of God, thus causing God's life to flow into us, but it commissions us to be missionaries as well.

III. Today's Gospel is not only good advice; it is good news. Our ears and tongues were loosened in baptism, and we received courage to proclaim our faith in the sacrament of confirmation; yet why do so many Christians have so little to say in a indifferent and secularistic world that so sorely needs the light of the Gospel?

1) So many Christians remain like deaf-mutes in the modern world. It is because, even though their ears were opened in baptism, they never filled them with the Gospel message, nor do they reflectively meditate on the little they have taken in. Their faith is weak and ill-informed.

2) Courage to profess their faith was indeed given in confirmation, but the fear of proclaiming the Gospel arises from their culpable and woeful lack of knowledge of it. So many Christians are guilty of spiritual lassitude or torpor, and so they continue in ignorance of their faith.

3) For many Christians the Gospel goes in their ears but not into their hearts. It is like the seed that falls on rocky or thorny soil: they let the cares and concerns of the world and business interests choke it off. The word of God just never grows sufficiently in them to bear fruit because of their lack of input. Their contribution to the spread of Christianity is nil.

IV. It is one thing to hear the good news, and another to respond to it. Both take effort, interest, and attention. God has sown the seed of faith in baptism; we must collaborate to make it grow. The Gospels are a gold mine of information and knowledge about Our Lord Jesus Christ. We must drink them in by reading, reflecting, and meditating on them. In this way, they become a vital part of us, and fill us with zeal.

1) "If any one thirst," said Our Divine Lord, "let him come to me and drink. . . . 'Out of his heart shall flow rivers of living water' " (Jn. 7:37-38). We can grow as much as we want to in our faith if we

dispose ourselves as the farmer disposes the soil to receive the seed. The challenge is that we must do our part, then God will do the rest.

2) Fulfilling our missionary obligation that comes from baptism is a natural desire for men and women of faith. Appreciating the good news, they will naturally want to spread it.

****

1) That we eagerly listen to the word of God and reflect upon it.

2) That we strive to particularize the Gospel message and apply it to ourselves.

3) That we eagerly proclaim the good news by our generous and compassionate actions towards others.

4) That the Lord fill us with a deep and lively faith and a zeal for souls.

5) That the ecumenical movement bring about unity in Christendom.

6) That all preachers of the word of God take their work seriously by preparing and reflecting on what they proclaim.

7) For peace in the world and an end to terrorism.

Saturday of the Fifth Week: Mk. 8:1-10

I. Today's Gospel makes it abundantly evident that Jesus' concern is not only with men's souls but with their bodily well-being as well. When Jesus' eyes fell upon human misery or need, there was an immediate response of compassion. Here people have been following Jesus enthusiastically for three days. Most of them used up what little provisions they had with them.

II. It is so true that the soul is least likely to listen when its companion, the body, is suffering from or experiencing hunger.

1) When a human being is worried about his/her daily survival or the survival of his/her family, concern for getting food, clothing, and lodging becomes an all-consuming preoccupation, and such a person becomes little disposed to listen to or benefit from the Gospel.

2) When William Booth, the founder of the Salvation Army and a popular London Evangelist, was criticized for spending more time getting food, clothes, and lodging for the impoverished people of London than in preaching the Gospel, he answered, "Before I can

preach the Gospel to the hungry, they must be fed; otherwise they will not be disposed to listen."

III. Viewing the situation, Jesus asks His Apostles about their own provisions, "How many loaves have you?" "Seven," they replied. Jesus knew before asking His Apostles that they surely did not have sufficient food with them to feed some four thousand people.

1) Jesus asked His Apostles this question to put them on notice that they had an obligation to do their part, however small it might be, and then God would do the rest.

2) St. Augustine sums up this so poignantly when he put it: "Without God we cannot; without us God will not." A similar proverb that we all learned when we were children has it: "God helps those who help themselves." In short, God wants us to do our part always, because we are all members of His Mystical Body and have an obligation to help our brothers and sisters in need.

3) Even though we are but mortal human beings, God deigns to use us as His instruments in bringing the good news to others as well as manifesting His compassion to those in need through us, the members of His Church.

IV. We are all called upon to act like Good Samaritans and not pass human misery coldly by. It is not enough to express sympathy for those in misery; God calls upon us to give a hand to alleviate that misery, and then He will extend His Hand. God never works miracles until all human resources have been exhausted. So often people criticize God for allowing so many people to starve in Third-World countries. The question should be put to them as well as to ourselves: "What are you doing personally to help alleviate that need?"

1) We live in an age when people are afraid of getting involved. There have been murders and assaults committed before the eyes of bystanders who refused to lend a helping hand, not even by at least calling the police.

2) Minnesota enacted legislation in the early 1980s which would hold witnesses to crimes liable to some legal recriminations if they do not offer help to the victim of a crime, at least by calling the police. This is a case where the state legislated a law of human compassion.

V. Seeing the compassion of Almighty God expressed in His Son, Our Lord Jesus Christ, can we ever doubt that God's Providence is watching over us every day of our lives?

1) It is good and beneficial to recall from time to time all the wonderful things God has blessed us with, not only in the material and physical spheres, but in the spiritual sphere as well. Above all, we should give God, our Father, special acts of gratitude for sending us His own divine Son, Jesus, to be our Savior and Brother and to make our eternal happiness secure.

2) We should make it a practice to thank God for such things as our faith, our health, our families, our daily bread, etc. By frequently expressing our gratitude, we dispose the Lord to be generous to us in our time of need.

****

1) In our seeing the compassion of Our Lord Jesus Christ, that God may drive out of our hearts all coldness and indifference toward others, especially the less fortunate in our community.

2) That we maybe generous to the poor.

3) That we frequently reflect upon the things God has given us and be effusive in expressing our gratitude to Him.

4) That our government respond to the hungry in our own country and in the Third World.

5) The multiplication of the loaves is also a symbol of the Eucharist, the Body of Christ, which is multiplied daily the world over; may we strive to prepare for our reception of the Eucharist in the Masses we attend.

Monday of the Sixth Week: Mk. 8:11-13

I. Isaiah had already given the signs of the Messianic presence: "Then the eyes of the blind shall be opened, the ears of the deaf unstopped; then shall the lame man leap like a hart, and the tongue of the dumb sing for joy" (Is. 35:5-6).

1) In Jesus, these miracles were multiplied many times over. What more could the Pharisees want? They were looking for some magical wonder that would have no immediate usefulness other than to satisfy their curiosity and pride. It is improbable that they would

have accepted Jesus as the Messiah even if Jesus had performed some magical feat.

2) Their own prejudices had already fabricated the kind of Messiah that would be acceptable to them. Such a Messiah would have to be completely different from the humble and meek Jesus who stood before them with His simple band of uneducated fishermen.

3) For the Pharisees, Jesus was not sophisticated enough, not political enough, not the one who was to be their military leader. He was not the one that they expected would come to free Israel from the Roman occupation and make Israel the most powerful and prestigious and wealthy nation in the world.

II. Needing signs is an indication of a lack of faith. What Jesus was saying and doing should have moved any honest and sincere person.

1) Pride and arrogance prevented the Pharisees from seeing and hearing, as Isaiah had foretold: "Hear and hear, but do not understand; see and see, but do not perceive" (Is. 6:9). They had closed their minds to the objective truth before them.

2) To accept Jesus — that is, to receive the gift of faith — childlike openness and simplicity were required. They lacked such requirements. Miracles or no miracles, Jesus was unacceptable to them, and that was it. They would concentrate now on getting rid of Him.

3) According to St. Bernard, wisdom (faith) comes to those who acknowledge their sins and praise God for His goodness and mercy. The proud Pharisees were not about to acknowledge their sinfulness.

III. Pride and arrogance blinded the Pharisees and continues to blind many people in the world today. Sensuality and a love for material things will also blind people spiritually.

1) To many people, Jesus is a very compassionate and lovable Person, but His message is too difficult. Many people accept Jesus, but on their own terms; that is, they water down the message of His Gospel. "There is nothing wrong with Christianity," said G.K. Chesterton; "it is that many people find its message too difficult." "It is not that Christianity has been tried and found wanting," said Chesterton, "It has been found difficult and left untried." We should

frequently ask ourselves: "Do I accept Jesus on His terms or on my own?

2) It is true that the Gospel of Our Lord Jesus Christ is difficult for those who seek the sensual and self-gratifying pleasures of a hedonistic secular world. The cross of Our Lord will continue to be a stumbling block to such people.

3) As with the Pharisees, the miracle they need is something that will bring them to see the emptiness and meaninglessness of the lives they are pursuing.

IV. The world about us is full of signs of God's presence, His love, and His omnipotence. God is always faithful. To seek signs from Him is insulting and indicates a lack of faith. God is present to us as an ocean surrounding a boat. The sheer power of His presence sustains us and the universe in existence.

1) Human beings frequently seek signs from others: lovers want signs of love like affection or the giving of gifts. We look for signs in nature for possible storms or earthquakes, and this is logical, for we simply cannot intuit these dangers.

2) With God we have the manifest sign of His goodness and mercy as is evidenced in the life of Our Lord Jesus Christ, God incarnate. In Him, the only acceptable attitude is our faith and confidence in His goodness and providence. Signs of His goodness and providence abound in nature; we are literally surrounded by them.

3) The Bible gives us all we need to know about God. There will be no more formal revelation. What God has left us in sacred Scripture is more than enough for us to really come to know and love and establish an intimate relationship with Him.

****

1) That we may be more responsive to the universe about us and use its wonders to make us mindful of the presence of God and thus frequently praise Him and thank Him for all He has done for us.

2) That God increase our faith and strengthen all those whose faith is weak.

3) That all members of our families persevere in the faith.

4) That the Lord give us a love for sacred Scripture, and that we

use the Bible daily to increase our knowledge of God so as to be motivated more to love Him.

5) For an increase in vocations to the priesthood and religious life.

6) For peace in the world, especially in the Middle East and in Latin America.

7) That people be more ecologically sensitive to the world we live in.

Tuesday of the Sixth Week: Mk. 8:14-21

I. Our first reaction to today's Gospel might be, "How imperceptive the Apostles were!" They had by now seen so many miracles and heard Jesus speak on many topics; yet their minds still seemed moored to mundane things and to physical rather than spiritual needs.

1) Their preoccupation was for their provisions. Upon boarding the boat, they observed that they had only one loaf of bread, certainly not enough for all aboard.

2) In spite of the fact that Jesus tries to raise the level of their conversation, they still persist with their immediate physical need until Jesus has them recall the fact that they witnessed two miracles involving the multiplication of bread for thousands of people.

3) They fail to see that the Bread of Life is in their very midst, and that with Him they lack nothing whatsoever.

II. Jesus is in so many words telling them, "Your first concern and preoccupation should always be the message of the Gospel and the food necessary for your souls." When Jesus questions them about the two miraculous multiplications of the loaves, they still fail to see His real message.

III. Many people fail to capture God's message because they listen with ulterior motives and interpret it for their personal interest or for physical and mundane needs.

1) When Elisha the prophet told Naaman the leper, general of the army of the king of Syria, to wash seven times in the Jordan river to be cured of his leprosy, Naaman scoffed at such a message. Why should he wash in a little river like the Jordan when he had the Abana and the Pharpar rivers in his own country which were better and much more prestigious than the Jordan. Fortunately, his servants

convinced him to do as Elisha instructed; he did so and was cured (2 K. 5).

2) When the rich young man came to Jesus to ask Him what further things he might do to earn eternal life, Jesus told him to give his possessions to the poor and join His band of disciples. The young man could not "see" the why of this; he wanted Jesus to have said something more to his liking. He could not see because he was too attached to material possessions. He consequently lost a golden opportunity. How differently history would have remembered him if he had said yes.

IV. How true it is, we choose to hear what we want to hear and pretty much shut out the rest or what is uncomfortable for us to hear. Because of this, much truth is lost to us.

1) When Jesus asked His Apostles, "Who do you say that I am?" Peter responded for the rest and told Jesus that He was the Messiah, the Son of the living God (cf. Mt. 16:13-16). Then Jesus told His Apostles that He was going to be delivered over to the elders, scribes, and chief priests and be put to death. Peter did not want to hear that message, and Our Lord chastised him for this saying to Peter, "Get behind me, Satan! For you are not on the side of God, but of men" (Mt. 16:23).

2) Whether we want to hear or not, God's message will never be tailored for our individual tastes or personal convenience, for only truth will set us free and make us really grow, even though the truth is painful to take.

3) God's message can only be heard by sincere, humble, disinterested, and detached people. Our motive in listening to the word of God should be not "What do I want to hear?" but "What is God really trying to tell us?"

4) Abraham Lincoln said, "I am not bound to win, but I am bound to be true. I am not bound to succeed, but I am bound to live up to what light I have. I must stand with anybody that stands right: stand with him while he is right and part with him when he is wrong" (*Treasury of the Art of Living*).

5) Jesus tells us, "Strive to enter by the narrow door," referring to the hardships involved in carrying out the teachings of the Gospel. Even though part of the Gospel message may be difficult for us, our consolation should be: Nothing is impossible with God, for He never

lets us go things alone. He is always there to help us shoulder the burden.

6) Let our disposition always be: "Lord, speak, for Your servant is listening."

****

1) That we may always be preoccupied with trying to discern what God's will is for us.

2) When listening to sermons, that we not let the speaker's appearance or personality deter us from listening to what God wants us to hear.

3) That the Lord bless us with sincerity and openness.

4) Before reading sacred Scripture, that we pray that the Holy Spirit will inspire us to capture God's message for us.

5) That we always keep our priorities straight and seek first the kingdom of God.

6) That the Lord deliver us from all pride and self-deception.

Wednesday of the Sixth Week: Mk. 8:22-26

I. A tree planted near a river's edge will never dry up for lack of moisture; neither will it overdrink from its abundant source of water. Its root system will take in what it needs. Jesus is that abundant source who will give to those in spiritual and physical straits what they need and in proportion to that need. He would not work miracles needlessly.

II. Most of Jesus' miracles were instantaneous, but in the case of this blind man this was not so. Neither was it so in the case of the deaf-mute, whose cure was narrated by St. Mark in the previous chapter.

1) Perhaps an instantaneous miracle done for this man would have been quickly forgotten, ill-appreciated, or would have made little impression on the man's faith status.

2) Jesus takes the blind man aside, outside the village, as if to perform this miracle in secrecy. This is another instance of Mark's interweaving thesis of the "Messianic secret" in his Gospel: Jesus is slow to reveal His identity because the people were not ready for it yet; so Jesus repeatedly cautions the people who receive miraculous

80

healing from Him to keep the miracle secret. He does not want the people to seek to make Him king.

3) Jesus wanted His miracles to deepen the faith of these people, especially the people who witnessed them. Jesus performs this miracle in stages. Some hold that the degree of healing corresponded to the stages of the blind man's faith.

4) Quite likely Our Lord also took the man apart from the crowd with just His disciples present to teach them a lesson. They were to learn that spiritual enlightenment is usually a gradual process. This was certainly so with the disciples, and so it will be for all of us (*A Catholic Commentary on Holy Scripture*).

III. The blind man is a typical case of an open person collaborating with the grace of God to grow in faith. Jesus first placed spittle on the man's eyes, a standard procedure among doctors of the East in Jesus' day. "Do you see anything?" Jesus asks. "I see men; but they look like trees." This indicates that the man at one time did have sight. The conversation heightens the man's belief in Jesus. Then Jesus lays hands on the man's eyes, and his vision is perfectly restored.

IV. Over and over again in the Gospels Jesus remarked that faith in Him allows God's wonders to take place in one's heart.

1) The deepest healing we all need is the healing of our relationship with God, and this only grows in proportion to the intensity of our faith.

2) Just as Jesus took the blind man outside the village, away from the noise and distraction of the crowds, so too we must come away from the noise and distraction of the world in which we live to spend time alone with Our Lord, who eagerly awaits us in the interior of our souls. Only by this private interpersonal conversation with this Divine Guest of our souls can we hope to put ourselves into that state wherein we become disposed to receive an increase of faith and knowledge. It is there, in the inner core of our souls where our Divine Guest and Spouse of our souls touches us to open the eyes of our hearts, that we may see clearer and clearer with each divine visit and touch. Only in this way will our relationship with God take on more and more meaning and grow.

V. When we come apart from the noise and bustle of the world and fix our minds and hearts on Jesus, we become like the tree planted near the river's edge, drawing the waters of divine grace as we need them, taking what we need in proportion to our need in our spiritual growth process.

1) We will never exhaust that river of grace, no matter how much we may drink. Neither will God permit us to drink more than we are disposed to receive, for He will not permit His grace to be wasted.

2) We must go to Jesus to have our own spiritual blindness and ignorance healed. In order to do this, He will take us out of the town as He did with the blind man, to get us away from distractions, so that we can concentrate on Him and on what He is saying. This can only be done in the solitude required of true mental prayer. There in the interior of our souls, Jesus will reveal Himself little by little, not instantaneously, but slowly in a stage-by-stage growth process.

****

1) That we may be generous to God with our time, carefully setting time aside to be alone with Him each day.

2) That the Lord heal us of our own spiritual blindness, thus enabling us to improve our relationship with Him.

3) That we may possess a growing hunger to hear the word of God and to reflect on it.

4) For an increase of vocations to the priesthood and religious life.

5) For all those who are experiencing serious doubts or a crisis in faith.

Thursday of the Sixth Week: Mk. 8:27-33

I. There are sixteen chapters in St. Mark's Gospel; here in the eighth chapter — that is, halfway through Mark's Gospel — Jesus is well into His public ministry. Here Jesus questions His own Apostles about His identity. Jesus wants to see "where His Apostles are at" and how much they have really grasped of His identity and mission.

1) If the truths that Jesus came to reveal and teach were going over the heads of the Apostles, how much more so would this be for the people?

2) For them to have heard and seen so much thus far and not to have grasped who He really was and what He was about would be disheartening to Jesus.

II. Jesus was quite aware of the prevalent notion in the Jewish mentality of what the Messiah would be like. The common notion was that the Messiah would be a great military leader who would smash his enemies into extinction and make Israel the most powerful and prestigious nation on earth. He would free Israel from its Roman oppressors and keep it free forever. Israel would become the center of the world.

III. With such notions even in the minds of the Apostles, Jesus wanted to see if they really accepted Him and what He was trying to impress of His real identity and mission on their minds: namely, the suffering servant predicted by Isaiah, who would take away the sins of the world through His suffering and death (cf. Is. 53:1-6).

IV. Turning toward His Apostles, Jesus directs the question to them: "But who do you say that I am?" A solemn moment of silence reigns, and then Peter steps forth as the spokesman for the rest, "You are the Christ, the Son of the living God." In St. Matthew's account Jesus responds to Peter's answer, "Blessed are you, Simon Bar-Jona! For flesh and blood has not revealed this to you, but my Father who is in heaven" (Mt. 16:17). Peter had this knowledge by divine illumination and infusion.

V. What a relief and joy this must have given to Jesus to see that His Apostles were finally coming around to seeing Him for who He really was. Still, Jesus had to keep repeating that hard lesson which they did not want to hear: "That he must go to Jerusalem and suffer many things from the elders and chief priests and scribes, and be killed, and on the third day be raised."

1) In spite of Isaiah's suffering-servant Messiah prophesy, the Jews and even the Lord's Apostles did not want to accept the notion of a suffering Messiah. They would not let that register on their minds. Jesus was going to establish His kingdom, and they wanted to be important officials in it.

2) Jesus had to now prepare His Apostles for the climax of his Messianic mission — the redemption of fallen humanity through the crucifixion. What a difficult task indeed.

VI. Like the Apostles, we all have our own image of Christ. One common error is to choose those elements and characteristics of the life and work of Our Lord Jesus Christ which are attractive to us and relegate to the background other aspects of His life and teaching which are less attractive or perhaps might even be painful to us.

1) We all love the image of the Jesus who goes out as the Good Shepherd in search of the stray sheep; similarly, we love the image of the Jesus who weeps at the grave of Lazarus or who consoles the widow of Nain. The Jesus, however, who tells us that we must love our enemies, that we must turn the other cheek or go the extra mile or forgive seventy times seven times, or that we will perish unless we do penance, that we must take up our cross daily and follow Him — this is the Jesus who is hard to accept, whom we tend to gloss over.

2) We must accept the whole Jesus together with His doctrine if we expect to have part with Him. We must take care not to get an isolated image of Christ as someone apart, since He identifies Himself with His Mystical Body, His Church, and when we touch others we touch Him. Our image of Our Lord Jesus Christ and our relationship to Him must be integrated with our brothers and sisters in the world in which we live.

****

1) That we never be detoured by the false ideals of this world which are a variance with those of Our Lord Jesus Christ.

2) That God give us, as He gave His Apostles, the gift of wisdom, so we may see and understand the truths of our faith, and bear witness to them in our daily lives.

3) That we may come to see Jesus in all our brothers and sisters, and see that what we do to them touches Jesus Himself.

4) That we always keep the image of Jesus Christ in a prominent place in our homes.

5) That all people may come to see that Jesus is Messiah, Lord, and Savior.

6) That we do all we can to spread the good news of the Gospel to others.

Friday of the Sixth Week: Mk. 8:34-9:1

I. From the standpoint of Jesus' human nature, there can be no doubt that the suffering involved with His forthcoming agony and death made Him apprehensive. It looked dismal and horrendous, but Jesus was absolutely sure it was the only way to final victory. In His divine nature He knew that this was the decree of the Blessed Trinity which He, as the second Person of the Trinity, shared in a very intimate and integral way.

II. It is the daily lesson of experience that tells us that the great things even in this life will cost us.

1) A young person realizes that a profession like medicine, law, or engineering can give one a comfortable living; nevertheless, he/she also recognizes that getting there will indeed take time and involve much sacrifice and work.

2) Victory, Churchill told his war-weary people, would come only through blood, sweat, and tears.

III. So much of this evident wisdom is envisioned in Jesus' statement: "Whoever would save his life will lose it; and whoever loses his life for my sake and the gospel's will save it."

1) The world will not remember the people who conserved their lives by taking all kinds of security measures and thus advance to a great old age because of their wise protective precautions, prudent exercise, and good nutrition.

2) The world will, however, remember the people who lost their lives spending them for the benefit of their brothers and sisters. People like Father Damien, Tom Dooley, Dorothy Day, Albert Schweitzer, Florence Nightingale, Maximilian Kolbe, and Mother Teresa are venerated because they gave of themselves for the benefit of others.

3) We naturally honor people who risked their lives to save others: firemen who brave raging flames to rescue people, soldiers who dodge bullets to save wounded buddies, and people who go to the aid of victims of violent crimes — all of these kinds of people we naturally esteem and admire.

4) What woman does not risk her own life in bringing a child into this world? This is one of the reasons we all honor our mothers.

5) A person may elect to take a job that will bring him/her more money and comfort instead of one that would pay less but be of much more service to one's brothers and sisters in the world; yet the position that places one in the service of others is more meritorious in God's eyes.

IV. "What does it profit a man if he gains the whole world and loses or forfeits himself?" (Lk. 9:25).

1) Jesus is asking: "Where are your values really at?" "Where are your priorities?" Gaining eternal life must be our top priority.

Common sense should dictate this. Yet how easy it is to become blinded to our sublime end by being swallowed up in the attractions of this passing world and the seductions of the devil.

2) Carrying out the principles of the Gospel may not bring you fame or material fortune. On the contrary, it may well make you the butt of criticism and the object of persecution; yet in the long run, you will be the ultimate winner.

3) The praise and applause of men and women is short and empty, whereas the esteem of God is everlasting.

4) Cardinal Wolsey summed it up so well on his deathbed: "Would that I had served my God as well as my king."

5) Let our criterion of values and judgments be by the light of eternity and not that of time.

V. Our Lord Jesus Christ assures us that if we are ashamed to carry out His Gospel or to be identified with Him, He will be ashamed of us when we stand in judgment. Christianity may well cost us, but its rewards are immensely more enriching than the cost. God never asks us to go things alone, much less difficult things. He will share in our trials and our victories.

****

1) That the Lord give us the courage and strength to live up to our faith in this difficult secular and materialistic world.

2) That we always make our criteria of evaluation those principles coming from light of the Gospels instead of those from the world.

3) That we be generous and daring with our time, talents, and resources in the works of charity.

4) For all of those who are weak in their faith and who are apt to give in to the opinions of their peers rather than follow the light of the Gospels and the principles of their faith.

5) That we espouse good causes even though they are unpopular and may bring about criticism and even persecution by our peers.

6) That we respond generously to those who call upon us in the time of crisis or need.

Saturday of the Sixth Week: Mk. 9:2-13

I. In today's Gospel, we see something of the drama of the

passion, death, and resurrection of Our Lord Jesus Christ. In the previous chapter, Jesus had cautioned His Apostles about his forthcoming sufferings, death, and resurrection. In today's narration, chapter nine, St. Mark gives an the account of the transfiguration or manifestation of the divinity of Jesus. Jesus is balancing the scandal of the cross with the glory of His transfiguration. It is as if Jesus is preparing His Apostles for the shattering experience of His crucifixion by giving them a clean and convincing impression of His divinity plus the corroboration of His heavenly Father's statement: "This is my beloved Son; listen to him."

II. In the transfiguration scene, Moses and Elijah are seen talking with Jesus. Elijah had a unique place in Jewish biblical history. He was supposed to return immediately before the appearance of the Messiah. He was to cleanse and prepare Israel for the coming of the Anointed One.

III. The Apostles were slow learners. Even though Peter answered Our Lord's previous question about His identity, the Apostles still clung to the common Jewish idea of what the Messiah would be like — one full of might and power, like a military hero, a new David.

1) When Jesus asked His Apostles, "Who do you say that I am?" Peter answered, "You are the Christ. . ." (Mk. 8:29). The Lord commended Peter, and then followed up by saying that the Son of Man was to suffer, be delivered over to His enemies, be put to death, and then after three days rise again (Mk. 8:31).

2) Such a prediction clashed in their minds and was a complete contradiction of the Apostles' idea of the Messiah.

3) Peter answered correctly that Jesus was the Messiah, and to bolster that conviction, Jesus takes Peter, James, and John to Mt. Tabor and there reveals His glory and divinity to them. There too Moses, the giver of the Law, and Elijah, the greatest of the Old Testament prophets, appear with Jesus, bearing testimony to Him and to His mission.

IV. Coming down from the mountain, Jesus again refers to His death and resurrection. He is slowly impressing upon the minds of His Apostles the inevitability and necessity of His crucifixion.

1) To the question about Elijah coming before the Messiah, Jesus answered, "Elijah has come and men treated him as they willed."

Jesus was referring to John the Baptist, who was an Elijah figure. What the Jews did to Elijah in the person of John the Baptist, they would also do to Jesus, and subsequently to the Apostles themselves.

2) This too would be the lot of the Apostles and all faithful followers of Jesus. When truth confronts error and deceit, there will always be a clash. Devout Christians will inevitably clash with those who prefer the darkness of sin.

V. The glory of the Transfiguration is darkened by the reality of the Cross. This message, the doctrine of the Cross, the Apostles did not want to hear about. They wanted things as they would like them to be. They wanted Jesus to go on doing the wonders He was doing and to establish His kingdom wherein they might share in its grandeur and glory and enjoy the popularity and acclaim of the people.

1) How true this is with most of us. We refuse to see things as God does; we continually try to see them the way we want them to be.

2) We know Christ is God, and that the glory of the Transfiguration is the reality of heaven; nevertheless, it is difficult to accept that the cross of Jesus Christ must be a vital part of our lives in whatever form God permits it to come, be it sickness, emotional problems, family difficulties, death of a loved one, loss of employment, setbacks in business, criticism, or even the treason of friends.

3) It is through the cross of Jesus Christ that we come to see the glory of the risen Lord. If we refuse the crosses of life, they will come anyway, and we will gain no merit from them, but if we embrace them with love, they become easy and a source of merit and happiness, for the Lord's yoke is sweet and His burden is light. Simon of Cyrene did not want to help Christ carry His Cross, but once he was put to it no one could take it from him. It changed his life. So it will be for us who learn to shoulder the crosses of life with loving resignation. It will change our lives and become the cause of our happiness, peace, and joy.

****

1) That we learn to accept things as God has ordained them for us.

2) For an increase in the virtue of faith and the gift of charity.

3) For all those who are suffering from physical and emotional trials.

4) For parents who have to deal with drug addiction among their children.

5) That all the members of our families persevere in the faith.

Monday of the Seventh Week: Mk. 9:14-29

I. "This kind cannot be driven out by anything but prayer and fasting." Earlier in Mark's Gospel, we are told that Jesus gave power to His Apostles to cast our demons. Here, later on in his Gospel, we see the Apostles powerless to cast out the devil possessing the boy in today's narration.

1) We might therefore logically ask, "What happened to this power given to the Apostles?" The power had obviously become ineffective because they had become careless in their prayer lives.

2) Like neophytes, they became overzealous and presumptuous. They were like children with new toys, caught up with enthusiasm, and were not maturing in the power the Lord had given to them; nor had they given sufficient heed to the instructions that Jesus had given them in applying this power over demons.

3) Something of this happened to many priests and sisters after the Second Vatican Council. They had become caught up with a new wave of enthusiasm for working in the inner cities, of identifying more and more with the poor and marginated. In their enthusiastic involvement, they had forgotten to nurture and nourish their own prayer lives. The unction of religious life and of the priesthood had dried up for want of a prayerful relationship with God. As a consequence, many of them left their God-given vocations to become laicized.

II. How quickly we can lose our perspective. How easily the powers, talents, and charisms that God has given to us become so many tools we use to advance our own personal cause and to enhance our own image.

1) Prayer will give us the wisdom and balance and zeal to enable us to use the gifts God has given us for His honor and glory rather than our own.

2) Spiritual gifts and charisms are delicate blessings, which of

their very nature are given for God's glory and for the sanctification of our own souls and those of our brothers and sisters in the world.

3) The gifts of healing, tongues, prophecy, discerning spirits, interpretation of tongues, clairvoyance, miracles, administration, leadership, etc., are all God-given to build up the body of Christ, the Church, and not to build up our own image or ego. They can easily be abused unless we keep close to God in our prayer lives, for then the Spirit will guide and inspire us as to when, where, and how we are to use our God-given gifts. If we do not have a meditative and prayerful contact with God, we will quickly fall victim to our own pride and perhaps even lose these gifts.

4) Constant communion with God will give the prudence necessary to sharpen and bring these gifts to the maturity God wills them to have within those upon whom He deigns to confer them to build up His Body the Church.

III. Jesus observed the weak faith of the boy's father as being insufficient to obtain the favor he was requesting, so He challenges the man's faith by saying, "If you can! All things are possible to him who believes." The man responds by confessing his weak faith: "I believe; help my unbelief!" With that, Jesus works the miracle of casting out the devil from the boy.

1) Many miracles are worked through prayer — that is, prayer made in deep faith and confidence. Conversely, many potential miracles are not worked because of a lack of faith, confidence, and persistence.

2) The lesson here is that faith is a gift, and like all other gifts it intensifies or diminishes through our prayer lives and desire for union with God. We have but to ask and the Lord will increase our faith, but we must take care to ask with persistence and earnestness.

****

1) That we frequently ask God to increase our faith.

2) That we may be filled with the spirit of optimism and confidence in our prayers, believing that we will receive what we petition for.

3) That we examine our own gifts and talents in prayer and beg God for light to see our gifts and to use them well.

4) That we have the humility to acknowledge that gifts are not

90

acquired but are generously given to us by God, and that we never act as if we obtained them on our own.

5) That, whatever gifts we have, we use them for God's honor and glory and for the sanctification of our own soul and that of our neighbor.

6) For all Christians of little or no faith, that God invigorate and quicken their faith.

Tuesday of the Seventh Week: Mk. 9:30-37

I. "If any one would be first, he must be last of all and servant of all." The Lord demands humility of all of His followers. It is a necessary foundation for learning the spiritual life and for building any meaningful relationship with God. Jesus has said, "Learn from me; for I am gentle and lowly in heart. . ." (Mt. 11:29).

II. Humility brings light, knowledge, and truth; it is not a sanctimoniousness, nor is it a denial of the good qualities and talents we possess. It is rather a frank evaluation of ourselves and a recognition of the good qualities we possess together with the gifts and talents God has given to us. It is a recognition of such gifts and talents as God-given and not as acquired by our own efforts.

III. While recognizing our good qualities, gifts, and talents, humility also forces us to recognize our evil propensities and shortcomings. In seeing the talents and gifts of others, humility makes us see our own spiritual, intellectual, artistic, and social limitations. Yet while recognizing such limitations, humility aids and prevents us from being envious of others because of the endowments they possess.

IV. God is truth, and humility is walking in truth. The devil is the master of deceit and revels in falsehoods and deceptions. Humility put him to flight. The humility involved in confessing one's sins pains and infuriates him. He does his utmost to keep people away from the sacrament of penance and reconciliation.

1) The higher the tree grows, the deeper the roots that must penetrate into the ground to sustain it in its upright position. The same holds in the spiritual life: the higher the spiritual edifice, the deeper into the depths of humility one must plummet.

2) St. Teresa of Jesus said that the most perfect gift one could ask of God in the spiritual life is the gift of humility. Asked by a religious one day what it was he considered the most important

91

virtue in religious life, St. Francis de Sales answered unequivocally by writing in large letters on the blackboard: H-U-M-I-L-I-T-Y.

V. The virtue of humility abounded in Our Lord Jesus Christ. He, being the Son of God, was born in a stable. He lived an obscure life for thirty years. He selected uneducated fishermen to build His Church. He sought to serve the poor and afflicted, sinners, rejects, and lepers. When He worked miracles, He frequently demanded silence. He fled from the crowds when they wanted to make Him king. He washed the feet of His Apostles. He insisted that He came into this world to serve and not to be served. He was rejected, treated worse than Barabbas, a murderer. He was mocked, scourged, and crucified. Indeed, the road Jesus traveled in His life on earth was studded with humiliations.

VI. The life of Jesus was one continual act of humility. "Learn from me; for I am gentle and lowly in heart."

1) Jesus tells us if we wish to be first we must learn to be the last and the servant of all. This was the very lesson He gave and experienced. After washing the feet of His Apostles, Jesus said to them, "You call me Teacher and Lord; and you are right, for so I am. If I then, your Lord and Teacher, have washed your feet, you also ought to wash one another's feet. For I have given you an example, that you also should do as I have done to you. Truly, truly, I say to you, a servant is not greater than his master" (Jn. 13:13-16).

2) When we look at the really great figures of history, we must conclude that they were men and women who served rather than being served. By the time Albert Schweitzer was thirty years old, he was regarded as an intellectual in Europe, an outstanding theologian, and a leading authority on Johann Sebastian Bach. He wanted to serve. He spent the next seven years studying medicine, and after graduation he left for Africa to serve one of the most backward tribes of all of Africa. He spent the rest of his life serving the lowly of this world.

3) It is in serving others that we serve Christ Himself, and we humble ourselves when we serve others who are not as well off as we are or who hold less prestigious positions than we do. In the final analysis, it is Christ we serve when we serve others.

****

1) That the Lord bless us with the virtue of humility.

2) That we anticipate the needs of others, serving them warmly and cheerfully.

3) That the Lord permit us to see ourselves as He sees us.

4) In our confession of sins in the sacrament of Penance and Reconciliation, that we not seek to excuse ourselves or rationalize our sins.

5) When we are criticized, that we do not snap back, but rather accept it as a salutary humiliation and penance.

6) That we never think that we are better than others just because God has given us more talent than they have.

Wednesday of the Seventh Week: Mk. 9:38-40

I. The thrust of the Second Vatican Council was Christian unity: that all Christians might be one under one shepherd, as Christ wanted it. As a consequence of the Vatican Council's drive toward Christian unity, a new and optimistic sense of tolerance was engendered, and a great respect for individual consciences.

II. St. Augustine once said, "Where there is certainty, there is obligation; where there is doubt, let liberty obtain; but in all things let charity reign."

1) The great scandal in Christianity is the many sects claiming Jesus Christ as their savior. Their beliefs, liturgy, and discipline differ. The Christian flock is scattered, and there are too many shepherds. This same Jesus Christ, whom so many of these Christian sects claim to be their Lord and Savior, clearly indicated that He wanted one flock and one shepherd (Jn. 10:16).

2) All Christians must be true to the mandate of the Savior in this matter and honestly strive for Christian unity. Leaders of the many Christian sects have a special obligation in promoting Christian unity.

III. If unity is to be achieved among the many Christian sects, tolerance, understanding, and patience must reign in discussions and dealings with our separated brethren.

1) There will be beliefs and tenets with which one may not agree; nevertheless, one must respect the right of another to hold such beliefs and tenets when they honestly believe them to be true.

2) Tolerance is of its very nature unbiased, but it does demand honesty, openness, reverence for individuals and for truth. It does not

respect deceit or prejudice. Tolerance is based on love, compassion, and concern for each individual's right to search for truth.

IV. No one individual or community has a monopoly on truth. Truth is like a diamond: it has many facets for reflecting veracity, just as a diamond reflects new dimensions of its beauty when it is viewed from different angles. The wholeness of its beauty is not seen straightaway. We often do not see the wholeness of a given truth; rather, we see facets of it.

1) As Catholics, we believe that the Holy Spirit will guide the magisterium of the Church, and particularly the Holy Father, from leading the Church into error in the areas of faith and morals. Christ did not give the Church a monopoly on truth. The Church as a living body is always learning as she courses the corridors of time and is constantly confronted with new knowledge. The Holy Spirit, however, will protect His Church from error and enlighten its supreme pastor in the areas of faith and morals for the sake of the sanctification and salvation of souls.

2) Truth is one, but, alas, like a diamond it has many facets and angles to it. One can never have it totally in one's grasp. To believe so is to cease to learn.

3) In the area of faith, one must believe that he/she has the maximum of truth possible in his/her creed or body of belief, because one's salvation will depend on one's sincere pursuit of truth in those vital areas of faith and morals.

4) In the final analysis, we will be judged on our consciences, consciences that we have striven to enlighten with the light of truth as we honestly strive to see and embrace it.

V. In 1949, Pope Pius XII corrected the narrow notion that salvation was impossible outside the Catholic Church. He said, in effect, that for those who honestly and sincerely believe, in good faith, what they hold to be the truth and follow their consciences in their conduct and moral behavior, they will be saved (Denzinger, 3871).

1) One's conscientious convictions are the important thing, and these must always be respected, for conscience is a sanctuary where God meets His sons and daughters in their daily lives. The obligation, however, to seek truth and to enlighten conscience always obtains.

2) The basis for tolerance must be charity: love of God and love of neighbor, together with a realization of the magnitude of truth. An honest, upright person's conscience will bear testimony to his/her life and conduct.

3) Miguel de Cervantes lived during the period of the Spanish Inquisition; yet he wrote, "Many are the roads by which God carries His own to heaven."

****

1) That we may all hunger for truth so that our consciences may be ever more enlightened and informed.

2) That we strive to appreciate where the other person is coming from.

3) That the Lord deliver us from arrogance when we express our views.

4) That we strive to bury all grudges and vindictiveness.

5) That the Lord bless us with patience and empathy in dealing with people holding divergent views.

6) That we treat all people, regardless of their beliefs, with warmth and kindness.

7) Through the intercession of Mary, the Mother of the Church and the Mother of all Christians, that all her sons and daughters might be brought into one flock under one shepherd.

Thursday of the Seventh Week: Mk. 9:41-50

I. "If your hand causes you to sin, cut it off. . . ." In the Near East, it was common for people to use exaggerated speech to make their point or to make an impression on others. This is precisely the idiomatic tool Jesus used to impress upon His listeners the absolute necessity of avoiding evil in all its forms. Sin is a spiritual cancer that consumes and destroys.

II. In Muslim countries, punishments are designed to meet a physical identification with the crime committed. Serious thefts are punished by cutting of the culprits' hands. The person is thus stigmatized as being a thief.

III. What Jesus is saying through the use of hyperbole is, "Your goal is heaven, and it is worth all the sacrifices necessary to attain it." Sin and the proximate occasions of sin seriously jeopardize one's eternal salvation.

1) Hell is for keeps; there is no second chance. It is final, and it is forever. No sacrifice or suffering, however intense, can possibly come near to eternal separation from God. What separates us from God is serious sin.

2) Physical evils and illnesses are indeed sad. No one wants to see another consigned to a wheelchair for the rest of his/her life. Even though a given affliction might last a lifetime, such a duration is nothing in comparison to eternity. Physical evils can only have temporal repercussions. Spiritual evils have eternal consequences.

3) At Fátima, the Blessed Virgin Mary gave the children a vision of hell. A beam of light proceeded from her hand and penetrated into the earth. The children saw what looked like a vast sea of fire, in which were plunged, all blackened and burnt, demons and souls in human form. The heat of the flames raised them into the air as if without weight, and they would fall back in all directions, like sparks, into a huge fire, amid loud cries and horrible groans of pain and despair. This caused the children to shudder and tremble with fear. The scene lasted but a moment. The horror of it was such that the children said that they would have died if they were to behold it much longer.

4) To lose a hand or a foot is nothing in comparison to the horror of eternal damnation. Just as it is necessary to amputate a finger or a toe in order to save a hand or a foot, so too, sinful attachments and habits are cancers that must be cut off, whether they be people, places, or things. They threaten the life of God within the soul. Sin drives God out and places a soul in jeopardy of being eternally lost.

IV. Jesus speaks of salt and the need of keeping it in our hearts. Salt has two basic powers: it imparts savor to food, and in Our Lord's day it was used as a preservative for foods.

1) Jesus is saying that His followers must be like salt to lift up their environment, to season it with the savor of faith and virtue.

2) Evidence from studies taken in the United States indicate that the un-Christian lifestyles of many Christians constitute for the unchurched the chief obstacle to hearing and responding to the word of God.

3) The Gospel indicates that God will be very hard on those who

are saltless and give scandal by their bad example. Deeds are more powerful than words. The example of devout Christians was often the cause of the conversion of faithless and indifferent people. St. Augustine admitted that he owed his conversion more to the example of St. Ambrose than to his arguments.

4) Frederic Ozanam, the founder of the St. Vincent de Paul Society, had serious doubts about his faith as a youth. It was rekindled when he noticed the great physicist and pioneer of electricity André-Marie Ampère praying his rosary with intense devotion in a church in Paris.

5) Tertullian, one of the early writers of the Church, said that he and most of the converts of his day were converted to Christ not by books and sermons, but by observing how Christians lived and died.

****

1) That we be conscious of the environment in which we live and work, and of the effect we have on others by our example.

2) That parents may be aware of how their behavior and attitude affect their children.

3) That people in positions of authority give an example of fidelity in their commitment to their work.

4) That teachers inspire their students with Christian ideals.

5) That those who have compromised themselves for money or vain pleasures realize that they have betrayed God and themselves and come to detest such actions and behavior.

6) That we all strive to make reparation for our bad example.

Friday of the Seventh Week: Mk. 10:1-12

I. The sacrament of matrimony begins when a couple stands in the sight of God and declares: "We take each other until death do we part."

1) This obviously doesn't mean that at this solemn juncture their relationship has just begun. Surely this love began months and perhaps years before.

2) The sacrament of matrimony proclaims and blesses this relationship. In this sacrament, one's marriage becomes formally rooted in Christ, and He commits Himself to it in a similar way that He commits Himself to His bride, the Church.

3) The husband and wife become a sacrament, that is, a formal sign to the community that indicates a deep commitment and bond to each other, a commitment and bond that symbolizes and externalizes the union of Jesus Christ with His bride, the Church.

II. Through this sacrament a young couple really says, "I give myself totally to you to share in the pleasures, joys, and sorrows of our lives together. Whatever our lot, I pledge to mingle my life intimately with yours, to live, to love, to share, and to help each other grow and mature together" (John Thomas, S.J., *Beginning Your Marriage*).

1) On their wedding day, the couple professes before the altar of God to live out that glorious objective of pouring out their lives for each other in order to possess them in a more enriched way. In this way, they become the sacrament of matrimony for each other, a sacrament that is so intimately based on the love relationship that exists between Christ and His bride, the Church. It is a love that expresses itself in giving, sharing, enduring, a love that is totally based on self-sacrifice, of which Christ is the exemplary Model.

2) Marriage is a sacrament of self-giving; for this reason St. Paul likens the relationship between the spouses to the sacrificial love of Christ for His Church (Eph. 5:23-27). It is through this mystery of the sacrificial giving of spouses to each other that they will experience their own sanctification. This sacrificial love becomes a purification of their own souls as they go hand in hand through the trials and difficulties of wedded life together.

3) These trials become so many purifications that are, no doubt, analogous to the purifications or dark nights of soul that contemplative souls experience on their journey toward perfect union with God. The proper end and goal of the sacrament of matrimony is the mutual sanctification of the spouses. St. Paul alludes to this in his discourse on marriage in his letter to the Ephesians when he writes, "Husbands, love your wives, as Christ loved the church and gave himself up for her, that he might sanctify her, having cleansed her by the washing of water with the word, that he might present the Church to himself in splendor, without spot or wrinkle or any such thing, that she might be holy and without blemish" (Eph. 5:25-27).

4) This sacrament of matrimony is designed to generate the helps and graces the spouses will need as they go through life together.

The burdens and difficulties that crop up in married life are lightened because they are split in half when such trials are shouldered together.

III. In today's Gospel, Jesus moves to correct a deteriorating situation that existed in His day: the frequency and ease of obtaining a divorce. The ease with which the marriage bond was broken was due to a liberal interpretation of chapter twenty-four of the book of Deuteronomy. Jesus quotes this Mosaic regulation and gives the reason why Moses made this exception for permitting divorce, i.e., because of the hardness of heart of the people. Jesus immediately adds that this was not at all in the divine plan for matrimony, which He reiterated was a permanent and sacred bond that was unbreakable from the beginning.

IV. Jesus further sanctifies marriage by making it a sacrament that becomes a three-way commitment: between God, the husband, and the wife.

****

1) That married couples realize that God is committed to their marriage and will help them to overcome all their difficulties.

2) That couples divest themselves of selfishness and really try to look to the other's good and happiness.

3) That couples pray together and reflect on the Scriptures for inspiration and guidance in their marriage.

4) In the area of limiting the number of children, that couples not resort to artificial contraception, vasectomies or other bodily mutilations, but rather generously undertake a natural method of family planning.

5) That married couples be open and honestly communicate with each other about all aspects of their married lives.

6) That God bestow peace and tranquillity on all married couples.

Saturday of the Seventh Week: Mk. 10:13-16

I. Charles Dickens wrote of children, "I love these little people, and it is not a slight thing when they, who are so fresh from God, love us."

1) Perhaps what makes a child so attractive is the beauty of its innocence, its openness, its trust and complete lack of sophistication

or pretentiousness, its unashamed dependence on parents and elders, and its unbounded sense of wonder and fantasy.

2) They have these qualities because they are fresh from the hand of God. These are qualities we all admire. Why do we lose them as we grow from childhood to adulthood and into old age? Much of the answer must come from the evil to which we are inevitably exposed, which we all come to call the "realities of life."

3) Yet the Lord tells us that these are the qualities necessary for entering into the kingdom of heaven. If children have them because they are fresh from the hand of God, getting close to God will undoubtedly restore them. This is done through grace and the sanctification of the soul.

II. Perhaps it is because a child doesn't know evil that it is slow to impute evil to a cunning adult. Yet the child has an uncanny way of sensing the presence of evil.

1) When a child shies away or runs away from an adult, it often indicates that there is a certain harshness, meanness, impatience, or intolerance in that adult; or the child intuits that that particular adult doesn't like children.

2) On the other hand, a child has a guileless and overwhelming confidence in the adults he/she loves. This is particularly so of parents. They feel that their parents can literally do anything. This is obviously the type of confidence God wants us to have in Him when we pray.

III. The simplicity of a child has a power to touch and move hearts, even hard hearts. Father Raymond, the Trappist monk and spiritual writer, narrates an account of a six-year old child about to undergo an operation to remove her tonsils. The surgeon told the little girl that he was going to help her to go to sleep for a while. Whereupon the child knelt on the operating table, and in all simplicity said, "If I am going to go to sleep, I must first say my night prayers." She proceeded to say them vocally. This touched the surgeon deeply. He had ceased practicing his faith. The little's girl's innocence and simplicity moved the doctor to put God back into his life.

IV. "Whoever does not receive the kingdom of God as a little child will not enter into it." We cannot return to our mother's womb, but we can be reborn in the Holy Spirit to be imbued with the virtues which children possess.

1) Unless we receive the message of God as conveyed to us in the Gospels with the openness, simplicity, confidence, and wonder of a child, it will never really become a vital part of us, and thus we will not be able to enter into the kingdom of heaven.

2) We simply have to take the Gospel to heart as a little child is accustomed to do with parents when they speak seriously to him/her. Our openness to God's message coming to us through the words of Our Lord Jesus Christ in the Gospels must be total and not eclectic — not picking and choosing those parts and passages that are agreeable to us.

V. Children do not harbor grudges. They are quick to forget past offenses committed against them. To enjoy any meaningful relationship with God, we too, like children, must forget our grudges.

1) Our Lord tells us that we must generously forgive those who have offended us. The Lord's Prayer lays this down as a fundamental requirement for forgiveness of our sins and constructing a relationship with God, our brothers, and our sisters.

2) Children are the precious examples of those who are most acceptable to their Heavenly Father. We must put on their virtues to get close to God, and thus to obtain the eternal crown won for us by Our Lord and Savior Jesus Christ, the Lover of little ones.

****

1) That God give us the simplicity and openness of children.

2) That we go to God our Father with a childlike trust and confidence when we pray.

3) Like children, that we do not harbor grudges or hatred.

4) That we strive to give some of our time to children when opportunity arises to serve these little people fresh from the hand of God.

5) That parents especially teach their children to pray and not give them bad example.

6) That parents dutifully raise their children in the faith and engender in their hearts a filial devotion to their heavenly mother, the Blessed Virgin Mary, and to their guardian angels.

101

Monday of the Eighth Week: Mk. 10:17-27

I. If Christians really practiced Christianity there would be no need of preaching it. "It is not that Christianity has been tried and found wanting," said G.K. Chesterton; "it has been found difficult and therefore not tried."

II. The rich young man admired Jesus. He was so enthusiastic about Him that when he saw Jesus he ran up to Him and threw himself at His feet.

1) The Jewish people of that time believed that wealth was a sign of God's favor on a person who possessed it, and undoubtedly this young man thought that God's favor was on him. The young man certainly was faithful in keeping God's commandments. For this reason Jesus admired him and offered him a place among His Apostles.

2) His goodness, however, did not go very deep. It was the goodness of respectability; that is, he hurt no one, was just in his dealings with others, and yet was not apt to go too far out of his way to attend someone in need. There is no doubt that he was very attached to his wealth. Jesus looked at him with love because of the young man's fidelity.

3) Jesus responds to his natural goodness and, looking at him, invites him to greater sanctity. He challenges him to perfection and urges him to do something much more positive and electrifying, to go beyond the Ten Commandments, to give his wealth to the poor and to follow Him. Jesus is urging him to practice the evangelical counsels.

III. How much did that young man really want Jesus and the message that He was preaching? Was he willing to detach himself from his wealth, or was he too attached to his wealth? Money has a tendency to corrupt those who have large amounts of it. This prompted Jesus to say: "How hard it will be for those who have riches to enter into the kingdom of God!"

IV. Today's world places a high value on wealth, worldly careers, and pleasures. The communications media constantly drum this message to millions every day, and like the rich young man who was given a vocation, many young people find it very hard to sever themselves from the world and its goods to follow Christ in a call to the priesthood or the religious life. As a result, the Church is hurting from a lack of vocations to serve the people.

1) Jesus is not condemning wealth, but He sees how susceptible people are to letting themselves become enslaved to it and blinded by it.

2) The worldly-wise may know the value of material things but fail to see their true value in their relationship to eternity. Only a healthy detachment and a spirit of poverty will engender the wisdom that will allow us to see these things as God sees them.

3) It is the rare person who has such largess and detachment that they will enable him/her to tower above his/her wealth and make that wealth his/her servant.

V. The young man went away sad, as many do today in the face of a call from Jesus to follow Him as a disciple in a vocation to the priesthood or religious life, precisely because of their attachment to the goods of this world. Much of the blame for this can be laid at the feet of the media for brainwashing young people to this hedonistic philosophy since they were toddlers.

1) Deprogramming them will be a difficult catechetical task, but the word of God and His grace have the power to disabuse them of the illusions created by wealth, material things, and ephemeral pleasures.

2) Our Lord Jesus Christ gives us the most effective tool in getting young people to say "yes" to a vocation to the priesthood or religious life: "Pray . . . the Lord of the harvest to send out laborers into his harvest" (Mt. 9:38). The sheer force of the many fervent prayers of the faithful, together with sacrifices and sufferings born graciously and generously and other voluntary penances, will win the graces necessary to overcome the strident and deceptive voices of today's secular, raucous, and materialistic world.

3) Parents have a special edge in disposing their children to be open to a vocation to the priesthood or religious life. From their children's early years, parents must supervise their children's access to television. They should read to them and get them to read passages of sacred Scripture and lives of the saints to engender in them an idealism that will make them more disposed and open to say "yes" to God's call to His service.

****

1) That the Lord deliver us from avarice.

2) That we remember that our eternal bank account will depend not on what we amass here on earth, but on what we have given to others in need.

3) That young men and women will reject worldly attractions and respond to the call of the Good Shepherd to serve Him in the priesthood or religious life.

4) That God bless us with a poverty of spirit and a healthy detachment from material things and pleasures.

5) That parents instill in their children a high esteem and regard for a priestly or religious vocation.

6) That we be generous with our time and talent in serving our brothers and sisters in the community.

7) For all of those who are suffering from the throes of poverty and hunger, that their wants be responded to by their more affluent brothers and sisters.

Tuesday of the Eighth Week: Mk. 10:28-31

I. One cannot help but reflect on how pragmatically worldly-minded the Apostles were at this stage in Our Lord's ministry. They were looking to cut out their portions of this new kingdom Jesus was talking about establishing.

1) Their ambitions were worldly, and their interest was fixed on some sort of remuneration measured by prestige and possessions.

2) Jesus still had a way to go in setting their priorities straight. It would be a while before the Apostles would grasp the notion of a spiritual kingdom on earth.

II. Indeed there would be remuneration in this world, and it would be a hundredfold. These would be the priceless gifts and fruits of the Holy Spirit, like wisdom, understanding, counsel, charity, peace, joy, prudence, mildness, patience, benignity, etc.

1) But with the giving of these gifts comes an admixture of the cross, as Our Lord stated: "Truly, I say to you, there is no one who has left house or brothers or sisters or mother or father or children or lands, for my sake and for the gospel, who will not receive a hundredfold now in this time, houses and brothers and sisters and

mothers and children and lands, with persecutions, and in the age to come eternal life" (Mk. 10:29-30).

2) Amid all those rewards enumerated, Our Lord adds, "with persecutions." This is precisely because this, too, mystically speaking, is also a reward, for through it the soul is purified and is drawn closer to God; there is nothing more rewarding on this earth than a close and intimate relationship with Our Lord Jesus Christ. There can be no merit or growth without sharing in the cross of Our Lord Jesus, and this was the message that was difficult for the worldly-minded Apostles to learn. They had yet to become detached from this world with its attractions of wealth, pleasures, and prestige.

3) Jesus' invitation to follow Him is indeed attractive and adventurous, but not easy, for He Himself calls the road to salvation the "narrow" way (cf. Mt. 7:14, Lk. 13;24).

III. When we look at the myriad examples of those whose goals were completely worldly — so many examples of actors and actresses, Hollywood stars who were in and out of three or four marriages, who literally consumed their lives in high and fast living — we can't help but conclude that their lives were indeed worldly and spiritually empty. It is certainly not the way to prepare to leave this world.

1) On the other side of the spectrum, we see those who have given up their lives for others and who have in so doing carved unforgettable images on our memories.

2) Tom Dooley voluntarily spent his life and talent as a doctor for the poor in Vietnam and Laos. He once wrote: "Inside and outside the wind blows . . . but there are times when the storm around me doesn't matter . . . a wider storm of peace gathers in my heart. What seems unpossessable I possess. . . ."

3) Mother Teresa generously follows the Lord and spends herself on people this world rejects. What peace and joy it gives her! She experiences the hundredfold reward in this life for her generosity.

4) Abraham Lincoln wrote: "I desire to so conduct the affairs of this administration that if, at the end, when I come to lay down the reins of power, I have lost every other friend on earth, I shall at least have one friend left, and that Friend will be down inside of me."

IV. St. Paul sums up the value of material things in his letter to the Philippians: "But whatever gain I had, I counted as loss for the sake of Christ. Indeed I count everything as loss because of the surpassing worth of knowing Christ Jesus my Lord" (Phil. 3:7-8). He rated material possessions as "loss for the sake of Christ" precisely because they tend to bog one down on one's way to union with God.

1) God's gift of wisdom enables us to grasp the things of time in the light of eternity.

2) Jesus tells us that following Him will indeed cost us, but He will not be outdone in generosity even in this life. His hundredfold is not an exaggeration.

****

1) That the Lord bestow upon us His gift of wisdom, which will enable us to evaluate things in the light of eternity and not of time.

2) That we may be generous and responsive to the graces and inspirations of the Holy Spirit acting within us.

3) That we become sensitive to the needs of people in our community and offer our time as the need arises.

4) Trials and persecutions will come, as Our Lord warns us, but when they do, that we may be mindful of offering them up in union with Jesus Christ crucified.

5) That we reflect on the Gospels each day, so that the philosophy of Our Lord Jesus Christ might be emblazoned on our minds.

Wednesday of the Eighth Week: Mk. 10:32-45

I. When the Apostle Peter asked Jesus what the recompense would be for having left all to follow Him, Jesus promised a hundredfold reward in this life, together with persecution. It would be through the cross that the rewards of inner peace, joy, and happiness would come to those faithfully following Him.

1) Jesus repeatedly reminded His disciples that the Son of Man would be handed over to the elders and chief priests and be put to death.

2) How slow they were to learn! They would not get a firm understanding of what Jesus said until they received the Holy Spirit on Pentecost. James and John asked for positions of honor, to sit on His right and left hand in His kingdom. Jesus warns them that what is to happen to Him will also be their lot in this life. They obviously

still had the idea of Jesus as a Messiah with worldly power who would still establish an earthly kingdom, and they wanted prestigious positions in it.

II. Jesus cautions His disciples against ambition. They are not to lord it over anybody, but rather become the servants of all. Indeed if one wishes to become first in His kingdom, he/she must become the last and least of all.

1) Ambition is in all of us; it is the driving force behind self-love. It is the basic cause of much evil and has brought about wars among nations. Its root cause is pride. T.S. Eliot once remarked that most of the trouble in the world is caused by people wanting to be important. Ambition has an appetite that seems never to be satiated.

2) It is a blessing to be content with little things. How much happier we would be, and how much better we would execute our ordinary tasks!

III. "Ask not what your country can do for you, but what you can do for your country" (John F.Kennedy). What is this saying but that we should serve rather than seek to be served?

1) Great men and women were literally the servants of their brothers and sisters in the world: Mother Teresa, Maximilian Kolbe, Dorothy Day, Abraham Lincoln, Mohandas Gandhi, Albert Schweitzer, etc.

2) It is for giving and serving that history ultimately judges men and women to be great. Ambition seeks to be served, wants to use and abuse others.

3) Ambition ultimately destroys one's happiness and peace of mind, and it can even literally destroy the person. It is a creeping fungus that is never satisfied until it consumes the whole of its host. Shakespeare illustrates this in his drama *King Lear*. Lear's ambitious daughters, Goneril and Regan, vie for their father's kingdom and are both destroyed. His unselfish daughter, Cordelia, who did not seek it, ultimately becomes its possessor.

IV. The fall of Lucifer and his angels was due to ambition, the ambition to possess and to govern.

1) In Shakespeare's *King Henry VIII*, Cardinal Wolsey on his deathbed cries out to Cromwell, "Cromwell, I charge thee, fling

away ambition: / By that sin fell the angels. How can man, / Then, hope to gain from it?"

2) No one gets to the top of a building without first starting at the bottom. If there are only a few steps we may succeed in jumping over them, but the higher we must climb the more difficult it becomes to reach the top by skipping over steps; we simply must take each step at a time. This is eminently true in the spiritual life. Union with God is a slow and difficult climb. It is only reached by patiently collaborating with the inspirations of the Holy Spirit, and by learning the difficult path of humility and service.

3) True greatness springs from humility. As our Savior says: "Learn from me; for I am gentle and lowly in heart" (Mt. 11:29).

4) Genuine love is self-giving, not self-seeking. Our paragon must be Our Lord Jesus Christ, who said: "The Son of Man . . . came not to be served but to serve, and to give his life as a ransom for many" (Mk. 10:45).

****

1) That we examine our own personal ambitions to see if they are in keeping with the light of the Gospel.

2) That we reflect once in while to see if we are using people for our own ends.

3) That God bless us with the virtue of humility, allowing us to see our strong and weak points, and give us the knowledge of how we may employ them in serving Him and our brothers and sisters in the world.

4) That we reflect on our own selfishness and ask God's pardon.

5) That we be generous in giving our time to serve the elderly and the shut-ins who have no one to serve them in their needs.

Thursday of the Eighth Week: Mk. 10:46-52

I. "Jesus, Son of David, have mercy on me!" Bartimaeus cries out the holy name of Jesus, begging Him to alleviate his condition.

1) Through the holy name of Jesus our sins are forgiven, our sicknesses are healed, and our sufferings are born cheerfully and fruitfully. Bartimaeus wanted to place himself under the mantle of Jesus' compassion, where he knew he would find healing, so he cried out the holy name of Jesus.

2) St. Bernard said of the name of Jesus that it was "honey to the mouth, music to the ear, a shout of gladness to the heart! ... O blessed name ... this is the glorious name that instructs hearts when it is thought of, cures when it is invoked." (Juan Arintero, O.P., *Song of Songs, a Mystical Exposition.*)

II. Bartimaeus was reduced to the state of begging for his daily bread. Being blind, he was unable to support himself. He was totally dependent on the compassion of others. We can easily see why he cried out after Jesus in desperation.

1) Despite the rebukes of the crowd, his moment of liberation had come, and he was not to be denied. "Son of David, have mercy on me!" Jesus orders that Bartimaeus be brought before Him and asks what he wants Him to do.

2) "Master, let me receive my sight." Jesus responds, "Go your way; your faith has made you well." Once again it is the faith of the individual that moves Jesus to respond to his request.

III. In Bartimaeus we see the necessary qualities of prayer:

1) He showed unbounded confidence in Jesus.

2) His petition was not vague or conditional, dependent on other things; he wanted one thing, his sight, in order to be able to lead a normal life again.

3) His faith was genuine and deep: not only did he cry out the holy name, but he added testimony to his faith by calling Jesus "Son of David," a term used in reference to the Messiah, the Promised One of Israel.

4) Bartimaeus showed persistence: no one was going to succeed in silencing him or deny him the opportunity to approach Jesus his Savior. How often we quit our prayers if we are not heard immediately, or if some obstacle easily discourages us from persisting with perseverance in our prayer. Bartimaeus's persistence is a manifestation of his faith.

5) Bartimaeus was humble: he had a need and was a completely dependent person; he was not afraid to make this confession of his dependency public.

6) Bartimaeus's response to the miracle Jesus granted him was a profuse manifestation of gratitude; his gratitude was spontaneous and real, and it prompted a commitment of loyalty. The Gospel tells us

that Bartimaeus followed Jesus up the road. In all probability he became a disciple of Jesus.

IV. St. Bernard writes of the holy name of Jesus, "What is there that does more to restore the senses, to encourage virtue, to confirm good habits, to sustain holy desires, and to promote chaste affections and thoughts than this holy name of Jesus?" (Arintero, Ibid.). St. Bernard states, "Whatever you may write, it cannot delight me unless I read in it the name of Jesus. However you may argue or converse, your words cannot give me pleasure unless I hear in them the name of Jesus. For Jesus is sweetness to the taste, music to the ear, and joy to the heart" (Louis Martinez, *El Espiritu Santo*).

V) The Church concludes all of her prayers through the holy name of Jesus. Our Lord Himself tells us, "Whatever you ask in my name, I will do it" (Jn. 14:13). A traditional belief holds that God is not only invoked by the name of Jesus but is already present in the invocation. If Jesus is made present through the words of sacred Scripture, He must certainly be present in His holy name.

VI. St Bernard writes, "There is nothing which curbs the path of anger, which deflates the haughtiness of pride, heals the wound of envy, extinguishes the flame of lust and moderates the thirst for avarice as the devout invocation and memory of this sweet name" (Arintero, ibid.). May we always have recourse in the holy name of Jesus.

****

1) That frequently throughout the day we invoke the holy name of Jesus.

2) His name is, as sacred Scripture describes, "oil poured out" (Song 1:3); when we pronounce it mentally or orally, that we do so meaningfully and lovingly.

3) That those who take this name in vain might cease doing so.

4) That we all take the faith, confidence, and persistence of Bartimaeus to heart, and pray with like qualities.

5) That the Lord increase our faith and perseverance in our prayers.

6) Under and through the holy name of Jesus, that Christians might become one flock under one pastor.

7) That we be mindful to express our gratitude to Almighty God for all the favors He has bestowed on us and on our families.

Friday of the Eighth Week: Mk. 11:11-26

I. "The Church is you," said Pope Pius XII in one of his audiences. The physical structure of a church edifice may indeed be as impressive as the Temple in Jerusalem in Our Lord's day. Too often we have beautiful churches whose members, the Christian community, bear little fruit.

II. St. Mark includes the account of the cleansing of the Temple with the episode of the withered fig tree. There is a salutary relationship between the two. The money changers, like the barren fig tree, gave no fruit; on the contrary, they were using religion to cheat the people who came to the Temple to worship. Jesus cleansed the Temple of those members who were abusing it. They were not bearing the fruits of true religion which the Temple evoked.

III. Traditionally, the fig tree symbolized Judaism, because the Jews were not ready to receive Jesus at the time of His visitation to them.

IV. Prophetically, the cleansing of the Temple challenged the too easy familiarity some of the Jews were manifesting in the Temple precincts.

1) Jesus was angry at the commercialization and exploitation of the pilgrims who came to the Temple to pray. They were being fleeced by the money changers and the vendors of animals for sacrifice.

2) All of this commercialization was being done under the guise of religion. It all amounted to a desecration of the house of God.

V. Many people are like the barren fig tree. They look promising at a distance, but their faith is weak and they produce no fruit.

1) Jesus quotes the prophet Jeremiah (7:11), who decried the Jews for using the Temple as a refuge and cover-up for their evil doings. Jeremiah said: "Behold, you trust in deceptive words to no avail. Will you steal, murder, commit adultery, swear falsely, burn incense to Baal, and go after other gods that you have not known, and then come and stand before me in this house, which is called by my name, and say, 'We are delivered!' — only to go on doing all

111

these abominations? Has this house, which is called by my name, become a den of robbers in your eyes?" (Jer. 7:8-11).

2) Many Christians may indeed attend church regularly, contribute toward its support, recite prayers, and go on living lives which are the complete opposite of what their attendance at church would normally indicate. Churchgoing can never buffer, appease, or assuage evil. What should underlie all church attendance is sincere sorrow for sin.

3) Like the barren fig tree, such churchgoers bear no real fruit. You and I are the Church, the living community of God, and we must bear fruit or we will hear the words of the Lord addressed to the Church at Laodicea: "I know your works: you are neither cold nor hot. Would that you were cold or hot! Because you are lukewarm, and neither cold nor hot, I will spew you out of my mouth" (Rev. 3:15-16).

VI. Church buildings cannot serve as cover-up for true worship of the heart; rather they are centers of reconciliation and worship. Worship should be a sincere expression of our love and fidelity to God.

1) Our Lord tells us that before our gifts can be acceptable on the altar, we must first seek reconciliation with our brothers and sisters whom we have offended (cf. Mt. 5:24).

2) Isaiah says that true religion consists in clothing the naked, breaking the shackles of injustice, feeding the hungry, and sheltering the homeless (cf. Is. 58:6-8). These are the fruits that spring from a truly religious heart. Such worship is pleasing to God, and the Lord hears such worshipers when they cried out to Him.

3) Whenever we come to worship in church, we should endeavor to examine our consciences to see if we are at enmity with any of our brothers and sisters. Our Lord clearly laid this down as a fundamental requirement for acceptable sacrifice and worship when He said, "If you are offering your gift at the altar, and there remember that your brother has something against you, leave your gift there before the altar and go; first be reconciled to your brother, and then come and offer your gift" (Mt. 5:23-25). Worship of God can only be acceptable and efficacious if it is suffused with genuine charity.

****

1) That we use the church and not abuse it.

2) That the church may become truly a house of prayer and worship.

3) That we be mindful of our duty to make our religion fruitful by striving to carry out the Gospel in our everyday lives.

4) When opportunity presents itself, that we make visits to Jesus Christ in the sacrament of the altar to be alone with Him in prayer.

5) That we refrain from unnecessary conversation in church.

6) For peace in the world and unity among Christians.

7) That we strive to eradicate all hypocrisy in the expression of our religion.

Saturday of the Eighth Week: Mk. 11:27-33

I. No one can remain indifferent to the truth; of its very nature, it produces a reaction: that of acceptance or rejection.

1) Jesus acted in truth, and hence with authority, when He drove out the money changers from the Temple.

2) Confronted with the truth of the just action of Jesus, the chief priests and the experts in the law were stunned and overwhelmed. They did not and could not criticize Jesus' action. Dumbfounded, they ask, "By what authority are you doing these things, or who gave you this authority to do them?"

II. Jesus put them between the horns of a dilemma: "Was the baptism of John from heaven or from men?" If they were to reply by saying that it was from heaven, they would be admitting to John's divine call and commission. They didn't accept John because of his open criticism of them. He called them hypocrites and a "brood of vipers." If they were to respond to Jesus' question by answering that John's baptism was from men, they would incur the wrath of the crowd, because the people regarded John highly and recognized that he was a prophet. They decided to answer the question by saying, "We do not know." They simply evaded the truth.

III. Like truth, genuine holiness causes one of two reactions: either acceptance and admiration or rejection and disdain.

1) When Pilate asked Jesus, "What is truth?" the answer was staring him in the face. Pilate's reaction was to try to escape his dilemma — that is, the fear and threat of the Jews on the one hand

and the fear of killing an innocent man on the other. He evaded the truth by trying to wash his hands of Jesus' death.

2) Our Lord said in effect, "Either you are for me or against me: No man can serve two masters; for either he will hate the one and love the other, or he will be devoted to the one and despise the other" (Mt. 6:24). Leading lukewarm Christian lives is in many ways evading the truth. If we are really for Christ, we will be committed to Him and strive to put His Gospel into practice in our daily lives. Then our lives will be truthful, and this profession of truth will affect others; it will provoke a similar reaction in others as it did with the contemporary enemies of Jesus. "If the world hates you," says Our Lord, "know that it has hated me before it hated you" (Jn. 15:18). "If they have persecuted me, they will persecute you. . . ." (Jn. 15:20).

IV. Sanctity is a manifestation of truth in the life of an individual. Holy people are sure of themselves; they are secure and are not likely to cave in under pressure. Sanctity is a profession of truth; it has leadership qualities about it and is not afraid to stand up and be counted, regardless of the criticism.

1) Thomas More professed the truth he believed in, and he would not buckle under the pressure of the king, nor to the pleas of his family.

2) Mahatma Gandhi did not buckle under the might of the British empire. He addressed the injustices and the oppression of British rule. He spoke with moral authority backed by a holy life, and he ultimately won independence for his people, but not without suffering much criticism and pain.

V. Holiness compels admiration and moves people to a conversion of heart.

1) Few people who confronted Padre Pio walked away indifferent. They felt compelled to look at themselves in a more serious light. Many of those people who spoke with him felt that this contact was a source of their conversion.

2) Authority in the hands of holy people is respected and honored. In the hands of tyrants and self-seekers, it is despised.

3) Truth, like holiness, challenges all of us. It compels us to face up to the consequences of being exposed. Truth challenges us to confront it and come to terms with it. The alternative is to evade it or run away from it.

114

4) The only face we can wear when we confront truth is that of humility, always being open to the possibility of error and of being ready to ask pardon when authority offers to justly criticize the faults and errors it sees in us.

****

1) That we may be always open to the truth in a spirit of humility and courage.

2) That we neither evade nor cover up our wrongdoing to others.

3) That we be quick to ask pardon for known faults committed against others.

4) That we always cultivate a desire to grow spiritually and therefore not be afraid of honest criticism.

5) That we may be open to charitable and fraternal correction and thus continue to grow in the spiritual life.

6) That those in authority use their authority justly and meekly, and not compromise themselves by taking bribes.

Monday of the Ninth Week: Mk. 12:1-12

I. This is a parable of how Israel constantly rejected the prophets and in the end finally killed the Prophet of prophets, the Messiah. The vineyard stands for Israel; the owner of the vineyard is God; the tenants are Israel's religious leaders; the servants are the prophets, and the beloved son is Jesus (*Jerome Biblical Commentary*).

1) The parable manifests God's patience and how enduring it is; yet it also shows that God's patience has a boiling point, and that God will eventually mete out justice.

2) Killing the heir was a way of getting possession of the vineyard. In Israel, land left without an heir passed on to the first occupant (Maertens-Frisque, *Guide for the Christian Assembly*).

3) The vineyard, Israel's birthright, is taken away, for its owner, God, comes to take it from the ungrateful tenants; that is, the Jewish people. The Kingdom of God, the vineyard, now is extended to the Gentiles.

II. The parable is about God's generosity and patience, and about the selfishness, ingratitude, and meanness of men. Out of sight, out of mind. The tenants assumed that because the owner was so far away, they could carry on as they pleased.

1) Because people do not see God, they feel that they can do as they please and somehow God will ignore it all.

2) The moral of this parable is that freedom begets responsibility, and our responsibility is to turn in a good stewardship, for the Lord wants us to produce.

III. The generosity and trust of Almighty God is shown in creating us and placing us in a world where we have at our disposal all we need materially, and now through Our Lord Jesus Christ, we have all we need spiritually to glorify God and sanctify and save our souls.

1) Our first response to such generosity and trust in us should be gratitude. Most of us are ungrateful, as Our Lord revealed to St. Margaret Mary: "Behold the Heart that loves men so much and is so little loved in return."

2) So many people fail to realize the great gift that God has bestowed upon them in creating them and raising them to the heights of being His sons and daughters with a sublime destiny. The response is one of indifference and irreverence.

IV. Our gratitude to God for creating us and sending His Son into the world to redeem us should be unbounded, and we should frequently show our appreciation to Almighty God for His tremendous generosity toward us, His sons and daughters.

1) St. Paul never wearied of rendering thanks to God for all that the Lord did for him, in spite of being confronted with constant hardships. In eleven of the fourteen epistles, the apostle is profuse in lavishing his gratitude on Almighty God. He urges us to always give similar thanksgivings.

2) It was ingratitude and indifference that wrung from Our Lord's lips those awful woes: "Woe to you Chorazin! woe to you, Bethsaida! for if the mighty works done in you had been done in Tyre and Sidon, they would have repented long ago. . . . But it shall be more tolerable in the judgment for Tyre and Sidon than for you" (Lk. 10:13-14).

3) St. Bernard says that gratitude is like a fertilizer that renders the soil fruitful, whereas ingratitude is like a searing desert wind that dries up the wellsprings of virtue. St. Vincent de Paul strove to spend as much time in thanking God for a favor received as he did in beseeching God for that favor.

4) How quick God is to respond to grateful souls. St. Augustine

says that the shortest and most perfect prayer is *"Deo gratias*, thanks be to God!" Gratitude melts the heart of Our Lord Jesus Christ and literally disposes God to bestow more favors and graces upon grateful sons and daughters.

5) God created you and me to share in His life and in beatific bliss. It is not that He needs our gratitude, but He demands it as a proof of our love. Gratitude softens the heart and quickens our love for God. Let us remember that God is very responsive to grateful souls and is cold toward ungrateful and indifferent people.

****

1) That we may be always grateful to God for having created us and redeemed us, and that we express our gratitude frequently, even daily.

2) That one of our frequent short prayers may be "Thank You, Lord."

3) Each night before retiring, that we include in our prayers a prayer of thanksgiving for the day that passed and for the graces and blessings God bestowed upon us during that day.

4) When we awaken in the morning, that we may say, "Thank You, Lord, for another day to grow in Your love."

5) That we may be generous in almsgiving as an expression of gratitude for God's generosity toward us.

6) That parents instruct their children on the importance of expressing their thanks to Almighty God and to others who do them good turns.

Tuesday of the Ninth Week: Mk. 12:13-17

I. "Render to Caesar the things that are Caesar's, and to God the things that are God's." Our Lord here sets down the fundamental principle necessary for the survival and operation of both Church and State. Both are necessary entities which must be supported and respected in order that God may be honored and served, and mankind protected and provided for.

1) In totalitarian states, martyrdom is sometimes the only way to go in order that God may not be subordinated to the state. It was the price Dietrich Bonhoeffer had to pay because he would not respect Nazism.

117

2) Franz Jägerstatter, a devout Austrian farmer, was executed by the Nazis on August 9, 1943. A father of three young children, Franz refused to serve in Hitler's army because he sincerely believed the Nazi movement was wrong and immoral. He was imprisoned, but he steadfastly refused to change his mind. His letters from prison reveal a man of deep faith, high principles, and extraordinary character. The Catholic chaplain who assisted him on the day of his execution said that he would never forget the joy shining in the young man's eyes and the confidence with which he lived his final hours. The chaplain said, "I say with certainty that this simple man is the only saint I have ever met in my lifetime." Franz refused to submit to Caesar when Caesar was wrong.

3) St. Thomas More endured a similar clash with King Henry VIII of England. He refused to accept Henry's arrogant claim to be head of the Church in England because the king was usurping the role of the pope. Even in the face of death, Thomas More was steadfast and died a martyr rather than submit to Caesar's wrongdoing.

4) In Poland, many young men have been blackballed and denied good-paying careers or entrance to state universities if they entered the seminary; yet the seminaries in Poland have been full. People who attend church in Cuba are denied opportunities of advancement in their employment. How extremely grateful we should be here in America for our freedom, the Constitution's respect for God and religious liberty.

II. Jesus tells us to render to Caesar those things that are lawfully Caesar's and to give God His due. Jesus here asserts that the state has rights, yet it must not exceed its bounds.

1) If it weren't for the state, where would we be? It gives us security and places order in society, and affords us all the opportunity to pursue our goals in life. Anarchy can only bring chaos. The state protects our lives, our possessions, and our homeland. Such an institution should be venerated and given the support it needs to carry out its duties. The Fourth Commandment requires this.

2) Here in our country, we all have a participatory role in government. Our voice can be heard on the legislative floors of state and federal governments. Our job is not finished when we elect our

representatives. When a piece of legislation comes up that would be unjust, we must make our voices heard by contacting our representatives either by phone or by mail. Not to do so would make us guilty of omission.

III. The image of government may well be printed on its money, but God's image and likeness are inscribed on our souls. He has first claim on us, and our first duties must be to Him, even if this means offending government.

1) Patriotism is virtuous. Patriotism demands that we love our country and its government, and that we support and cherish them. Just as the Church is you and me, so too our government is you and me. A constituency cannot be separated from its representatives. Both demand active participation.

2) Patriotism should be a matter of personal pride. In our country we have much to be proud of, thanks to our founding fathers and the men and women who have made heavy sacrifices to keep it free. Although our founding fathers kept Church and State as separate dominions, they did recognize the need for religion to provide and mold the caliber and character of citizens necessary to keep the nation free and strong.

****

1) That God direct our president and the members of congress in all their deliberations.

2) That we always show our love and devotion for our country.

3) That we make our voices heard in government so that favorable and just legislation may be passed.

4) That we may be conscientious in our duties to our federal, state, and local governments.

5) That we frequently pray for our representatives that the Lord will guide and direct them in their deliberations.

6) That our justice system may come to realize the unspeakable crime that abortion really is, that it is nothing more than taking the lives of our future citizens.

7) For all the men and women who died for our country.

Wednesday of the Ninth Week: Mk. 12:18-27
I. The Sadducees were a small, aristocratic, wealthy party. Most

of the priests belonged to the Sadducee party. They tended to collaborate with the Roman occupation in order to retain their wealth and privileges.

II. The Sadducees differed with the Pharisees on a number of issues.

1) They accepted only the first five books of the Old Testament, the Pentateuch. They would not accept or be guided by the oral law which was the guiding norm of living for the Pharisees, nor would they accept the traditions of the ancients.

2) They did not believe in bodily resurrection or immortality of the soul, because according to them there was no proof for this in the Pentateuch, the five books of the Old Testament ascribed to Moses. They did not believe in angels or spirits. In the modern world, they would be considered secularists and humanists.

III. They approached Jesus with a question designed to make the resurrection of the dead look ridiculous.

1) The Jewish law of levirate marriage held that the brother of a deceased man should marry his widow to continue the family. The child that might be born of this union was to be considered the son or daughter of the deceased brother.

2) In this way the family of the deceased would continue and the property of the deceased would remain in the family (Barclay, *The Gospel of Mark*).

IV. Jesus proceeded to pull the rug out from under the feet of the Sadducees by citing the source which they believed in, the Pentateuch, the book of Moses. He cites Exodus 3:6, where God calls Himself the God of Abraham, the God of Isaac, and the God of Jacob. These men had long since died. The implication is clear. God is not a God of the dead but of the living. Therefore, Jesus is saying that these patriarchs are still alive. If this be so, then these men are immortal. The soul then is immortal.

1) When the Sadducees cited the levirate law requiring marriage of a deceased brother's wife, they presented a picture of heaven as a prolongation of life on earth. Jesus corrects them here, by saying that in heaven there will be neither married people nor giving in marriage. We will be like the angels. Here we get an inkling of what our glorified bodies will be like. They will be "angelized." Our corporeity will be made spirit-like.

2) The Muslims or Muhammadans believe that heaven is a place of physical luxury, full of all sorts of bodily pleasures. The American Indians also believed in a material heaven — the happy hunting grounds.

V. We all fall into errors when we picture heaven with earthly or material symbols. They all fall far short of what eternal life is like. St. Catherine of Siena had a vision of heaven, but couldn't describe it. There was no physical image with which to compare it.

1) Heaven is a basking in the beatific vision, and who can describe God in His splendor and beauty? When St. John of the Cross had a vision of Christ, he tried to write a description of Our Lord as he was conversing with Him. When the vision was over, he looked down at what he had written. He filled the whole page with the word beauty.

2) Even St. Paul could not describe what he had seen when he was granted a vision of heaven. He concludes, quoting Isaiah, "What no eye has seen, nor ear heard, nor the heart of man conceived, what God has prepared for those who love Him" (1 Cor. 2:9).

3) God is faithful to those who serve Him, and there is a blank spot in His heart until all of His children come home.

4) When St. Bernadette Soubirous lay dying, she spoke with regret of those people who do not sufficiently desire heaven. "As for me," she said, "that will not be my case. Let us determine to go to heaven. Let us work for it, suffer for it. Nothing else matters."

5) St. John in his first epistle writes: "Beloved, we are God's children now; it does not yet appear what we shall be, but we know that when he appears we shall be like him, for we shall see him as he is" (1 Jn. 3:2).

****

1) That the Lord may fill us with a lively hope.

2) That we think from time to time about heaven, especially when we are swamped with earthly problems.

3) That we all receive the grace of the last sacraments before death.

4) That no member of our families die outside of God's grace.

5) For all of those who have lost their faith, that they may recover it and be filled with hope.

6) That we all cultivate a deep devotion to the Blessed Virgin Mary so that she may protect us from the insidious attacks of the devil and from a sudden and unprovided death.

7) For all of our deceased relatives and friends, that they may soon be in paradise.

Thursday of the Ninth Week: Mk. 12:28-34

I. Jesus had just dealt with the trap set for Him by the Sadducees on the question of paying tribute to Caesar when He was approached by a scribe of the party of the Pharisees who asked Him which was the first of all the commandments.

1) By Jesus' time the rabbis had enumerated some 613 precepts of the Law, 258 commands, and 365 prohibitions (*Catholic Commentary on Holy Scripture*). These were classified into grave and light obligations. There was no end to the additions by way of interpretation of the scribes and Pharisees.

2) Added to this tendency toward expanding the Law, there was also the tendency to summarize it in a general statement or principle. Jesus does just this by making the whole import of the Law be based on the principle of love of God and love of neighbor. Both of these commandments, the love of God and the love of neighbor, were central in Israel, but their combination into a single moral principle appears to be original with Jesus (*Jerome Biblical Commentary*). Jesus cites the first commandment from Deuteronomy 6:4, "Hear, O Israel, the LORD our God is one LORD; and you shall love the LORD your God with all your heart, and with all your soul, and with all your might"; then He quotes the second commandment from Leviticus 19:18, "You shall love your neighbor as yourself," and He put them together as the operational principle of the whole Law of God.

II. Love of neighbor in the Old Testament interpretation meant love of one's fellow Jews. By Jesus' time it included the resident alien. It was perfectly permissible to hate the Gentiles.

1) By uniting these two commandments, Jesus extends the limited Jewish sense of neighbor to include all men and women without reservation. True and sincere love of God will manifest itself in love for one's fellow human, brother or sister. The reverence we show one another is a thermometer of our love of God.

2) To the question put to Jesus, "Who is my neighbor?" Jesus responds by giving the parable of the "Good Samaritan." The implication of this parable is that our neighbor even includes our enemies. The Samaritans were traditional enemies of the Jews.

III. St. John states, " If any one says, 'I love God,' and hates his brother, he is a liar; for he who does not love his brother whom he sees, cannot love God whom he has not seen" (1 Jn. 4:20-21) There is an obvious incongruity in such behavior.

1) St. Augustine asks, "How can you love and kiss the Head while you trample upon the members?"

2) When a deaf and blind little girl, Helen Keller, asked her exemplary teacher Anne Sullivan, "What is love?" Miss Sullivan drew her close to her heart and said: "It is here," pointing Helen's finger to her heart. . . . "You cannot touch love, but you can feel the sweetness that it pours into everything."

IV. You can give love away and never suffer any loss of it within yourself. In fact, the more you give of your love and affection to others, the more you grow in love. You literally come to possess more of it.

1) Love cannot remain abstract. It demands relationships, respect, and caring. For love to be productive and outgoing, it must begin with oneself — a love and respect for oneself, for the way God made us, with the many or few talents and gifts He has endowed us with.

2) Psychologists like Eric Fromm tell us that people who don't love themselves are incapable of loving others. Yet our intrinsic worth comes from the fact that God loves us as we are, no matter what we do, whether we achieve or fail, sin or serve.

3) There are not kinds of love; there are only degrees of love. God loves us more or less depending on the sincere love we bear for Him and for our brothers and sisters.

****

1) That frequently during the day we lift up our minds and hearts and tell God that we love Him with all our hearts.

2) That we bury all ill will and rancor we may tend to harbor toward a brother or sister.

3) That we be quick to serve others and anticipate their needs, especially the members of our own families.

4) That we not forget our brothers and sisters in purgatory, praying often for them.

5) As a mother has the charism of uniting her sons and daughters, let us pray to our Blessed Lady that all Christians become one under the one shepherd, the Vicar of Christ.

6) For peace in the world, and end to the arms race, and the conversion of the Soviet Union.

Friday of the Ninth Week: Mk. 12:35-37

I. The title "Son of David" is indeed the popular title for the Messiah, but this title got the popular connotation of the Promised One being like David, a great military leader and liberator of the Jewish people, one who would break the Roman yoke of occupation in Israel.

1) At the time of Jesus, the title, "Son of David," had highly nationalistic overtones. Jesus wanted to disabuse the people of the notion that the Messiah was coming as a military leader and liberator from foreign military occupation.

2) By throwing out the question "How can the scribes say that the Christ is the son of David?" Jesus wants to show His physical relationship with David, a necessary qualification of Messiahship, while at the same time point out that the Messiah is Lord, and therefore above and independent of David.

II. Jesus does not deny that He is son of David in physical ancestry. He is claiming much more than physical relationship. He is saying that not only is He David's son, but He is David's Lord.

1) The word "Lord" is the English translation of the Greek word *kyrios*. Jehovah is the English hybrid translation of Yahweh (McKenzie).

2) Jesus is claiming to be what He really is: Lord, God, and Messiah, who existed as God before David although, as man, He is a descendant of David.

III. Jesus is trying to bring home the idea that He is not a military or political Messiah.

1) The kingdom He is establishing is the kingdom of God on earth, a kingdom of love, peace, and grace.

2) This kingdom, while on earth, will coexist with evil but will not be destroyed by evil.

IV. His teaching will reveal that He is equal to God, for Jesus proclaimed His identity with God. The mind of Jesus is the mind of God. The words of Jesus are the words of God.

1) Jesus' role of obedient servant of the Father does not make Him subservient to the Father. His obedience springs out of pure love of His Father. It shows the perfect harmony there is in His equality. The will of the triune God was that the Son would become the redeemer, a role of obedience that is a product of a tremendous love and humility. This obedience would lead Jesus to death — death on a cross, a penalty that was considered below the dignity of Roman citizens.

2) David, in Psalm 110, calls the Messiah "Lord." In the Eastern mentality, it was inconceivable that a father would allot the title "Lord" to one of his sons (Thierry-Maertens, op. cit.). David, then, under the inspiration of the Holy Spirit, is calling the Messiah God.

V. No one goes to the Father except through Jesus. The Father is the giver of eternal life, which Jesus, the Messiah, is about to restore through the redemption. When we accept the way of life Jesus offers us, however difficult it may be, it will infallibly lead to happiness.

1) The closer we enter into relationship with Our Lord Jesus Christ, the closer and deeper our relationship to God the Father and to God the Holy Spirit, and even to our brothers and sisters in heaven, in purgatory, and on earth.

2) It is a relationship that transforms us, wherein selfishness becomes generosity and warm service to others; hatred and rancor become loving concern; hostility is transformed into friendship, and anger to meekness and kindness.

3) The natural tendency of love is to unite the lover with the beloved, to make the two one. Through love, God so unites us to Him that we participate in His very nature and life.

****

1) That we make frequent acts of faith in Jesus Christ, acknowledging Him as our Lord and God.

2) That we ask God often to increase our faith.

3) That we say frequently and meaningfully, "Thank you, Lord, for Your incarnation, passion, death, and resurrection."

4) That we strive to sharpen our faith by a daily reflection on some passage from sacred Scripture.

5) For all those who are drifting or who have lost their faith.

6) That all men and women will come to acknowledge Jesus Christ as their Lord and God.

7) For peace in the world and an end to the arms race.

Saturday of the Ninth Week: Mk. 12:38-44

I. The Temple was divided into four courts: the Court of the Gentiles, the Court of Women, the Court of Men, and the Court of the Priests. In the Court of Women, there were thirteen collection boxes called "trumpets," because they were in the shape of trumpets (Barclay, op. cit.). Into these trumpet-like receptors, people deposited contributions voluntarily. Each one of these thirteen trumpets were earmarked for different Temple needs, like money for candles, fuel, vestments, utensils for the altar of sacrifice, etc. It was into one of these trumpets that the elderly widow put her two small copper coins worth about a penny.

1) Generally one of the priests was stationed by these collection boxes to announce the amount of money being placed into them (Prat, *Life of Christ*). We can imagine heads turning as the amount deposited by the widow was announced. Yet she courageously ignored that and proceeded to give the little she had to live on.

2) Jesus singles her out for her generosity and her faith in God for she gave all she had. She was obviously throwing herself into the arms of divine providence. Jesus turns to His disciples and says, "Truly, I say to you, this poor widow has put in more than all those who are contributing to the treasury. They all contributed out of their abundance; but she out of her poverty has put in everything she had, her whole living."

II. The Old Testament is replete with praise for almsgiving. The prophets put it on a par with fasting and sacrifice. For the Jewish people, almsgiving is among the three pillars on which a good life is based; the other two are prayer and fasting.

1) From the book of Sirach (Ecclesiasticus) we read: "Kindness [alms] to a father will not be forgotten, and against your sins it will be credited to you; in the day of your affliction it will be remembered

in your favor; as frost in fair weather, your sins will melt away (3:14-15).

2) Almsgiving was clearly seen as a salutary reparation for personal sins. In the book of Tobit, we read, "It is better to give alms than to treasure up gold. For almsgiving delivers from death, and it will purge away every sin" (Tob. 12:8-9).

III. All almsgiving is meritorious, even when given from one's excess, but when almsgiving costs us, it becomes more meritorious. Jesus singled out the widow because she gave at a huge sacrifice. She gave of her substance. She in a way symbolizes what Jesus Himself will do: give His very self for us. This cost Him dearly, but it was needed for our redemption.

1) When a woman gives birth she participates in creation and shares with God the giving of her very substance — herself — and she risks her life in doing so.

2) Few people give sacrificially; that is, at a real cost to them. Generally it is out of their surplus. For those who do sacrifice, the reward is great even in this life.

3) The Lord will not be outdone in generosity, and no one ever died in the poorhouse for almsgiving. We will never experience need for having given. How much the rich young man lost by clinging to his wealth when Our Lord asked him to make a heroic sacrifice!

4) When one gives of one's substance, he/she in a very real way places him-/herself in the hands of divine providence as to the future. This was the case of the widow in today's Gospel. She thrust herself into the "darkness" of faith.

5) The poverty that abounds in the world about us offers us an ample opportunity to detach ourselves, to give at a cost to ourselves, and thus lay up abundant treasure in heaven. As St. Ambrose said, "The stomachs of the poor, the houses of widows, the mouths of children are the barns which last forever."

IV. Ultimately, we will only really possess eternally what we give of ourselves, our time, our talents, and our material goods.

****

1) That the Lord give us the true spirit of generosity.

2) A Roman proverb goes: "He gives twice who gives quickly"; that we respond graciously and generously to those in need.

3) That we may become more citizens of the world by sensitizing with people suffering in other areas of the world.

4) That we share our time and company with the lonely and elderly.

5) That wealthier nations feel more responsibility toward the poorer nations of the world.

6) That we not abuse money in lavish waste or on things we do not need.

Monday of the Tenth Week: Mt. 5:1-12

I. In proclaiming the beatitudes, Jesus was setting up goals and values that would challenge those of the world and make saints out of us. The beatitudes are full of paradoxes and are absolutely opposite to the values of a materialistic society that is also a victim of media that strive to make us consume more.

The beatitudes are a map of the Christian road to happiness while shouldering the cross; happiness, wisdom, and divine comfort come to those who know how to accept and practice them.

1) How can the sorrowful, the hungry, the poor, and the persecuted be blessed and happy? The hungry and the thirsty are those who hunger and thirst for God and for justice and peace in the world.

2) The poor in spirit are those who constantly manifest their dependence on God for everything.

3) The persecuted are those who suffer unjustly for accepting and living up to the Gospel of Jesus Christ. It well may be that insult awaits the person who insists on Christian chastity. Mockery awaits the person who practices Christian love and forgiveness. Persecution and sneering criticism may await the person who insists on doing an honest day's work in industry.

4) Those who live the beatitudes are those who are living witnesses to Jesus and His message, to the point of heroism. The person who is called upon to bear a material loss, the loss of a friend or a job, or to bear the injustice of detraction or slander against him/her because he/she will not compromise the principles of Jesus Christ — such a one has the promise of Our Lord Jesus Christ that He will be closer than ever to such stalwart son or daughter when such a person may feel abandoned by his/her fellows.

II. To be blessed is to feel a deep hunger for God, while at the same time acknowledging our weaknesses and emptiness without Him. The term "blessed" means to be filled with happiness and joy — spiritual gifts of God given to generous souls, who in the eyes of the worldly may seem foolish, but who in God's eyes are wise.

1) The beatitudes are in effect saying: "Oh, the bliss of being a Christian! The joy of following in the footsteps of Our Lord and Savior Jesus Christ!" They are sacraments of peace and joy, optimism and happiness, for not only do they point to heavenly bliss, but while we are still on earth they give us drafts of the sweetness of heavenly bliss.

2) They speak of the joy which one possesses even while passing through the pain of a disease or through the grief of a great loss. It is the joy that shines through tears that the worst of adversaries can never take from us. It is the victory of blood, sweat, and tears, the sweet yoke and the light burden of the cross.

3) "Blessed are those who mourn" refers to those who are truly sorry for their sins and who lament at seeing so much evil in the world, and at seeing God so blatantly offended.

4) "Blessed are the meek" refers to those who strive to put their passions and appetites under the gentle control of reason enlightened by faith, and this is reflected in a blessed gracefulness in their interactions and relations with others.

5) "Blessed are the pure in heart" refers to those who possess that simplicity of heart and mind that makes their overriding objective, in all that they do, to do it for the honor and glory of God, and to please Him in all their undertakings.

6) Poverty of spirit detaches us from servitude to material things and makes us realize our utter helplessness and real poverty in facing the difficult challenges of life, and our complete dependence on God.

III. Those who practice the beatitudes are peacemakers insofar as they actively strive to make the world a better place to live in, not by evading issues, but by meeting them and bringing them to a happy conclusion in the light of the Gospel. As Abraham Lincoln once said: "I would like it said of me when I die that I always strove to pull up a weed and replace it with a flower wherever I thought the flower would grow."

****

1) Although they may cost us dearly to practice, that we nevertheless strive to live the ideal of the beatitudes.

2) Through poverty of spirit, that we strive to check our desires for unnecessary things and readily give what we don't need to those in need.

3) That we frequently manifest our sorrow for our sins and lament the fact that God is so much offended.

4) That the Lord bestow upon us the meekness necessary to keep our passions and appetites under the control of reason.

5) That we all strive to be genuine peacemakers, especially in our own families.

6) That the Lord engender within us a deep hunger and thirst for God and the things of God.

7) That we make a serious effort at building social justice in our country and abroad.

Tuesday of the Tenth Week: Mt. 5:13-16

I. By Divine Providence you and I have been placed in the world at a certain time and place to be the salt and leaven for that period and place in the history of the human race.

1) We have been given life, talents, and a mission by Almighty God, and He wants us to return a good stewardship of our lives in this world, for we will never have an opportunity to repeat it again.

2) We cannot go through life in this world just marking time or with irresponsible indifference. No man is an island; we affect people for better or for worse.

3) Salt is a catalyst; it cannot remain indifferent in a given liquid. It invariably gives savor to that liquid. By the mandate of our baptism and the gift of faith, we too must give the flavor, tang, and zest of that faith to others with whom we live, work, and associate. If our faith doesn't have that salt to it, it is an indication that it is a weak faith, and as such it should cause us a justifiable alarm that should reawaken our desire for God to rekindle it with a new fervor.

4) If Christianity were really practiced, the problems of the world would much more readily be solved. The truth is that too many Christians do not have the salt of a lively, living faith within them.

II. No one will make his/her mark in the world by passing the buck. The fervent Christian doesn't run away from problems; rather, he/she seeks to solve them by facing them courageously. A great sin of our age is the sin of omission and indifference.

1) Mahatma Gandhi once said: "I would suggest first of all that all of you Christians must begin to love more like Christ. If you would come to us in the spirit of your Master, we could not resist you." "It is not that Christianity has been tried and found wanting," said G.K. Chesterton; "it is simply that it has not been tried."

2) St. Gregory the Great said if the Gospel were practiced by Christians there would be no need for sermons. Good example gives off powerful light and challenges others to imitate it.

3) Two of St. Francis' friars turned away two thieves who came to the door seeking food and lodging. When St. Francis, who had just returned from begging for food for his friars, learned of this, he made the two friars take the sack of food and go out in search of the two men they had turned away. They were not to return until they found them, and when they did find them, they were to kneel before them and beg pardon for their uncharitableness. The two thieves were so moved that they went to St. Francis and asked to be admitted to his new order of Franciscans. Francis accepted them, and they persevered until their deaths.

III. Our Lord tells us that we must be lights in this world, like cities built on mountaintops which cannot help but be seen.

1) Our light and our salt will be our lives and our deeds. Will they give savor and light to the environment in which we live and work and really serve to affect the lives of the indifferent?

2) Every day we will be challenged to put the Gospel into practice. What you do and how you conduct yourself will be the sermon you literally preach that day.

IV. The English writer John Ruskin left us with a splendid image of what Jesus wants us to be in our world. In Ruskin's time there was no electricity. City streets were illuminated by gas lamps. Lamplighters had to light them at night with their torches. One night when Ruskin was looking out of his window of his study, he noticed the streetlamps going on one after another as the lamplighter made his way up and over the hill and disappeared on the other side. Ruskin tried to see him, but because of the mist and the darkness all he could see was the lighted torch going from streetlamp to streetlamp, leaving a trail of lights behind, and then disappearing into the night. He turned to a friend beside him and said: "That's a good illustration of a Christian. People may never have known him, never have met him, nor ever seen him, but they know he passed through the world by the trail of lights he left lit behind him" (Mark Link, S.J., *Sunday Homilies*). We may never do great things, but the testimony of our example should always leave a light behind us.

****

1) That our daily lives may be a source of light and savor to those who see us and deal with us.

2) That our example be an encouragement to the weak and fainthearted.

3) That we may not cower to human respect or peer pressure in our efforts to do the right thing.

4) That we may be compassionate and concerned people, sensitive to our brothers' and sisters' need for support in leading a good life.

5) For the gift of fortitude and wisdom to know the prudent way to act in putting the Gospel into practice in our daily lives.

Wednesday of the Tenth Week: Mt. 5:17-19

I. St. Augustine said of the Old Testament, "God wisely arranged that the New Testament be hidden in the Old, and that the Old Testament be made perfect in the New." The Old Testament is a preparation for the coming of the Messiah.

1) Our Lord said, "If you believed Moses, you would believe me, for he wrote of me" (Jn. 5:46). Jesus fulfilled the prophetic content of the Law while criticizing the Pharisees for their legalism and for killing the spirit of the Law by their endless interpretations and additions tacked on to the Law.

2) The Pharisees worshiped the Law rather than its Author.

II. Jesus reaffirms the Law and its purpose, namely the service of God and neighbor. Once interpretations or additions impede this fundamental end of the Law, they cease to have the force of law.

1) The basic Law of the Old Testament is the Ten Commandments. These are the broad principles of all law in reference to God and to society. These commandments are based on

love that is expressed in reverence for God and for our fellow human beings.

2) Our motive in keeping these commandments should be one of love, reverence for God and the things of God, and respect for our brothers and sisters and their possessions.

3) St. Augustine said, "Love God and do what you will." Obviously, real love will not offend the Beloved.

4) The first and principal fruit of love is its manifestation in obedience, dutifully carrying out the will of God as it is expressed in the Ten Commandments.

III. Napoleon once said that laws were made for ordinary people; he considered himself above ordinary people, and therefore felt that he was above the laws that bound them.

1) Most people, however, disobey God's law either through weakness or selfishness. When pride and arrogance are the motives for breaking God's law, the infraction is much more serious and delinquent.

2) Falls through weakness are much more pardonable and pitiable, and when the people who so fall are quick to acknowledge their weakness and guilt, they will more readily obtain the pardon of both God and man.

3) The Holy Father has said that many people in today's world have lost their sense of sin. This is an indication either of gross ignorance or of having hardened their consciences to sin by so many repetitious falls. Others just don't care. They have lost all fear of God. Some have reached the state where their consciences cease to bother them any longer. What a lamentable state, for they make their eternal salvation practically impossible.

IV. All laws are a recognition that people cannot live in harmony together without regulations. Our actions and conduct affect others. Reckless actions or sins hurt other people beside ourselves. When one steals, another suffers the loss. When industry conspires to raise prices unjustly, the consumer suffers an unjust loss. When we speak about others, their reputation is affected for better or worse. When we do not recognize the sanctity of human sexuality, we reduce our brothers and sisters to mere animals and worse.

1) The Ten Commandments were not given to prevent us from enjoying life; quite the contrary, they are infallible guidelines to

happiness in this life. They are wisdom in action. A businessman of questionable ethics once said to Mark Twain, "Before I die, I mean to climb to the top of Mt. Sinai and read the Ten Commandments aloud." Mark Twain replied, "I have a better idea. Why not stay here and keep them" (Sunday Sermons).

2) The Ten Commandments are from God and are a clear manifestation of God's will. To obey them out of love of God will bring the rewards of the Holy Spirit: joy, peace, kindness, gentleness, self-control, goodness, trustfulness, love and reverence for God and for our brothers and sisters.

3) St. Augustine spoke of the Ten Commandments as a ten-stringed lyre on which the Holy Spirit played, bringing the harmony of the divine order into our lives (Gerard Sloyan, *Rejoice and Take It Away*). The two tablets of stone containing the Ten Commandments are summed up in Jesus' twofold command to love God and our neighbor.

****

1) That God give us a deep reverence for His commandments and a greater appreciation and understanding of them.

2) That we may always be conscious that when we keep God's law we are manifesting our love for Him and for our brothers and sisters.

3) The consequences of keeping God's law are happiness, peace, and harmony in the world; that world leaders show their reverence and respect for God's Commandments when enacting civil laws.

4) That we be compassionate and help those who break God's commandments from the impulse of passion or peer pressure.

5) That young people see and appreciate the wisdom of the Commandments and the built-in rewards for keeping them.

6) That the plague of drug abuse may be broken.

7) That wealthy nations may see their obligation in charity to help out their unfortunate brother nations of the Third World.

Thursday of the Tenth Week: Mt. 5:20-26

I. Under the Roman occupation of Palestine, Jewish tribunals could not carry out death sentences. Apart from death, the toughest sentence to be meted out to a Jew was excommunication. This literally cut off a man from social life as a member of the Jewish community, and he would be banned from the Temple and synagogue services.

1) The Sanhedrin had this power, and the power to condemn to death, but they could not carry out a death sentence. Only a Roman tribunal could have the death sentence carried out. The Sanhedrin did excommunicate and had the power to have that sentence carried out.

2) Jesus goes to the core of the violations of God's law — the intention and desire of the person violating it. These flow from the human heart, which no one but God can see. God judges the sentiments of the heart more than exterior actions.

II. We see this same philosophy of Jesus applied to worship and sacrifices offered in the house of God. "If you are offering your gift at the altar, and there remember that your brother has something against you, leave your gift there before the altar and go; first be reconciled to your brother, and then come and offer your gift" (Mt. 5:23-25).

1) For Our Lord Jesus Christ, the observance of the law had to be an external manifestation of the heart. Not to commit murder, theft, adultery, etc., is fine, but Jesus is saying one must not even interiorly entertain such thoughts or desires, for these equally violate God's Law.

2) Since the end of the whole law is charity, God will render our worship of Him as null and void if we fail to reconcile ourselves with our brothers and sisters.

III. Men and women can only see external actions; consequently, civil legislators can only effectively legislate against external actions. God's Law governs even the heart, and when our hearts are good, we are good, and our actions become meritorious because of the good intention behind them. One's intention for observing the law or for performing an act of virtue is what really matters before God. Even more important than the magnitude of an action is the intention behind it.

IV. The Psalmist writes: "Great peace have those who love thy law" (Ps 119:165). What produces that happiness is the desire to please God when one fulfills the law.

1) Today, because of the materialistic society in which we live

and work, people need the support of good example to do the right thing, to do God's will and stand up to peer pressure.

2) Many people have the intention to do what they feel to be right, but they lack sufficient courage to carry their convictions out on the stage of life. They need our example, so they won't feel alone in doing the right thing. The Roman philosopher-playwright Seneca said, "It is a long journey to one's goal going by the direction of teaching and lectures; it is much shorter and easier through example."

3) Good example gives others a needed nudge or push. As Mark Twain put it, "Nothing stings so much as the annoyance of good example."

4) "Blessed are the pure of heart, for they shall see God" (Mt. 5:8) "If your heart be right," said St. Francis of Assisi, "then every creature is a mirror of life, and a book of holy doctrine." What is this but the virtue of simplicity which makes one so attractive to God. God enlightens people of pure heart — people whose intention behind their actions is to please God. He gives them the gift of understanding and knowledge to see His plan in people and things.

****

1) That we frequently examine our hearts to find if there is any evil lurking there and expel it.

2) That we strive to be at peace with our brothers and sisters so as to more worthily offer our worship of God when we assist at Mass.

3) That we be generous in forgiving others and not harbor grudges.

4) That we frequently examine the intentions behind our actions to see if we are really serving God or ourselves.

5) That we ask God's pardon for any duplicity in our past actions.

6) For families torn by jealousy and strife, that they be reconciled with each other.

7) That we all strive to please God in what we do today.

Friday of the Tenth Week: Mt. 5:27-32

I. Fornication and adultery in thought, desire, and action are equally forbidden by the sixth and ninth commandments.

1) Our bodies, writes St. Paul, are temples of the Holy Spirit. They are destined for glorification.

2) In his letters to the Corinthians, the Galatians, and the Ephesians, St. Paul states that adulterers, fornicators, and sodomites will not enter the kingdom of heaven.

II. When God created Adam and Eve, they had perfect control over all of their appetites and senses.

1) Perhaps control over one's sexual appetites is the area that has suffered the most damage as a consequence of Original Sin.

2) The virtue of chastity has as its objective the restoring of our sexual drives back to the dominion and control of reason.

3) St. Thomas Aquinas argues that chastity disciplines the bodily senses and orders them to be subject to reason to enable a person to more readily and easily contemplate God.

4) Chastity then frees the mind to meditate and reflect on spiritual things and eternal truths without being badgered or interrupted by unruly passions and desires.

III. In heaven we will be contemplating God in all His splendor, and our glorified bodies will also share in this beatific vision. There, all our mental and bodily faculties, passions, and desires will then have as their objective to feed on God as He is in His beauty and majesty without any need or feeling for sexual gratification as we know it here on earth.

1) St. John of the Cross states that even here on earth when our bodily and spiritual faculties are all purified, they all collaborate and merge in a harmonious way to hunger for God as their natural object and focal point of interest. They will all seek their individual and total gratification and satisfaction in Him.

2) Our Lord Jesus Christ assures us that in the kingdom of heaven all sexual activity will cease, for there we will be as the angels (Mt. 22:30). Angels, as we know, have no physical bodies and do not reproduce themselves.

IV. Chastity is a delicate virtue because it strives to restore control, harmony, and beauty to a beautiful but unruly human faculty.

1) St. Francis de Sales called chastity a lily among the virtues because it makes men and women likened to the angels, since nothing is beautiful really that is not pure, and the purity of chastity in human beings has its own particular beauty and glory.

2) What makes children so attractive is in large part due to their

innocence, and chastity in adults restores the attractiveness of innocence.

V. If there is any virtue today that is bombarded and belittled by the media, it is chastity.

1) Many psychologists encourage violations of this virtue by suggesting fornication and masturbation as means to alleviate sexual pressures. Chastity urges control through prayer, avoiding occasions of sin, and the discipline of mortification.

2) Modern theater and movies are at an all-time low in their ribald, crude dialogue and provocative scenes. They justify this as being a realistic reflection of reality. Little consideration is given to the consequences these scenes and dialogue might have on their audiences. They certainly are not making any constructive contribution to the building of character in their young viewers. Furthermore, this obscene material is ultimately harmful to the nation.

3) Our Blessed Lady indicated at Fátima that many people are losing their souls because of sins of impurity.

VI. Temptations against chastity are no respecter of persons nor of age. We need the help of the sacraments. Frequent confession, Holy Communion, and the spirit of constant prayer are very powerful aids in strengthening the virtue of chastity in all of us.

1) The maxim "Idleness is the devil's workshop" has special relevance to maintaining chastity. Being healthily occupied in productive work or in reading is a great asset to protecting this delicate virtue.

2) Devotion to the Blessed Virgin Mary and to St. Joseph is also a very good practice in building and protecting chastity, for they are its exemplars and will certainly help anyone who asks their protection and help.

3) Let us all have frequent recourse to prayer, mindful of our Savior's words, "Watch and pray that you may not enter into temptation" (Mt. 26:41).

****

1) That God bless us with the beautiful gift of chastity.
2) That we direct our hearts to a more fervent love of God.
3) That our devotion to our Blessed Lady grow in fervor.

4) That we strive to avoid persons, places, and reading materials which would be an occasion of sin for us.

5) That those who remain away from confession because of shame or fear receive the grace to use this sacrament of reconciliation more frequently.

6) For parents, that they be blessed with the wisdom and the tact needed to instill in their children healthy attitudes toward sex and an esteem for the virtue of chastity.

Saturday of the Tenth Week: Mt. 5:33-37

I. Oaths are taken especially in court testimony to guarantee the truth of one's statements. Oaths exists to insure and protect the truth. In today's Gospel, Jesus is making a plea for truth, that we may be truthful always without the necessity of taking oaths.

1) Truth is an absolute necessity for the harmonious working of any society. Deceit frustrates confidence, impeding growth and progress.

2) We should not have to add oaths to our statements and transactions to assure their truthfulness. Oaths should not be taken except in serious matters.

II. In today's Gospel, Jesus inveighs against the use of sacred language for frivolous ends. The taking of the holy name of Jesus in vain is wrong; or worse, the employment of the holy name of Jesus in evil conversation is degrading. It is an irreverence. The holy name should always be employed with reverence and with a consciousness of its being used.

III. Jesus is the living truth. He said, "I am the way, the truth, and the life" (Jn. 14:6). While on earth, Jesus proclaimed truth, and looked with love on people who sincerely hungered for truth. When He left this earth, He promised to send the Holy Spirit to guide us along the road of truth.

1) No one will receive the gift of faith if he/she is basically dishonest, for faith is supernatural truth and demands a foundation of sincerity and truthfulness. Deceit stifles faith and true self-knowledge.

2) Truth challenges us to be true to ourselves and to others as well. It challenges us to come clean, to recognize our virtues and our

weaknesses, to recognize our talents and limitations, and to be ourselves.

IV. Whether we realize it or not, God hears our speech and witnesses a lie whether or not we call upon Him to witness it. Jesus warns us to say "yes" when we mean yes, and "no" when we mean no. This is a plea for sincerity and truth.

1) "You will know the truth, and the truth will make you free." (Jn. 8:32). Truth liberates. It frees us from the servitude of ignorance and passion.

2) To satisfy one's passions, the temptation is to rationalize truth or compromise it to justify a wrongdoing. Love of truth helps to dispel the blindness of human passions.

3) Our Lord called the devil a liar not only because he is the father of lies but because most of his temptations are sugar-coated lies. Our Lord cautions us to pray always so as not to be hurt or deceived by temptations.

V. Some people will lie for the flimsiest of reasons in order to escape the slightest reprimand if they have done something wrong or evil. This is preferring to offend God by lying rather than to receive a reprimand from a fellow human being.

1) Cheating is also lying, and many resort to this in exams or in job applications.

2) Some pay for phony documents or licenses or degrees in order to practice a profession for which they are not qualified. A license or degree is a permission or an award for a true status or capacity. Society needs honest communication in order to fill positions which need qualified people to serve the public.

VI. Sincerity and truth are virtues which require fortitude to practice. The prophets spoke the truth and were persecuted for it. Our Lord Jesus Christ spoke the truth and was crucified for it. The martyrs faced death rather than deny their identity as Christians. Lying is cowardice. God is truth, and He is truth's reward. To live the truth, to tell the truth will cost us, and perhaps dearly, but it is bearing witness to Our Lord Jesus. The Lord walks with truthful souls. The Psalmist says as much: "No man who practices deceit shall dwell in my House; no man who utters lies shall continue in My presence" (Ps. 101:7).

****

1) That we place a high priority on being sincere and authentic.

2) That we strive to be truthful in family circles and especially between husbands and wives.

3) That we always use the holy name of Jesus with reverence.

4) That we refrain from doubletalk.

5) That we be honest in our business dealings.

6) For fortitude and courage to speak the truth when it is required.

7) That governments of nations be honest in their negotiations with other nations.

Monday of the Eleventh Week: Mt. 5:38-42

I. In today's reading, Jesus quotes the ancient law of "talion," *Lex Talionis*. It was a law of retaliation: "An eye for an eye and a tooth for a tooth."

1) It appears in the ancient Babylonian Code of Hammurabi, the king of Babylon (1792-1750 B.C.). This code of laws was one of the greatest of antiquity.

2) This retaliatory code found its way into the Book of Exodus, where it states: "You shall give life for life, eye for eye, tooth for tooth, hand for hand, foot for foot, burn for burn, wound for wound, stripe for stripe" (Exodus 21:23-25).

3) This law was to serve as a practical means of stopping or limiting evil perpetrated by others in a society that did not have effective police enforcement.

4) It was not to institute a vendetta mentality that would lead to limitless bloodletting, for a community accepted and expected that a crime would be repaid by the injured person's family, but not to exceed the damage incurred.

II. Jesus, after citing the law of revenge, abrogated it, and instituted His new law of love, even a love that was to include one's enemies. Charity must be the end of all law, even justice. A Christian's vengeance must still be charity, for only charity can restore healing. St. Paul in his letter to the Romans reiterates Jesus' teaching: " 'If your enemy is hungry, feed him; if he is thirsty, give him drink; for by so doing you will heap burning coals upon his head.' Do not be overcome by evil, but overcome evil with good" (Rom. 12:20-21).

1) Jesus is urging us to defeat evil by goodness. When one takes you to law for your shirt, Jesus counsels, give him your coat as well. Should anyone press you into service to go a mile, Jesus states that we go an extra mile in offering our services.

2) "Give to him who begs from you, and do not refuse him who would borrow from you"; that is, those who are hard put to it and need immediate aid.

3) We are to turn the other cheek. This means being patient in bearing with evil that we cannot change, for only such a behavior will bring about good. It will prick the consciences of those who are perpetrating the evil. St. Augustine states that God is patient with evil people precisely for the motive of ultimately making them good, for His patience leads the sinner to repentance (*Corpus Christianorum, Series Latina*, Sermon XVIII).

4) Today greed instead of charity rules the hearts of many Christians, who for the flimsiest of reasons will sue their neighbor for financial gain. This is so often nothing but greed and selfishness.

III. The expressions "taking care of number one," "every dog has his day," "I won't forget," etc., really harbor a spirit of vengeance that is totally un-Christlike.

1) It is paying evil for evil, tit for tat. This is the very thing that Our Lord condemns in today's Gospel, for it is nothing more than the world's philosophy of vengeance.

2) There is nothing more Christlike than rendering good for evil, helping rather than sinking opponents, and forgiving and forgetting. What better way is there for conquering our enemies than by loving them? It ultimately wins them over.

3) Karl Menninger, the renowned psychiatrist, said: "No matter how glorified or how piously disguised vengeance as a human motive may be, it must be repudiated by each and every one of us. Unless we the people, the man on the street, the housewife in the home, can give up our delicious satisfaction for vengeful retaliation on scapegoats, we cannot expect to preserve our peace, our public safety, or our mental health."

4) Not to react vengefully is Christianity practiced heroically. It

cannot help but pay the debt of our own sins, reap a huge reward in heaven, and ultimately contribute to the salvation of our enemies.

****

1) That we never harbor grudges.

2) That we forgive those who have offended us from our hearts.

3) That we strive even to forget past grievances committed against us.

4) That governments strive to bury their differences for the cause of peace.

5) For an end to the arms race and the conversion of the Soviet Union.

6) That we strive to attain to the ultimate in Christian charity by repaying good for evil.

Tuesday of the Eleventh Week: Mt. 5:43-48

I. The Old Testament commands the Jews to love their neighbor, but the neighbor was interpreted as referring to one's fellow Jews, and by extension to resident aliens.

1) It is easy to love one's friends; what merit is there in that? The merit comes when it costs us to love, and this is the case with loving one's enemies. They, too, are made in the image and likeness of God, and God loves them. They are the products of His creative hand.

2) God seeks the salvation of all men and women, and will work toward this end until we all die. This is symbolized in His allowing the rain to fall and the sun to shine indiscriminately on the just and unjust alike.

3) The Christian sense of neighbor must go beyond family, relatives, and friends to include everyone.

II. Jesus introduces a disarming way of love, the "graduate-level" response. He teaches that we are to respond to evil with good, to endure evil and injustice rather than inflict it as a response or retaliation. Enduring hardships unjustly afflicted is an excellent penance. It is one of the beatitudes. By responding to evil with good, we heap live coals upon our enemy's head. Such a response should jar the conscience of the one perpetrating the evil, and could be a start for a genuine conversion. St. Stephen's prayer for his persecutors won the conversion of Saul of Tarsus.

III. To comprehend Jesus' new commandment of loving enemies, we must see beyond the evil done by its perpetrator and decry the evil rather than abhor the person guilty of it, for evil we should always detest.

1) It is not the response of non-resistance that Jesus is espousing as much as it is the response of positive good in the face of evil. This good becomes the active agent in touching the heart of the evildoer.

2) The response of one insulted is to offer the other cheek as an act of love. This is obviously not the normal reaction. It is a heroic Christian response that will literally shock its perpetrator to the core, to touch whatever bit of good there may still be in him/her, and shake him/her into the realization that he/she is ultimately hurting him-/herself by doing such an evil. When a taunter picked up a stone and threw at the face of Benedict Joseph Labre, the saint picked up the stone tinged with his blood, looked kindly at his persecutor, and kissed the stone.

3) This is a challenge of grace rather than vengeance. It is the overwhelming response of good to evil that sends out a strong message of repentance.

4) A lawyer who had a violent dislike for St. Francis de Sales, the bishop of Geneva, would let no chance pass by in which he might slander the saintly bishop. One day Francis met him on the street and said to him, "If you had removed one of my eyes, I should not have ceased looking at you in all good faith and love with the other." It became proverbial in Savoy that it was necessary to offend Francis in order to receive every sort of favor (Couannier, *St. Francis de Sales and His Friends*).

IV. Love of one's enemies seems like wild logic and is very difficult to put into practice. It demands a deep and generous trust in Our Lord Jesus Christ. It is exceedingly meritorious and rewarding. St. Francis de Sales liked to tell the story of an experience he had as a student in Padua, Italy. The Paduan students acted like bandits and wandered around the city armed at night, provoking fights. One of these bullies attacked and killed another young man; then horrified, he rushed off to hide in a friend's house. The friend's mother was there awaiting her son's return. Distraught, the murderer confessed what he had done, not knowing who it was he had killed. She was sorry for him and promised to hide him. A knock came at her door, and a group carried in the body of her son who had been killed a brief while earlier. He had been killed in the street by a stranger (the young man she was hiding). Faithful to her promise, she kept the secret. Francis added that then she received a vision, where her son appeared to her shining like a saint. He had died in sin, but his mother's heroic charity and forgiveness had cleared his debt at one sweep (Ibid.).

V. When we strive to love even our enemies, we come to imitate the love our Savior taught in its highest degree. He died for friend and enemy alike for the sole unselfish motive that we all might attain to the bliss of heaven.

****

1) When we are provoked, that we pause before responding, lest we say something that will further aggravate the situation.

2) That we strive to remove all rancor and ill will from our hearts.

3) That we may be quick to forgive and even strive to forget all that might aggravate our relationships.

4) That the Lord give us prudence and tact to enable us to deal with provocative people.

5) That we pray for those with whom we are having difficulty.

6) That a true spirit of dialogue might reign among nations in order to seek peaceful solutions to their differences.

Wednesday of the Eleventh Week: Mt. 6:1-6,16-18

I. One thing Our Lord detested in the Pharisees was their hypocrisy. They were great ones for doing things to be seen by others.

1) In performing any good work, our intention should be to please God and to glorify our Heavenly Father, to seek His praise and not that of other human beings.

2) We are to become lights and examples to others by the fruit of our work, but Jesus cautions us not to blow our horn before doing a virtuous deed. Our intention must be pure; otherwise our reward will be that of men and not of God.

3) If one prays to be seen and esteemed, such a person is praying hypocritically and preying on people. So too with fasting; although it

is a laudable penance and an excellent mortification, Our Lord warns us against vanity and an external show of piety.

II. Humility is the foundation of any solid spiritual edifice. Purity of intention is the first fruit of humility. Jesus said, "Learn from me, for I am gentle and lowly in heart" (Mt. 11:29). St. Augustine said that humility is so necessary for Christian perfection that among all the ways to reach perfection, the first is humility, the second is humility, and the third is humility.

1) Humility in the spiritual life is like a hub of a wagon wheel; all other virtues flow from it to the outer rim like so many spokes of the wheel. St. Teresa calls it the greatest gift of grace God can bestow on us.

III. Humility is truth. With it, one strives to see oneself as God sees one. It does not rationalize one's sins and faults. There are three basic rungs in the ladder of humility: 1) to consider oneself a sinner worthy of chastisement and disdain; 2) to actually rejoice when one is rebuked or insulted or demeaned, believing that one is worthy of such treatment and should be thought little of; and 3) the humble person tries to hide his or her virtue or good works, and if he/she cannot readily do so, then he/she quickly attributes such a good work to the grace of God or to the merits of another person.

1) St. Francis wept so bitterly one night that Brother Elias asked why he wept so. The saint replied that he was the worst sinner in the world. Brother Elias asked how he could possibly believe such a thing. St. Francis replied that if any other person received as many graces as he did, he would be a far better man.

2) When our Blessed Lady was told by the Archangel Gabriel that she was chosen among all women to be the Mother of God, she replied that she was but His handmaid.

3) St. Bernard exclaimed one day: "O my God, what do we expect to reap if we seek to appear great in the eyes of men? What does it matter whether we are ridiculed, regarded as insignificant by men, if in Your eyes we are great and without fault? Oh, will we ever understand this truth and thus arrive at the peak of perfection!" The saints had but one desire — to be unknown and regarded as inferior by everyone (*Spiritual Diary: Selected Writings and Examples of Saints*, St. Paul Editions).

4) St. John Vianney said humility is to all other virtues as a chain

is to a rosary. Take away the chain and the beads scatter. Remove humility and the other virtues vanish.

IV. In the practice of any virtue, one's primary motive must be to please God, and not to perform any good work to be seen by others, or to hunger for the praises of other men and women.

1) Our Lord counsels us to seek the lowest place, to seek to serve and not to be served.

2) To consider ourselves servants in relation to God is easy, but to consider ourselves as servants of others is very difficult. To be showered with praise is naturally consoling. Not to defend ourselves when we are criticized or even maligned or held in contempt is very difficult; yet this was the practice of the Savior Himself.

****

1) That the Lord bestow the grace of humility on us.

2) In our good works, acts of virtue and piety, that we may be conscious of our intentions and desire to please God.

3) That we avoid doing things to win the applause and esteem of others.

4) That we strive to serve rather than be served.

5) That we strive to offer up as a salutary penance any insults or humiliations of which we might be the victims.

6) That we strive to form the good habit of prefacing our prayers of petition with an act of contrition.

Thursday of the Eleventh Week: Mt. 6:7-15

I. Just about everybody prefers quality over quantity. This is eminently true in the matter of prayer. Jesus tells us when we pray we are not to "heap up empty phrases as the Gentiles do; for they think that they will be heard for their many words." Jesus is positing sincerity, humility, and trust as primary requisites of good prayer. Since our Heavenly Father knows what we want, there is no need to go on explaining and describing things to Him. He wants us to go to Him as a child goes to his/her father and sincerely and earnestly ask Him what we want without beating around the bush.

II. Jesus goes on to show us how to pray in the Lord's prayer. We have learned this prayer since we were very young, and no doubt we have been saying it every day, possibly several times a day. Quite probably the words fall automatically from our lips without our reflecting upon them. It is rich in meditative content. St. Teresa would tell her nuns, when they were at a loss for something to meditate on, to say the Our Father and reflect on each word or phrase of it. She could hardly get past the first line of it without going off into ecstasy. The very reality of being able to address God as our Father should spark a real confidence in Him.

III. St. Augustine said of the Lord's Prayer, "The very effort we make in praying the Lord's Prayer calms the heart, makes it clean, and renders it more capable of receiving divine gifts."

1) It calms the heart because God makes us feel as one of the family by the mere fact that Jesus told us to address God as our Father. The opening line of the Our Father is one of adoration and gratitude that we have God as our father. Our gratitude is expressed by hallowing His Name and being grateful for being members of His kingdom that Jesus came to establish in our hearts.

2) When a child approaches a loving father, there is that feeling of calm and confidence that his/her father will hear him/her. St. Augustine felt that a devout recitation of the Lord's Prayer would bring about the forgiveness of one's sins, hence the calming effect of the Our Father. This is further augmented by asking that our wills be in harmony with God's will. This is the case with the angels and saints in heaven, and consequently there is seraphic peace there.

3) Since we are all God's sons and daughters and members of His family, it is only logical that if we expect God to forgive us our sins, for He is a forgiving and loving Father, then it follows that we must forgive those who have offended us. This is precisely what God wills. Forgiving others is also a necessary ingredient for an effective prayer of petition, for Our Lord tells us, "When you are offering your gift at the altar, and there remember that your brother has something against you, leave your gift there before the altar and go; first be reconciled with your brother, and then come and offer your gift" (Mt. 5:23-25).

IV. Only evil can rob us of God's kingdom. God reigns from our hearts; therefore, we pray that God deliver us from evil and from temptation. Having prayed that God's will be done on earth as it is in heaven, and having expressed our forgiveness of those who have offended us, and having asked God to forgive us our sins, now writes

St. Augustine, we become more capable of receiving divine gifts. Among those gifts is the greatest we have, Jesus Christ in the Eucharist, our true daily bread, the Bread of Heaven.

V. Jesus cautions us not to rattle on in our prayers. We must now remember that we are addressing a very special Father. Before beginning our prayers, we should place ourselves in the presence of God, humble ourselves before His divine majesty, and beg pardon for our sins. With reverence let us realize that we address the all-powerful triune God; let us also feel privileged in realizing that He is our loving Father, who is most gracious to His children, especially those who strive to do His will.

****

1) When we pray, that we do so with attention and seriousness, and not rattle off words unconsciously.

2) Before asking for petitions, that we examine our consciences to see if we harbor any ill-will toward others.

3) That we be quick to forgive and forgive generously.

4) That we always strive to know God's will and to put it into practice in our daily lives.

5) That we pray the Lord's Prayer becoming more conscious of its rich meditative content.

6) For a deeper faith and confidence, and persistence in our prayers.

Friday of the Eleventh Week: Mt. 6:19-23

I. Our treasure is where our hearts lie. Our true interests are what we really spend our time and energy on. Our Lord tells us the eye is the lamp of the body, and if our eyes are good, our bodies will be filled with light. Faith is the eye of the soul, and grace is the light which enters into it. The grace of God is the treasure that enriches the whole soul. If our faith is deep and intense, the eyes of our soul will respond to that supernatural light just as our physical eyes respond to sunlight. Through this light of faith, our intellects become illuminated to understand a situation involving the implementation of acts of virtue, and our wills will be moved to pursue the good suggested by the Holy Spirit.

II. Today's Gospel contrasts temporal treasures with spiritual treasures. We cannot buy happiness with material wealth; much less is heaven so negotiable.

1) Heaven cannot be purchased, not even by personal holiness. It is a sheer gift of Almighty God, but God has revealed that He will only bestow it on souls that cooperate with His graces, and thus grow in holiness, and as a consequence dispose themselves to receive the priceless gift of heaven. This side of heaven, happiness can only be obtained through spiritual possessions — that wealth accumulated through the practice of virtue, especially through the self-sacrificial practice of the queen of the virtues — charity: giving to and serving others.

2) Ernest Hemingway won the Nobel prize and the Pulitzer prize. He had a home in the Sawtooth Mountains in Idaho, a beautiful apartment in New York, and a luxury home in Venice, yet he put the barrel of a shotgun to his head. He really was not happy or fulfilled.

III. Jesus tells us not to spend time and energy in laying up an earthly treasure, where moth and rust consume and thieves can break in to steal. Obviously moths cannot eat gold or coins. In the East in Our Lord's day people equated fine clothing with wealth (Barclay); they were synonymous; in this sense, moths can eat wealth; therefore we should not put our hearts on such tenuous and ephemeral wealth.

1) St. Ignatius Loyola used to repeat the words "what does it profit a man if he gains the whole world and loses or forfeits himself?" (Lk. 9:25) to Francis Xavier when they were both students at the University of Paris. Francis Xavier had his eyes fixed on a lucrative career. Finally the words of that cited Scripture passage come home to him, and he joined St. Ignatius to begin the Jesuit Order. Francis Xavier went to India and to the Far East preaching the Gospel and winning many, many souls for Christ.

2) St. Paul said: "It is no longer I who live, but Christ who lives in me" (Gal. 2:20). Anything else was a poor investment to him. In the end, we must leave money, things, and all physical possessions behind us.

3) "The sons of this world are wiser in their own generation than the sons of light" (Lk. 16.8). How many people spend their lifetimes in spending time and energy to amass a fortune, and how little is spent in amassing merit before God.

IV. C.S. Lewis said that "If you read history, you will find that the Christians who did most for the present world were those who thought most of the next. It is since Christians have largely ceased to think of the other world that they have become ineffective in this world. Aim at heaven and you will get earth thrown in. Aim at earth, and you will get neither."

V. We should strive to make things and possessions work for us to amass treasure in heaven. Charity broadens one's faith; it makes it grow, thus enabling the eyes of our souls to see things more clearly in their relationship to eternity. Generous people have a deeper faith than miserly, egocentric, or selfish people. Just as the practice of charity increases our faith, so does selfishness cause one's faith to dry up and fade away.

1) Almsgiving should be part of our daily lives. This does not only include money but serving others with our time and talent.

2) Meditative prayer and spiritual reading will sharpen the eyes of our souls.

3) Making our living is one thing and a necessary one. Making our relationship with God is another. One should plan one's employment as a practical means of amassing treasure in heaven and improving one's relationship with God. This opportunity of so enriching ourselves presents itself while we are still alive on this earth, but it all ceases with death. St. Paul exhorts us all who are now living: "Behold, now is the acceptable time; behold, now is the day of salvation" (2 Cor. 6:2).

****

1) That we always try to see things of space and time in their relationship to eternity.

2) That we never separate but rather integrate our business lives and our spiritual lives.

3) That we learn to use things and possessions to earn spiritual rewards.

4) That we never become blinded by nor hunger for luxury goods.

5) That we be generous in almsgiving and in giving of ourselves in serving others.

6) That those who suffer from hunger may obtain the necessary food for themselves and their families.

Saturday of the Eleventh Week: Mt. 6:24-34

I. Mammon comes from the Arabic and Hebrew and signifies wealth or material possessions. In a broader sense it refers the our threefold adversaries: the world, our passions, and the devil, all of which are capable of bringing us to ruin.

II. Johann Wolfgang von Goethe (1749-1832) wrote the famous dramatic poem *Faust*. He spent sixty years in writing this masterpiece. Faust makes a contract with the devil, whereby the devil was to serve him for twenty-four years, and at the end of this period of time the soul of Faust was to be carried off by the devil forever. Faust chose to serve Mammon and gamble with his soul.

1) Many people bargain with evil while presumptuously thinking that somehow in the end they will have the best of both worlds and not lose out on either. God will, in their estimation, overlook their treason, and all will end up well for them.

2) Adam and Eve did just this, and struck out for all of us. We are still paying the price of their sin.

3) To live by presumption is reckless and risky. It blinds us to the reality of the danger of losing our soul. We are all tempted in one way or another by the world with its alluring riches, by our own passions, and by the devil; but to assume an attitude of bartering with these formidable foes with a daring presumption is downright foolish, irresponsible, and dangerous.

III. Our possessions must always be our servants and not vice versa. In the final analysis we really do not own anything in this world. At best, we have only the use of material possessions. We are their stewards, and are charged with responsibility for using them well. When men or women begin to hoard their possessions — that is, when their possessions begin to enslave them and be their constant source of worry — they become spiritually blind. In his letter to Timothy, St. Paul does not state that money is the source of all evil, but he does say that the love of money is the root of all evil. He writes: "For the love of money is the root of all evils; it is through this craving that some have wandered away from the faith and pierced their hearts with many pangs" (1 Tim. 6:10).

IV. In the latter part of today's Gospel, Our Lord speaks of the loving providence of God, and the evil of worry, since it is a lack of trust in a loving, provident Father. If God made the birds of the air and provides for them each day, how much more will He do so for us, who are much higher in the order of creation!

1) Birds work for their daily bread and hustle to feed their young; nevertheless, they do not store up food for an unforseen future. The flowers of the fields bloom for so short a time; yet in their brief beauty they reflect the beauty of God, the like of which cannot be reproduced by human hands.

2) God provides us with this beauty to cheer us up and as a reminder of our destiny: seeing permanent Beauty itself in the beatific vision.

V. Our Lord tells us not to worry about the future or what we are to eat or put on. Our Heavenly Father knows we have need of these things. He is not saying that we should sit back and it will all fall into our laps. Like the birds of air, we too have to work. What He is saying is that making the acquisition of wealth in defense of the future an overwhelming priority in our lives is an insult to God and His loving providence; it will bring us to ruin by ultimately cutting God out of our daily lives.

1) Worry is basically a lack of trust in God. It is the cause of so much unhappiness. It brings about mental and physical ruin. Coronaries, ulcers, and nervous breakdowns are in many cases brought on by senseless worry — the lack of trust in our Heavenly Father.

2) To brood over the past is ridiculous because it cannot be changed; to be apprehensive of the future is placing one's head into a wind of fears which so often are highly exaggerated as only a worried imagination can produce. It is all so much wasted effort and spent energy. "Enough, then, of worrying about tomorrow," says our divine Lord. "Let tomorrow take care of itself. Today has troubles enough of its own."

****

1) Worry often is a sin against the providence of God and against the virtue of religion; that we learn to cast ourselves into the arms of divine providence.

2) Our Lord tells us to be more concerned about seeking the things of God, which is also good mental health; that our priorities may always be God and our relationship with Him.

3) Our overriding preoccupation and concern should be knowing and doing the will of God, fearing Him and Him alone; that this may be our attitude and receive more of our time than senseless worry.

4) That the Lord fill us with a deep and vibrant faith and confidence in His generous and protective providence.

5) For all those who are suffering from anxiety and worry, that they may come to rest secure in God's loving providence.

Monday of the Twelfth Week: Mt. 7:1-5

I. What a remarkable guarantee Jesus gives us of a benign judgment after death if we are lenient in our judgment of others. Just as God forgives us as we forgive others, so too will He judge us as we judge others. Our charity has repercussions in heaven.

II. People are quick to see evil rather than good in a person. They see the speck in their brother or sister's eye, and completely overlook the plank in their own eye.

III. Our Lord Jesus Christ tells us to be perfect as our Heavenly Father is perfect. This is obviously a full-time job.

1) It is only when we reflect upon ourselves in meditative prayer that we are going to come to know ourselves with all our faults.

2) As a consequence of Original Sin, we are naturally proud and egotistical. We tend to seek to build up our own image and to aggrandize and exaggerate it at the expense of others, especially those who are more naturally gifted. It is easier to tear down rather than to build up.

3) Newspaper reporters prefer to seek the scandals and the crimes rather than the noble, compassionate, and charitable deeds performed by people. Why? because they feel people want to know more about the dirt of others than their good qualities.

IV. Such were the generous sentiments of St. Catherine of Siena that she counseled that even if our eyes beheld a person commit a sin, we ought not to pass judgment on that person. Rather, we should feel a sincere compassion for that person and offer the judgment to God accompanied by a humble and devout prayer for His mercy.

1) When we pass judgment on others, we are usurping the office

of God. This why God says, "Vengeance is mine, I will repay" (Rom. 12:19). In so many words He is saying to us, "Do not engage in judging others for what they may have done." We simply will never know the full facts of a situation together with the psychological conditions, nor the motivation a person had while doing something he/she should not have done, or failing to do something he/she should have done.

2) St. Francis de Sales said human judgments are rash "because every man has enough to do in judging himself without taking upon himself to judge his neighbor." He said that Simon the Pharisee judged Mary, when she entered the banquet hall to wash the feet of Jesus, to be a great sinner because she had lived as a public sinner for so long a time. Nevertheless, he accused her falsely because she was at that moment no longer a sinner, but a most holy penitent whom Jesus Himself declared to be clean and now virtuous.

3) The proud Pharisee thought the humble publican to be a great sinner, but wrongly so, for at that moment he was already justified, while the Pharisee was not, despite his profession and enumeration of the good works he performed.

4) In the Book of Job, God's wrath is turned against Eliphaz, Baldad, and Sophar because they judged Job rashly. Conversely, in the Book of Genesis, God's favor is bestowed on Jacob's son, Joseph, because he refused to judge his brothers who sold him into slavery to the Ishmaelites. He even wept when he saw them.

5) St. Augustine writes in his *Confessions* of two basic evils in man: severity toward one's neighbor, and indulgence toward oneself.

6) After being the victim of so much hate, venom, and insult, Our Lord's first words from the cross were. "Father, forgive them; for they know not what they do." Our Savior refused to judge them; rather, He begs for pardon for their obvious sins.

7) As St. John of the Cross put it, "In the evening of life, we shall be judged by our love." Let love invade our thoughts and judgments, and as this great mystic doctor put it, "Where there is no love, put love."

****

1) When we feel the temptation to judge or to criticize others, that we develop the habit of pausing and praying for them.

2) That we not repeat the gossip that was passed on to us.

3) St. James wrote: "If any man makes no mistakes in what he says he is a perfect man"; that we mortify our speech especially when the occasion arises to talk about others.

4) That we strive even to defend the absent.

5) When we are tempted to think the worst of another person, that we stop to search for the beam in our own eye.

Tuesday Twelfth Week: Mt. 7:6,12-14

I. Today's pericope is from the conclusion of the Sermon on the Mount. Treat others as you would have them treat you. This sums up the law and the prophets. It is the golden rule.

1) It is easy to be selfish and vengeful; it is hard to patiently endure harsh treatment, to turn the other cheek, or go the extra mile. For this reason, access to the kingdom of heaven is described as entering "by the narrow gate."

2) As for the salvation of souls, Our Lord was questioned by someone as He was making His way toward Jerusalem, "Lord, will those who are saved be few?" And He said to them, "Strive to enter by the narrow door; for many, I tell you, will seek to enter and will not be able" (Lk. 13:24). This clearly indicates that salvation is not an easy task. It is something at which we must sedulously work. Let us always remember that God created us without our help but He will not save us without our help. We must work at it.

3) Our Blessed Lady indicated to the children of Fátima, after they had been given a vision of hell, that many souls were going to hell for the careless lives they lead.

4) Today's Gospel narrative is the concluding part of the Sermon on the Mount. Jesus' teaching is demanding, but of course we are not alone, and, all in all, His grace is sufficient.

II. In today's society we hear such phrases as "Look out for number one," "Do your own thing," and "feel good about yourself." Is this not replacing kindness with egotism?

1) Kindness is something we can give away without suffering any loss; quite the contrary, we profit from acts of kindness. Kindness always enriches the giver of it. If it doesn't win over the one upon whom it is bestowed, it will prick his/her conscience.

2) It melts meanness in others, as St. Francis de Sales used to

say, "You catch more flies with a drop of honey than with a barrel of vinegar."

III. Kindness has an irresistible attractiveness about it. St. Augustine said that he owed his conversion to the influence of the bishop of Milan, St. Ambrose, not because of the eloquence of his sermons or arguments, but because of his kindness.

1) Emmanuel Kant, the great philosopher, speaking about death during his last illness, said: "If I knew for certain that this night would be my last, I would raise my hands and say, 'God be praised!' The case would be different if I had ever caused misery to any of my fellows."

2) If animals respond to kindness, how much more will we human beings do so? "Kindness has converted more sinners than zeal, eloquence, and learning" (Frederick W. Faber, cited from A. Castle, *Quotes and Anecdotes*).

IV. Kind people make eternal investments. God will not be outdone in kindness. Our Lord Himself tells us that we will basically be judged by the way we treat others.

1) Those who bear grudges and harbor vengeful thoughts cannot be at peace with themselves. Psychologically, it is bad mental health. One's countenance will lack serenity. The immediate reward of kindness is joy and peace.

2) Mahatma Gandhi liberated India by turning the other cheek with nonviolent protests. His persistent kindness won the hearts of his fellow Indians and finally the freedom of India from the British occupation.

3) Abraham Lincoln was criticized often for treating his enemies too leniently. His response to that criticism was, "In befriending them, I conquer them." He would say: "I want it said of me that whenever I came across a weed in life, I strove to replace it with a flower." He meant replacing meanness with kindness.

****

1) That we eliminate all ill will and all grudges from our hearts.

2) That we strive to increase our courteousness in our relationships with others.

3) That we be more thoughtful and considerate toward the elderly and the lonely.

157

4) That we bear with unkind remarks and not return them in kind; rather, that we offer them up in union with Jesus Christ crucified as an act of reparation for our own sins.

5) That we strive to anticipate the needs of others.

6) That we make more of an effort to be cheerful and to greet others warmly.

7) That we make an effort to be more hospitable and gracious.

8) That husbands and wives show special kindness toward each other.

Wednesday of the Twelfth Week: Mt. 7:15-20

I. St. Matthew wrote his Gospel for the Jewish people and the new Christian converts from Judaism. He wrote it to encourage the new Christian converts to hold on to their new faith even in the face of trials to come. To the Jewish people, Matthew set out to prove that Jesus is the Messiah, the ardently awaited One of the Jewish nation and of her people living in other lands — the diaspora.

II. Jesus warned against false prophets, who had been a perennial problem for the Jewish people through the years. Prophets generally wore a sheepskin mantle (Barclay). Our Lord had the Pharisees in mind here. They were false prophets because they did not practice what they were teaching; moreover, their motives were selfish: they were seeking to enrich themselves and to earn the esteem of the people by posing as men of God, when in effect they were voracious wolves dressed in a prophet's garb.

1) A true and forceful teacher is a dedicated person who lives what he/she teaches. The Lord lays down the principle for discerning true from false prophets — their fruits: what they do, how they live their daily lives.

2) All heresies have their elements of truth to them; otherwise they would not draw converts. In time, truth has her way of surfacing. Time, patience, and a critical eye will discern the errors.

III. A sound tree bears good fruit. It gets nothing in return for its fruit. It generously produces its fruit to give to human beings and animals as well.

1) A genuine person is a person of virtue across the board. Such a one is humble, a non-seeker of personal glory, whose paramount

158

objective is to give glory to God and to help others. It is the "I must decrease, He must increase" attitude of John the Baptist.

2) Those who prey on the open goodness of other people are wolves in sheep's clothing, false prophets. Greed and self-interest are their glaring qualities. Unlike the good tree which gives, they take. Like the bad tree, they can only give what is speciously good.

3) The phony cannot persevere in doing good works without tipping his/her hand. The self-seeker will eventually show his/her true colors. What one consistently does or fails to do ultimately reveals the inner person.

4) The intention of the person is much more important in the eyes of Almighty God than the outward excellence of the given work.

5) The higher the tree grows, the deeper its roots must penetrate into the ground. The deeper the humility with which a given work is done, the greater is that work and its worth in the eyes of God.

IV. Charity must be the foundation of all our intentions. We must do things, even our daily chores, for the motive of manifesting our love of God together with our desire to serve Him. This is done either directly with God as the immediate object of a given work, such as assisting at Mass and praying, or indirectly through our service rendered to God through our brothers and sisters in the world.

V. God so values the purity of intention with which we perform a given work, much more than the work or the success of that work. St. Francis de Sales once said, "In quantity our works may be extremely small, and they in no way are worthy of divine reward. But in quality they are, and this is by reason of the Holy Spirit, who dwells in our hearts by charity. He does these works in us, for us, and with us with such exquisite art that these very works which are wholly ours are still wholly His. Just as He produces them in us, so do we reciprocally produce them in and through Him, and just as He works them with us, we co-work with Him" (*Treatise on the Love of God*).

VI. We may not do great works in the eyes of other people, but we have it within our power to do great works for God if we dispose ourselves and arm ourselves with the right disposition, intention, and motivation, for this is what God seeks foremost in us. If we have them, He will do His work through us, work that will bear fruit, and we will be like good trees that will produce good fruit consistently.

****

1) When we rise in the morning, that we offer the Lord all our works to be performed that day as an act of worship and love.

2) That we really try to practice humility and strive to do things out of the pure motive of pleasing God and not for the esteem and praise of people.

3) Modern psychology tells us that we all need our strokes of affirmation; that we strive rather to seek the affirmation of God rather than that of other men and women.

4) That the Lord free us from all deceit and duplicity.

5) That we strive to be true and authentic to ourselves.

6) That businesspeople be filled with the desire to be honest in their dealings with their customers.

Thursday of the Twelfth Week: Mt. 7:21-29

I. The essence of Christianity is loyalty to Christ and fidelity in carrying out His teachings. The term "faithful" applies to Christians committed to live the Gospel even in the face of difficulty. "Not everyone who says to me, 'Lord, Lord,' shall enter the kingdom of heaven, but he who does the will of my Father who is in heaven" (Mt. 7:21).

II. Commitment is practically a taboo word in the modern world. People just do not want to be tied down. They want options that will permit them to opt out when the going gets rough.

1) For the Christian, there are no options with the Gospel; we must be committed to live the Gospel in all its demands. For this reason the road to heaven is said to be straight and narrow.

2) Our committed love of God and neighbor must be spelled out in deeds. Someone asked Mother Teresa why she worked so hard to eliminate poverty when she knew in her heart and soul that she would never totally succeed. She answered: "We are not called to be successful, but to be faithful."

III. In 1940, Hitler sent out an order that incurables and insane people were to be eliminated and no longer be a burden to the Third Reich. A Father Bodelschwingh was chaplain at Bethel, a hospital for the mentally ill. Three officials of Hitler's government came to the hospital and addressed Father Bodelschwingh: "Herr Pastor, the Führer has decided that these people must be gassed." The priest responded: "You can put me into a concentration camp if you wish; as long as I am here you will touch none of these patients. I cannot change to fit the times or the wishes of the Führer. I stand under orders from Our Lord Jesus Christ" (J. Foster, cited in *Quotes and Anecdotes*).

IV. We are all called to be saints, i.e., faithful followers of Christ, who has said: "Do not fear those who kill the body but cannot kill the soul; rather fear him who can destroy both soul and body in hell" (Mt. 10:28).

1) "Hell is paved with good intentions," goes the adage, precisely because intentions are not enough to get one into heaven. Committed effort in carrying out God's will is the password there. Heaven cannot be won by words and promises. Words and promises must blossom into fruits and deeds.

2) This is faith put into works, a faith that is alive and growing. Remember the lines from the song "Show Me" from the hit musical *My Fair Lady*? It goes: "Words, words, words. If you are in love, show me. Sing me no song; read me no rhyme; don't waste my time. Show me! Don't talk of June; don't talk of fall. Don't talk at all; show me!"

3) Many people are baptized and call themselves Christians, but their lives clearly do not measure up to the demands of the Gospel. These are not committed, faithful followers of Our Lord Jesus Christ. Faith is believing. Fidelity is carrying out those beliefs. Christians are called to be faithful; that is, they faithfully strive to carry out the word of God.

V. Fidelity demands courage to carry out our duties in the face of opposition and criticism. It means putting our faith into practice even in the face of hostile storms. It is this courage that will keep our house standing in spite of the lashing of the winds and torrents of storms.

1) While coral remains in the sea, it is soft and can easily be bent by a slight touch. When drawn out of the water and after being exposed to the sun, it hardens and becomes inflexible. So too for us: when we are in the atmosphere of the Church listening or reflecting on the word of God, we should be pliant, allowing God's word and grace to affect us, but when we face the world outside, let us be

inflexible like coral to a world that seeks to change our values or accommodate the Gospel to its standards.

2) God is saying in today's Gospel, "Show Me!" Let us remember Mother Teresa's words, "We are not called to be successful in our commitments, but to be faithful." Fidelity is the fruit and proof of genuine love.

****

1) That we profess our love for Our Lord Jesus Christ by our loyalty and fidelity.

2) That the Holy Spirit bless us with that holy fear — fear of offending God more than the threats and pressure of men and women.

3) That we may be generous in manifesting our love by our deeds.

4) That we be slow to make promises, but faithful in carrying them out.

5) That husbands and wives be faithful to each other and to their sacred vows.

6) That the Lord bless us with courage and fortitude.

Friday of the Twelfth Week: Mt. 8:1-4

I. In Jesus' days, lepers were treated like dead people. They were forbidden entry into Jerusalem or any other walled city.

1) On the open roads, they had to maintain a certain distance from non-lepers. They could not enter the temple. They were literally cast out and cut off from society.

2) No leper would dare to approach a scribe or a rabbi, but the leper in today's Gospel had faith and confidence in the goodness, understanding, and compassion of Jesus, so he came up to Him directly and knelt before Him. This was in clear violation of the Mosaic Law, as it was written down in the book of Leviticus (Lev. 13).

II. Even after his conversion, one thing St. Francis of Assisi found very difficult to do was to have to confront a leper. As he rode one day across the Umbrian plain, his horse balked. Francis wondered why, so he looked about to see what may have frightened it. Then he saw alongside of the dusty road a most hideous leper. His first impulse was to fly away at full gallop, but he rebuked himself and thought to himself, "Now is my opportunity to do something I don't like to do." Despite of the odor of the leper crouching before him, Francis drew near to personally place a bit of money into the poor unfortunate's hand, and even went as far as to kiss the bleeding stump of a hand of the leper. The leper showed his gratitude and kissed Francis in return. Francis remounted his horse and began to continue his journey. When he turned around to wave good-bye, the leper had vanished. Francis realized that it was the Lord Himself (Mark Stier, O.F.M., *Franciscan Life in Christ*).

III. All of us at some time or another must do difficult things, things that are repugnant to our nature; nevertheless, if it is part of our duty or our employment, we do them and do them quickly to get them over with.

1) It is when there is an option and our contract or employment doesn't demand it of us, it is then that we readily opt for the easy way out.

2) The doing of difficult things, even when such difficult things are repugnant to us, when there is no obligation for us to do them and there is an opportunity to walk away from them — it is then that our opting to do them becomes very meritorious and serves as a very profitable penance. This is the lesson Our Lord shows His apostles and ourselves in today's Gospel narrative. No doubt the Apostles, like their countrymen, would have loved to have run on and to have ignored the unfortunate leper, and in doing so would not have violated the Mosaic Law.

3) Jesus stretched out His hand and touched him. This said so much to the Apostles, since Jesus was in this instance defying the Mosaic Law, which expressly prohibited any contact with lepers, and especially physical contact. Jesus was saying in effect that when the Mosaic Law no longer serves the genuine needs of the people and the demands of the higher law of charity, it no longer binds, since charity is the end of all law.

4) Leprosy is a rare disease in our country. The elderly are in many ways treated like the lepers of old. They are herded into old-age homes, nursing homes, out of our sight and out of our minds. Nursing homes are not pleasant places to go into. The elderly need our compassion and love. What a meritorious thing it is to visit the elderly and offer to do chores for them that they cannot do, or just to spend time with them, listening to them and chatting with them to let

them know that they are not ostracized or completely cut off from society. If we live long enough, we, too, may very well be shunted off into nursing homes to be treated in much the same way as so many forlorn old people are treated. Could we muscle up enough patience and support from our own spiritual lives and resources to resign ourselves to life in a nursing home and maintain our equilibrium, while at the same time profiting from it spiritually, winning so many graces for ourselves and others by our constructive use of solitude and patient suffering?

****

1) When charity beckons us to do something difficult, that we may generously rise to the occasion.

2) That we treat the sick and the elderly with patience and kindness.

3) That we visit friends and relatives in hospitals or old-age homes.

4) For all those people who attend patients with communicable diseases, that in their generosity of service they do not contract those same diseases.

5) For all who care for the handicapped, retarded, and mentally ill, that they strive to serve Jesus Christ in their patients.

6) For all who are suffering from hunger, that nourishment be gotten to them.

Saturday of the Twelfth Week: Mt. 8:5-17

I. Centurions were the cream of the Roman army; they were handpicked men who led a command of one hundred men, a group called a century. A century was part of a Roman legion, which was composed of six thousand men (W. Barclay). The word "centurion" comes from the word century which means a hundred; a centurion was a commander of a hundred men. A centurion would be equivalent to a sergeant-major in a modern army. Though not a Jew, the centurion of today's Gospel was well-disposed to Judaism, for he had contributed toward building a synagogue in Capernaum (Lk. 7:5.) (*A Catholic Commentary on Holy Scripture*).

1) The centurion was a Gentile. Through his faith in Jesus and

164

Jesus' response of acceding to grant his petition, St. Matthew is showing that God's kingdom is opening up to the Gentiles.

2) Jesus is making it evident that His kingdom would not be the exclusive property of the Jewish people, and that the passport to it would be faith in Him, the "Messiah." The centurion is obviously open to Our Lord and would readily accept the Gospel message.

II. Jesus singles out the faith of the centurion and contrasts it with the faith of the Jewish people: "Not even in Israel have I found such faith."

1) "Faith," says St. Augustine, "opens the door to understanding; unbelief closes it." Reason can be deceived, writes the author of the *Imitation of Christ*; faith cannot. Let us always remember, however, that faith is a great gift of God, and it is basically through faith that we will be saved.

2) Charity, compassion, and generosity dispose one to be open to faith if one does not already possess it. For those who have the gift of faith, the practice of charity increases one's faith. There is a delicate interplay between charity and faith. Faith moves one to perform works of charity; while charity moves God to increase and intensifies one's faith. Isaiah says as much when he states, "To share your bread with the hungry, and bring the homeless poor into your house; when you see the naked, to cover him, and not to hide yourself from your own flesh. . . . Then shall your light [faith] break forth like the dawn. . ." (Is. 58:7-8).

3) We can see how the centurion's charity gave him a deep confidence in Jesus' ability to perform the miracle of healing for his slave. Slaves, according to Roman law, were mere chattels. An owner of slaves could do as he pleased with his slaves. He could sell them or even kill them if he so chose. This would be perfectly permissible. This centurion showed a love and compassion for his slave, whom he treated as a member of his household. Jesus knew this and was responsive to the request of the centurion.

III. Charity engenders faith; it disposes the Lord to bestow it ever more enrichingly. We cannot give without receiving, nor will the Lord be outdone in generosity. The more charity we bestow on others, the more enriched we become ourselves.

1) The deeper one's faith, the greater the works he/she will

perform. God will readily hear the prayers coming from a heart of deep faith.

2) The centurion's prayer of petition was coming from a man of deep faith which Our Lord Himself praised: "Not even in Israel have I found such faith. . . . Go; be it done for you as you have believed."

IV. The centurion's humility is also to be admired. His words were captured for posterity, and are repeated by all of us just before receiving Holy Communion: "Lord, I am not worthy that You should enter under my roof; only say the word and I shall be healed." No Jewish official had ever made a similar gesture of reverence or homage to Jesus.

1) The centurion's words had all the qualities of a perfect prayer of petition: faith, humility, confidence, and perseverance.

2) God resists proud and stingy people. Such people will never be endowed with a strong faith. In imitation of the centurion, let us always humble ourselves before God, especially asking pardon of our sins before addressing our petitions to Him.

****

1) That the Lord increase our faith.

2) That we always be alert to dispose ourselves by humility and works of charity to receive an increase of faith.

3) For all those, especially members of our families, relatives, and friends, who may have lost the faith, that through the intercession of the Immaculate Heart of Mary, they may receive this priceless gift.

4) That we ourselves may be instruments in bringing others the gift of faith.

5) For unity in the Church, that all Christians might be one.

6) For peace in the world and the conversion of the Soviet Union.

Monday of the Thirteenth Week: Mt. 8:18-22

I. "Teacher," said the scribe, "I will follow you wherever you go." Jesus' response was, "The foxes have holes and the birds of the air have nests; but the Son of Man has nowhere to lay his head."

1) Jesus is merely informing the scribe, "If you want to follow me, it will be tough going, so really think about it." The way would

be laden with many crosses and contradictions. It would not be a road to worldly prestige or comforts.

2) To be with Jesus is sweet paradise, but it has its built-in costly demands. Yet once committed, we are never to turn back.

II. Many people were enthusiastic about Jesus because of His miracles and the authority with which He preached. Enthusiasm very often is skin-deep. When it comes to making a commitment that costs and demands sacrifice, fervor soon fades away. Jesus did not want His followers to be deceived. He made it very clear that following Him would mean bearing crosses throughout life, even daily.

1) When Peter tried to make Jesus tone down His talking about His future sufferings and death, Jesus grew angry and said: "Get behind me, Satan!" (Mt. 16:23).

2) True love demands sacrifice. How true this is in marriage! Couples who really are devoted to each other show it so evidently by the sacrifices they make for each other with all the give-and-take that every marriage demands.

3) It is one thing to feel love on an emotional level, but to live it as a daily expression means paying its cost, which is often dear.

III. The message of today's Gospel is clear: Christianity is not easy; its commitments are demanding, but not impossible.

1) When one of the disciples asked permission to postpone his discipleship with Jesus until he had buried his father, Jesus responded, "Let the dead bury the dead." In the East, "burying" one's parent meant living with him/her until he/she died (*Jerome Biblical Commentary*). This could involve years.

2) When the grace of a call to follow Jesus is given, it must be responded to, or it will cease being given. God just simply will not waste His graces, which are often given in the form of inspirations.

3) "Many are called but few are chosen" (Mt. 22:14). All are called to follow Jesus and implement the spread of His Gospel, particularly by bearing witness to it in their lives, even in the face of difficulty. But alas, how many really do live it out? Look about in the world around you and see how many Christians are gobbled up by the world with all its comforts, pleasures, and enticements.

IV. Even though Jesus calls us to difficult things, the great mystery of it all is that when we commit ourselves to doing them, happiness, peace, and joy are always part of the package, for Our Lord assured us: His yoke is sweet and His burden light.

1) God did not will to take away all the consequences of Original Sin: death, sickness, suffering, and hardships of one kind or another; this is evident in the experiences of our everyday lives. Our Lord Jesus Christ did not intend to take away all our problems; rather, He showed us how to use them for our own spiritual growth. They help purify our souls, detach us from material things, and bring us closer to God. This is what our faith urges us on to do. Many of these trials are blessings in disguise.

2) St. Paul would find glory in nothing except in the cross of Our Lord Jesus (Gal. 6:14). St. Francis of Assisi gave us his idea of perfect joy: "More than all graces and gifts of the Holy Spirit, which God gives His friends, is to deny oneself and, for the sake of Christ's love, to suffer pain, injury, disgrace, and distress. For in the other gifts of God we cannot glory, because they are not our own but God's; whereas in the cross of trial and suffering we can glory, for it is our own" (Boylan, *This Tremendous Lover*).

****

1) That we may be truly enthusiastic in following Christ and cheerfully carry out our commitment to live His Gospel.

2) That our young people be enthusiastic and generous in responding to a vocation to the priesthood or religious life.

3) When our crosses become so heavy, that we then become more conscious of the presence of our Savior shouldering them with us.

4) That married people realize the importance of their commitment to each other and the permanence of their marriage to each other.

5) That we all come to truly appreciate the value in enduring trials, setbacks, and sufferings as salutary penances, sources and means of purifying our souls and drawing us closer to God.

6) That we frequently implore the aid of our Blessed Lady, especially through the rosary, to help us fulfill our commitments.

Tuesday of the Thirteenth Week: Mt. 8:23-27

I. The Sea of Galilee is some six hundred feet below sea level. This low Galilean basin creates a warm, comfortable climate. When the cooler air coming in off the Mediterranean nears the lake, it is sucked down through the gullies, ravines, and gulches on the western side of the lake. It becomes compressed in these gullies and picks up velocity. When the wind hits the surface of the lake, it churns it up into a raging storm, capable of overturning a sizable fishing vessel.

II. One such storm happened to the Apostles while Jesus was asleep in the stern of the boat. The Apostles were fishermen but found this storm too much for them, and they began to panic. With this, they awakened Jesus to protest that they were perishing. Jesus rebuked them for their little faith.

III. Among ancient cultures claiming belief in a single divinity, the sea was viewed as an enemy of God. Creation was often viewed as an outcome of a struggle between God and the forces of evil identified with the raging seas. Israel's culture was colored by such stories. "Thou didst crush Rahab [sea monster] like a carcass. . ." (Ps. 89:11). True confidence in the omnipotence of God was often expressed in terms of being rescued from the crushing power of the sea: "Let me be delivered," writes the Psalmist, "from the deep waters" (Ps. 69:15). With reason the Apostles say to one another: "What sort of man is this, that even winds and sea obey him?"

IV. Faith is not only believing, it is trusting in Him in Whom we have belief. It is the trusting aspect of their faith that Jesus criticizes.

1) Life will have many storms that threaten to inundate us: maybe one's marriage is going on the rocks; perhaps the health of a loved one is failing; a crisis arises that threatens one's career or employment; or someone we love has contracted Alzheimer's disease or is mentally ill. All of these threats are like so many waves breaking over the hulls of our souls. Jesus has the power to say to all these storms: "Hush, be still!"

2) Even when one of these tempests seemingly is getting ahead of us, let us remember the words of St. John Chrysostom, "God loves to manifest His power not at the beginning of our trials, but when we think all is lost. That is the time God chooses to come to our help." St. Francis de Sales also writes, "We must trust fully in God, and the more sincere and perfect our confidence is, the more will He have a special providence over us."

V. Sanctity lies in the paradox of two words: trust and distrust — trust in God, and distrust in oneself.

1) God does marvels to those who trust in Him. History has repeatedly shown that God selected weak, insignificant people to do great work for Him: the Blessed Virgin Mary, David, Gideon, Jeremiah, Isaiah, Francis of Assisi, Ignatius Loyola, Bernadette Soubirous, Thérèse of Lisieux, etc.

2) Distrusting God is an insult to Him and His providence over us. St. Margaret Mary's prayer of trust goes: "O Heart of Love! I place all my trust in You, for I fear everything from my weakness but hope everything from Your mercy."

3) Our Lord said to St. Catherine of Siena: "The more you abandon yourself to Me and trust in Me, the more I shall console you by My grace and make you feel My presence."

VI. The Sea of Galilee is notorious for its sudden storms. Life is much like this. Storms can arise suddenly without much warning: a sudden death of a loved one, an automobile accident, a reverse in fortune, the betrayal of a friend, loss of a job, ingratitude, and many other similar things. If we develop a spirit of prayer, we will experience the confidence that Jesus is present, even though it might seem that He is asleep within the cabin of our souls. Let us put our unbounded trust in Him.

****

1) St. John of God said: "Hope obtains from God as much as it hopes"; that the Lord give us the wherewithal to redouble our confidence in our prayers.

2) The Lord will try us to perfect our loving trust in Him; that we patiently persist in our petitions to Him.

3) That the Lord give us a light to see and abandon ourselves to His divine providence.

4) That those afflicted with drug abuse or alcoholism may blindly trust in God as they face and struggle through another day.

5) For all those who have lost the faith.

6) For an end to the arms race, an end to terrorism, and peace in the world.

Wednesday of the Thirteenth Week: Mt. 8:28-34

I. The shocking thing about today's Gospel is that this great miracle of Jesus did not inspire faith in the Gadarenes. Their possessions or the loss of them blinded them, preventing them from seeing the reality of the presence of the Messiah in their midst. Instead of being overwhelmed with joy at having the Messiah in their home territory, they ask Him to leave it.

II. The paradox of the passage is that the demons recognize Jesus' identity as the Promised One of Israel — the Messiah; the people of Gadara do not because of their self-induced blindness. The demons even call Jesus the Son of God: "What have you to do with us, Son of God?" Have you come to torment us before the time?"

1) The devils were referring to the hour when the prince of this world, Satan, would be overcome. This would come about through the passion and death of Our Lord Jesus Christ. Evil would be totally overcome at the end of the world.

2) The devils were subject to Jesus and would obey Him immediately; not that they liked to do so or opted to do so, but they simply had to obey God.

3) The Gadarenes refused to be subjected to Jesus or to obey Him basically because they were shocked over their financial losses when their herd of swine perished in the water below the cliff. The loss was considerable, for St. Mark's Gospel put the number of the swine herd at two thousand (Mk. 5:13).

III. Jesus came to the Gadarene territory, which lay about six miles inland southeast of the Sea of Galilee and is one of the towns of the Decapolis. The influence of paganism was quite evident there, since these people obviously ignored the Jewish prohibition against raising pigs. Jesus came there to offer these people the gift of faith.

1) The lesson is clear: People do let material possessions block the grace of God from working effectively in their souls. For this reason, many do not receive the gift of faith, or they fail to make any progress in it.

2) Many people literally sell their souls for a bit of this world's goods. The more attached to things we are, the more spiritually blinded we become.

3) The only real wealth is Jesus Christ, and what He offers — life in God and growth in our relationship with Him.

IV. The author of the hymn "Amazing Grace" is John Newton. He was a sea captain seeking his fortune in plying ships to the Americas loaded with slaves. The grace of God visited him, and the horror of what he was engaged in came home to him and struck him to the quick. He gave up the nasty and wicked business of slave-trading, and decided to become a priest. He worked as a priest in rural areas of his native England among uneducated people, whom he instructed through hymns he composed and sang. He would get the people to memorize these hymns and sing them.

1) "Amazing Grace" is the story of John Newton's conversion. It goes: "Amazing grace. How sweet the sound / That saved a wretch like me! / I once was lost but now am found, / Was blind, but now I see."

2) Unlike the Gadarenes, who objected that two men be liberated from devils who possessed them because it would cost them their swine, John Newton saw how his wealth was being made through a diabolical trade, and he decided to accept Jesus Christ and to follow His law of charity. He gave up the false wealth that was blinding him from seeing the Messiah and taking His Gospel to heart. The Gadarenes were too attached to their material possessions, and consequently couldn't see the Messiah who came to visit them and offer them faith and the means of attaining eternal life.

3) The lesson is very clear: Material wealth and our attachment to it can be very dangerous and blinding. We must always be detached and generous with what we have to prevent us from becoming enslaved to material possessions and consequently becoming spiritually blind to the higher riches and wealth of the spiritual life.

****

1) That the Lord give us the spirit of poverty whereby we will not be possessed by money, nor by the lure of things of this world.

2) That we be blessed with spiritual insight and wisdom not to allow people or things or comforts to impede our growth in the spiritual life.

3) That we be more conscious of the presence and the role of our guardian angels in our daily lives, and their role of protecting us from the devil and from physical harm also.

4) That our young people see the evil and the stupidity involved in drug-taking.

5) That all Christians who are blinded and enslaved by material

possessions and desires come to see the reality of Christ in their lives and take His Gospel to heart.

Thursday of the Thirteenth Week: Mt. 9:1-8

I. Illness in general is one of the many evil consequences of Original Sin. In the Israel of Jesus' day, people believed that diseases were directly related to one's personal sins. This notion of illness as being related to sin is unacceptable today, but perhaps not totally. AIDS and venereal diseases are frequently related to or are a consequence of one's personal sins.

II. Be that as it may, the paralytic in today's Gospel was thought of by the people and by the scribes and Pharisees to have been chastised with his paralytic condition because of some personal sin or sins.

1) Before any cure could be hoped for the man's sins must be forgiven, and Jesus undertook to do just that. Thereupon, the Pharisees made immediate objection, and in their minds they charged Jesus with blasphemy because only God can forgive sins.

2) Jesus was aware of what they were thinking, so He challenged the Scribes and Pharisees: "That you may know that the Son of Man has authority on earth to forgive sins," He said to the paralyzed man, "Rise, take up your bed and go home." The man stood up and went home.

3) Needless to say, the scribes and Pharisees were dumbfounded since they believed that no cure could be effected until his sin was removed. They certainly did not want to give any credence to Jesus. According to the logic they were working under, Jesus would have to remove the obstacle to health (physical affliction) together with its cause (which in this case would be the paralytic's sin) for the man to enjoy good health again. Jesus did so to the amazement of the dumbfounded scribes and Pharisees.

III. Jesus came to heal the whole person, body and soul, and He left His Church with the sacraments of the sick together with penance and reconciliation.

IV. Pope John Paul II has said that the modern world is losing its sense of sin. So many people do not realize the danger their immortal souls are in, and many of them perish for all eternity because they have become hardened to the reality of sin.

1) The salvation of souls is the supreme law, and we are all members of the Mystical Body of Christ. We must therefore help people to save their souls. Our Blessed Lady revealed to the children at Fátima that many souls were being lost because there was no one to pray and do penance for them.

2) In today's Gospel, we see that the paralytic was brought to Jesus by people who took an interest in him and wanted to help him. They brought him to Jesus. Perhaps it was these friends who aroused the man's desire to be taken to Jesus for healing. You and I can be instruments of God to encourage lax and faithless people, perhaps members of one's family or friends, to go to Jesus. We should always be disposed to pray for their conversion and to offer up penances for them.

3) A warm concern can break down barriers. Our loving and prayerful concern can make the alienated see Christ in us and come to the realization that they should do something about getting themselves straightened out with God.

4) St. James the Apostle writes, "Whoever brings back a sinner from the error of his way will save his soul from death and will cover a multitude of sins" (Jas. 5:20).

5) The faith will be extended to many more people, not by churches being filled with people but by people becoming full of God and zealous for the salvation of their faithless brothers and sisters. St. John Chrysostom, the great doctor of the Church, said, "I can't believe in the salvation of anyone who does not work for the salvation of his neighbor." For him, it was a far greater thing to convert a sinner than to give all one's riches to the poor.

****

1) That Christians realize there is such a reality as hell and that it is not impossible to go there.

2) The Blessed Virgin revealed at Fátima that many souls are being lost because there was no one to pray and do penance for them; that we always be mindful to pray for the conversion of sinners.

3) That people have an appreciation for the sacrament of the sick and not wait to the point of death before receiving it, but rather have recourse to it while they have a reasonable chance of recovery.

4) That the Lord fill us with a zeal for souls.

5) That we all die in God's grace and be armed with the Church's last sacraments before we leave this world.

6) For the success of th ecumenical movement, that all Christians be one united family.

Friday of the Thirteenth Week: Mt. 9:9-13

I. In today's Gospel, we get a clear example of Jesus breaking with Jewish custom and law by giving Matthew a vocation to the intimate band of the Apostles of Jesus. Like most tax collectors, who were also called publicans, Matthew was probably well off financially, but he was, like the other publicans, isolated and forced to lead a life that was unattractive except for the wealth he gained through his trade. In the mind of the righteous Jew, Matthew's profession, tax collecting, proclaimed his deep sinfulness. He was a constant reminder of the Jewish subjection to the pagan foreigners, the Romans, and he represented the worst form of collaboration by following a trade which typified injustice, oppression, and extortion. By calling Matthew to be an Apostle, Jesus vividly irritated Jewish sentiments and custom, but by the same token, He was showing the universal nature of His mission and kingdom.

II. The Pharisees were slaves to misguided priorities: they were extremely strict and fastidious in regard to ceremonial ritual and ritualistic washings to be observed before participating in the Temple sacrifices and even before meals, while the weightier demands of God's law went by the board.

1) They were so blinded by their observance of details of the Mosaic Law that they failed to see the requirements of the higher law of charity. Hosea, a prophet of the eighth century B.C., had criticized such blindness, and Our Lord Jesus Christ quotes this prophet's words concerning this inversion of values: "I desire steadfast love and not sacrifice" (Hos. 6:6). However good ritualistic sacrifices may be, in the eyes of God they are always inferior to the demands of the higher law of love and mercy.

2) The Gospel will further inculcate a more radical foundation of all the law firmly fixed on the underpinnings of charity and human compassion.

III. In Jesus' day, the Jewish people were divided into two basic groups, which we might describe by today's standards as the liberals and the conservatives. The conservative group would be led by the party of the Pharisees, while the liberal group, which espoused a much more liberal interpretation of the Mosaic Law, would more readily identify with the party of the Sadducees.

1) The conservative group, to which the Pharisees and scribes belonged, would have nothing to do with the common people, who were generally unlettered and unsophisticated. They were considered rabble and unlettered — the bottom rung of Jewish society.

2) The Pharisees considered associating or dealing with the common people as defiling themselves. Jesus regarded this as nonsense, and He manifested His detestation of such behavior and class distinction by accepting an invitation to dine with Matthew and his hated tax-collector friends.

3) Tax collectors were doubly hated because many of them fleeced the people and worked with the detested Roman government.

IV. Jesus was clearly breaking with such traditions and showed that His was a priestly ministry of mercy and of love.

1) He openly associated with the commoners and with tax collectors, and His reply to the criticism leveled at Him by the scribes and Pharisees was: "Such people need a doctor; healthy people do not."

2) Technically speaking, all sinners are sick people insofar as sin stifles or impedes their spiritual growth and their transformation into godliness, which is the ceaseless, tireless work and object of God's grace in our souls.

3) Jesus is lashing out at the self-righteousness of the Pharisees by quoting Hosea, the prophet, first, and then by adding a subtle criticism of His own: "Those who are well have no need of a physician, but those who are sick." Jesus is saying that those who are humble enough recognize their sickness — i.e., their sinfulness — and will call upon God the Supreme Doctor. Humble people will recognize their sinfulness, and will go to Jesus because they know that only He has the power to heal them by forgiving their sins.

4) The self-righteous, on the other hand, are like the Pharisees: they fall victim to their own pride, for they are virtually saying that they don't need a Savior, since in their own assessment and self-sufficiency they feel that they can take care of, or even heal,

themselves; consequently, they shut themselves off from God's help and ultimately cut themselves off from the kingdom of God.

V. We all need the great Physician of souls, Our Lord Jesus Christ, and we are our brothers' keepers. We therefore must show concern for all of our brothers and sisters, especially those who are cutting themselves off from God by the lives they lead. You cannot forgive them their sins, but you can bring them to Jesus, who will shower them with His mercy. You can talk to them, invite them to retreats, prayer groups, cursillos, encounters, etc. You cannot be the doctor; you can, however, be the nurse or the attendant who brings them to the source of healing through your loving concern and zeal for souls.

****

1) That we may always be blessed with the humility to recognize that we are sinners and have need of God's mercy.

2) That we not look down on or despise certain people because of the sins they commit; rather, that our attitude may always be to hate the sin while loving the sinner.

3) That the Lord fill us with a prudent and holy zeal for souls.

4) That we may be light and salt to other people by our loving kindness and warm concern.

5) That we do penance especially for wayward members of our families and for friends who have ceased to practice their faith.

6) For an increase in vocations to the priesthood and religious life.

Saturday of the Thirteenth Week: Mt. 9:14-17

I. In today's Gospel, Jesus demonstrates to the disciples of John the incompatibility of the old law of Moses with the new law of the Gospel.

1) Jesus is not condemning fasting by any means; what he is making evident is the incompatibility of the old order of the Mosaic Law with the new order of the Gospel, which must reign now as the kingdom of God is established on earth with the coming of the Messiah.

2) Jesus refers to Himself as the bridegroom. If there were any expression of joy, merriment, and feasting, it was shown at Jewish

weddings. Jesus is saying that His disciples now have reason to rejoice because He, the long-expected Anointed One, the Messiah, is among them. He is the Bridegroom of the human soul, and while He is physically and visibly present on earth, there is special reason to celebrate, but this state of things would be changed when the Bridegroom would be taken away; then His disciples would fast. Their joy would be turned to sorrow, for the honeymoon would be over. Like ourselves, they would be traveling with the resurrected and invisible Christ, but along a rocky road full of trials and persecutions and in many cases even martyrdom.

II. Jesus further illustrates the break between the old order and the new, and the impossibility of their even coexisting. The new law would simply supplant the old law. As in the parable of the new patch placed on an old garment and the new wine being placed into old wineskins: the new patch would only cause the old material to tear away more. Likewise, the new wine would burst the rigid, inflexible old wineskins because of the fermentation taking place in it.

III. Jesus is saying to the disciples of John that the new law of the Gospels has been inaugurated, and the Mosaic Law would not shape nor mold the Gospel. Jesus, the supreme Authority, would do this molding and structuring, for He is the excellent and perfect interpreter of the Law and the oracles of the prophets.

1) The old law, the Mosaic Law, now becomes obsolete and must give way to the new law of the Gospel.

2) This attitude of Jesus obviously scandalized the scribes and Pharisees and all those who strictly followed the Jewish law and customs.

IV. The Vatican Council has shaken many people with its many changes. Many people were hurt, and justifiably so, by the abuses of liberties that so many priests took with the liturgy.

1) Basically these abuses were due to false interpretations of the conciliar decrees and also to the sheer recklessness of priests and teachers.

2) The basic changes inaugurated by the Council must be good, for they are the work of the Holy Spirit, prodding us on to growth in truth. The Council has done so much to recognize the dignity of the human person and his/her duty to participate more actively in the

liturgy and the life of the Church. It urges all of us and all Christians to move toward uniting all the baptized into one flock under one pastor.

3) To grow, said Cardinal John Henry Newman, means to have changed, and to reach perfection means to have changed many times.

4) "Change," said John F. Kennedy, "is the law of life, and those who look only to the past or the present are certain to miss the future." Albert Einstein once said that everything is changed except the way we think.

5) With the Bridegroom among us, we cannot be static, even though Our Lord Jesus Christ is the same yesterday, today, and tomorrow. Our buoyancy must be like that of new wineskins for new wine, for the Holy Spirit moves within all us, and we must have the elasticity to move with Him who is truth and not limit Him by our rigidity, for this would only serve to frustrate the Spirit's designs upon us and His Church. Such rigidity can only be misguided, especially when it resists in spite of teachings of the Magisterium of the Church, expressed through her councils and through Christ's vicar, the Holy Father.

6) The changes Jesus brought about in His time were shocking to the Jews. Closed minds could not accept such changes. Let us not forget, Jesus speaks through the Magisterium of His Church, which He has promised to be with until the end of time. She will never leads us astray nor into error.

****

1) That the Lord give us the joy of sensing the reality of the presence of the Bridegroom, Our Lord Jesus Christ, in our hearts and souls.

2) That we frequently strive to communicate with this divine Guest of our souls.

3) That those who are especially plunged into sadness at the loss of a loved one may be consoled and comforted by a more palpable sense of the Lord's presence within them.

4) That the Lord give us the wisdom and the prudence to appreciate the need for healthy change and to recognize abuses when we see them.

5) That all priests, teachers, and parents recognize and obey the

teaching office of the Holy Father and the Magisterium of the Church.

6) In harmony with St. Francis, that we strive to change what must be changed, to accept what cannot be changed, and have the wisdom to know the difference.

7) For unity among all Christians.

Monday of the Fourteenth Week: Mt. 9:18-26

I. Over a 250 years ago, the English poet Alexander Pope coined what he called "the ninth beatitude." It goes like this: "Blessed is the man who expects nothing, for he shall never be disappointed." What moves us all to pray is the hope of getting what we set out to ask for. Hope makes us live for what we set our hearts on. It is one of the infused virtues that prompts us to ask our Heavenly Father for what we need. We get what we hope for, no more, no less. God has a big heart and is a generous giver. He is moved and conquered by persistent hope. We must not give up on what we set out for. Hope is the virtue that gives us confidence in prayer.

II. In today's Gospel, we are confronted with two people who are full of the hope that spawned an unbounded confidence that they were going to obtain the favors for which they approached Jesus. Jairus knew his daughter was dead; yet he felt deep down that Jesus could do the impossible: restore his daughter to life. The woman suffering from hemorrhage was shy. She seemed to be afraid to ask Jesus for healing in front of the crowd, yet her faith and confidence in Him were so strong that she thought that if she but touched but the tassel of His cloak, that would be sufficient to obtain healing.

III. Jairus, the synagogue leader, had a big obstacle to overcome in approaching Jesus, namely, the criticism of his peers. Most of the synagogue leaders belonged to the Pharisee party, most of the members of which opposed Jesus, because He criticized them and was breaking the Mosaic Law. If he resorted to Jesus for any favor, he could easily lose his position as president of the synagogue. His love for his daughter was forcing him to ignore any peer pressure or human respect.

1) Jairus would not approach Jesus unless he believed in Him beyond the point of curiosity just to verify the wonders Jesus was working among the people. Could such a miracle happen to his

family? The truth is Jairus believed that Jesus could and would do this for him; yet what he was asking was far beyond Jesus' other miracles, for once he was informed by his servants that his daughter was dead, his petition would be that Jesus restore his daughter to life.

2) Jairus knew in his heart and soul that Jesus was someone extraordinary in their midst, and that the Messianic era had begun in Him. The fulfillment of Isaiah's prophecy of the coming of the Messiah was realized in Jesus: "Then the eyes of the blind shall be opened, and the ears of the deaf unstopped; then shall the lame man leap like a hart, and the tongue of the dumb sing for joy" (Is. 35:5-6).

IV. The woman suffering from hemorrhage, which according to Mosaic Law rendered her and everything she touched unclean, was also barred from temple worship.

1) Her need was so deep for a cure, she spent all her money on doctors to no avail. She believed strongly in Jesus, and she had that important dimension of faith — confidence that Jesus would grant what she was seeking.

2) Indeed we get what we hope for, no more, no less. "Nothing," says St. Bernard, "shows the omnipotence of God like His rendering all-powerful those who hope in Him."

3) G.K. Chesterton wrote, "Hope means hoping when things are hopeless, or it is no virtue at all."

V. Most Christians believe in Jesus as the Savior of the world. They believe in what He taught, but their involvement, their relationship with Him, is skin deep. The consequence of this is that their hope and confidence in Him are also skin-deep, and so they get what they hope for — very little. They are discouraged in prayer before they start.

1) With the leader of the synagogue, Jairus, and the woman suffering from the hemorrhage, need drove them to Jesus as it does for all of us, but as with them let our hope and confidence be strong and our trust be on fire, so that whatever we ask for in prayer, as Our Divine Lord said, we must believe that we will receive it, and we will (Mk. 11:24).

2) Is Our Lord stingy? Or are we stingy in the confidence and hope dimension of our faith? Let us remember, the more ardently we hope, the more generously God will respond to us.

****

1) That the Lord increase our faith.

2) Though very often illnesses and moments of crisis are permitted by divine providence to befall us temporarily for our spiritual growth, that we may not be discouraged when we ask to be delivered from them.

3) That the Lord fill us with lively hope and a deep confidence in our prayers.

4) That our individual relationships with Our Lord Jesus Christ grow in knowledge and in love.

5) That we always be mindful of rendering profuse gratitude to Almighty God for all His favors, spiritual as well as physical.

Tuesday of the Fourteenth Week: Mt. 9:32-38

I. Today's Gospel shows Jesus in the role of teacher, preacher of the good news, and healer. When the opportunity presented itself, He would preach in the town's synagogues, expounding on the Scriptures and proclaiming His Gospel. The time was rapidly approaching when He would be banished from the synagogues. Then He would continue His mission in the marketplace, on the hillsides, and from the seashore.

II. Wherever He went, the needs of the people would tug at His Heart. His compassion for them in their affliction moved Him to action to alleviate their suffering.

1) It may well be said that Jesus could have spent as much time attending to the physical and spiritual needs of the people as He did preaching the word of God.

2) Many missionaries will say that it is hard to preach to or teach people with empty stomachs, or to those whose physical, emotional, or spiritual suffering are such a distraction to them that they cannot hear or concentrate on what the missionary is preaching or teaching.

3) William Booth, the British evangelist and founder of the Salvation Army, found that his evangelization program to the poor of London was getting nowhere. They could pay little attention to what he was saying because of their hunger. He realized that these people could not be preached to unless their hunger was satisfied, so He was moved to do something about it. He founded the Salvation Army to feed and clothe the poor in the hovels of London.

4) This, no doubt, was also the case with Jesus and the people with whom He was dealing. So that they might hear the word of God and make it a part of their lives, He set about curing the ill and those afflicted with demons or emotional and spiritual disorders.

III. The word compassion comes the Latin "*cum*," meaning with, and "*passio*," meaning suffering. It means to suffer *with* someone, to identify with the misery of another. The virtue of compassion makes us feel or experience another's plight. Compassion is like a sensitivity antenna that picks up the wavelengths of another's suffering. It then makes us feel for that person's plight. It stimulates us through the virtue of charity to do something to alleviate that person's plight.

IV. We all appreciate the compassion of another when we are in the throes of some suffering or difficulty. Gabriel Max did a painting called "The Last Token." It is based on a letter of a young Roman lady who was about to be consumed by the lions of the Colosseum. Her crime was her confession of being a Christian. The pagan crowd was cheering and urging the lions to attack the helpless girl. The unsympathetic crowd was sharing in this cold, brutal murder. At the moment the lions were about to pounce on her, a rose fell at her feet, thrown to her by some pitying unknown person among the thousands of spectators. The girl stooped to pick up the rose; then she raised her head to search the crowd to see if she could catch sight of that sympathetic and compassionate person who threw the rose, for she did not believe that there was even one compassionate person in that bloodthirsty crowd. Consoled by this act of compassion, she fixed her eyes on the rose and went off to her martyrdom and death with a smile on her young, beautiful face (Tonne, *Stories for Sermons*).

V. Compassion not only involves feeling another's plight or affliction; it means responding to that need in any way we can.

1) The contrast between Jesus and the Pharisees, the teachers and preachers of that day, is startling.

2) They called the people's attention to their religious duties, criticizing them for not fulfilling their obligations, but they did little or nothing to alleviate their burdens and their plight.

VI. The compassion of Jesus in the modern world will come, by and large, through you and me, the members of His Mystical Body.

1) By our baptism, we must proclaim the good news of the

Gospel, and what better way is there of doing this than to bring Christ's message to others with His compassion, manifested through our charitable concern for others?

2) The Lord depends on us human instruments, members of His Mystical Body, to get His message to the masses of people and to spread His compassion and charity. Jesus wills to continue His work through you and me; we are the arms and hands of His Mystical Body.

****

1) That we always show a warm, loving concern for others, especially those in less fortunate circumstances.

2) That our compassion may not rest with emotional sighs of pity, but that it may move us to alleviate affliction.

3) That our zeal for souls may take advantage of opportunities to evangelize and help deepen people's faith.

4) That the Lord bless His Church, especially in the western world, with abundant and worthy candidates for the priesthood and the religious life.

5) For all those suffering from incurable diseases, that they may be buoyed up by a lively faith and a fruitful prayer life.

Wednesday of the Fourteenth Week: Mt. 10:1-7

I. Israel, the Church of the Old Testament, was founded on its twelve tribes: Judah, Dan, Ephraim, Manasseh, Gad, Reuben, Simeon, Naphtali, Moab, Aser, Zebulun, and Issachar. Christianity is the perfection and fulfillment of Judaism. It too would be founded in a similar way upon the twelve Apostles, the foundation stones of the Church of the New Testament.

II. After the arrest of John the Baptist, Jesus led His disciples back to Galilee. St. Luke writes, "In these days he [Jesus] went into the hills to pray; and all night he continued in prayer to God. And when it was day, he called his disciples, and chose from them twelve, whom he named apostles" (Lk. 6:12-13). The word apostle comes from the Greek, and means one sent or a messenger. Jesus would shortly after send them out to preach the Gospel.

III. What is striking about Jesus' selection of the twelve Apostles is the variety of personalities and temperaments they had. Some of them had different and clashing ideologies.

1) Peter was outspoken and impulsive, while his brother, Andrew, was quiet and retiring.

2) Simon was a member of the Zealot party, which wanted independence for Israel and advocated violent means. It was like the I.R.A. in Ireland or the E.T.A. of Spain.

3) Matthew was a tax collector — a job that was held in contempt by the Jewish people because so many of the tax collectors were cheats and furthermore collaborated with the Roman occupation forces. We can hardly imagine Simon the Zealot working with someone like Matthew without coming to blows. Only the sheer force of Jesus' personality could unite such divergent people.

IV. Jesus was disposed to use such instruments to proclaim His Gospel, building His Church on them. Any industrial firm would go under in these circumstances, for the principles of good management were completely ignored by Jesus in His selection of these largely uneducated and disparate men. But then again, God has always confounded the worldly-wise and selected the insignificant of this world to do His great work, as St. Paul says in his second letter to the Corinthians: God's power is made perfect in human weakness (2 Cor. 12:9).

1) To top things off, Jesus even chose a cheat in the person of Judas Iscariot. At face value, this band of twelve was a motley crew; yet in spite of their lack of education, their disparate personalities and temperaments, they were enthusiastic and eager students of Jesus. They would, however, be slow to learn the real message of Jesus, since they were looking for a part in an earthly kingdom which they thought Jesus would establish.

2) Jesus called them, not for what they were, but because of what they could and would become in His hands, as they collaborated with the graces He would channel to them.

3) Jesus calls all of us to build up His Church. As with the Apostles, He doesn't ask for extraordinary people with all kinds of talents and degrees. He asks for ordinary people with willing and generous hearts. He will accomplish great things with such instruments.

V. Such is the Church, the Mystical Body of Christ, made up of all kinds of people held together and unified in Christ. God's graces can overcome differences in personalities and temperaments. What is needed are good will and generous, cooperative hearts disposed to cooperate with His graces; His presence will submerge our differences.

****

1. That the Lord make us patient and tolerant with the personalities and temperaments of other people, especially with the ones with whom we work.

2) That we may more willingly and enthusiastically do the things God calls us to do.

3) For unity in Christendom, that all Christians, especially religious leaders, strive to work hard and generously to bring about unity among all Christians, so that we all might be one flock under one shepherd.

4) For unity in all families that have split up because of internal squabbles.

5) That bishops, priests, and religious more generously serve the people of God.

6) For generous and enthusiastic vocations to the priesthood and to the religious life.

Thursday of the Fourteenth Week: Mt. 10:7-15

I. Jesus sent His disciples out not only to preach, but to heal the sick. He did not limit this power to the Apostles; He gave it to His Church, in which He still works through her sacramental system.

1) The disciples of Jesus were to heal the sick and raise the dead. We know that Sts. Peter and Paul accomplished such marvels, and so did saints throughout the centuries. Even here, much depended on the faith, trust, and confidence of the recipients.

2) When Jesus referred to physical death, He always used the word "sleep." On the other hand when He employed the word "death," He always used it to refer to eternal damnation. He spoke of going to awaken Lazarus, who had fallen asleep: "Our friend Lazarus has fallen asleep, but I go to awake him out of sleep" (Jn. 11:11). When Jesus entered the house of Jairus, ruler of the synagogue at Capernaum, to raise his daughter from the dead, He

said to the flute players and to those wailing: "Depart; for the girl is not dead but sleeping" (Mt. 9:24).

3) A person in grave sin is temporarily dead in God's eyes, for if physical death should ensue for a person in that state, then real death — eternal damnation — would be the consequence.

4) Jesus gave His Apostles marvelous powers, for when He sent them out He said, "Heal the sick, raise the dead, cleanse lepers, cast out demons." Many of these powers He has left to His Church. Although some saints have obtained from God the miracle of raising others from the dead, this is indeed a rare occurrence; nevertheless, the Lord has given His Church a far greater power, that of restoring the spiritually dead back to the life of grace through the sacrament of penance and reconciliation. Many physically ill people are restored to health through anointing, i.e., through the Sacrament of the Sick.

II. "You received without pay, give without pay." The Gospel is not for sale. Since the priceless things of life are free — the air we breathe, the water we drink, and the beauties of nature, the sky, the sea — how much more should the gifts of God be free for those who earnestly seek them!

1) The Apostles were to carry no money, since the people would support them for dedicating their full efforts to the spreading of the Gospel.

2) Preoccupation with supporting themselves by holding down a job on the side would impede the service the disciples were expected to give to the people, and it would diminish their availability and accessibility to the people who might need their services.

III. The Gospel of today goes on: "Whatever town or village you enter, find out who is worthy in it, and stay with him until you depart."

1) The Gospel is such an important message that there is nothing of more value on this earth, for it deals with eternal life and eternal death. It cannot be cast to swine — that is, to those who, out of contempt or disdain, refuse to hear it.

2) There is a note of urgency in this instruction of Jesus, for it will take time to teach the Gospel. Many people will want to hear it and understand it, so as to implement it in their lives. This will involve instructing them. All of this will take time.

IV. Jesus instructs His disciples to "shake off the dust from your feet" from any town that refused to listen to His Gospel. He continues, "It shall be more tolerable on the day of judgment for the land of Sodom and Gomorrah than for that town." Those who reject the Gospel are to be left to the judgment of God. The disciples and later bearers of the Gospel can be completely freed of all guilt of not fulfilling their duty to spread the Gospel when they are flatly rejected by hardhearted people who are closed to the challenge of the Gospel. This is symbolized by the shaking of the dust from their sandals.

1) The judgment of Sodom and Gomorrah will be easier since those cities never had the Gospel preached to them. Those who are indifferent or reject the good news of the Gospel lose a golden opportunity which may never be offered to them again. We only live one lifetime; we will not come back to repeat it and make up for gross mistakes. Sincere, humble, and open-hearted people will not reject the Gospel.

2) Our opportunity is one of not only listening to an occasional reading of the Gospel, but of growing in our knowledge and consequent love of Our Lord Jesus Christ through reflective reading and meditating on the words of sacred Scripture.

3) We cannot love what we do not know. The more our knowledge of God, the deeper will our love for Him be. Let us always be eager to learn more and more about God and the things of God. Let us take the words of St. Jerome to heart: "Familiarity with the Bible is the royal road to the knowledge and love of Christ."

****

1) That we may be ever eager to hear and reflect on the word of God.

2) That we may have an insatiable hunger for knowledge of God.

3) We may not be able to cure the sick or raise the dead, but we can give people in need the healing effects of our love and concern; that we may be generous with our time and our presence for others in need.

4) That we strive to awaken the interest of cold and indifferent people to a knowledge of God.

5) That we be moved to visit the sick and the elderly, doing errands and chores for those who are not able to do for themselves.

Friday of the Fourteenth Week: Mt. 10:16-23

I. Early Christianity was indeed a divisive force in the homes of Jewish and Roman pagan converts. Conversions to the faith ignited fires of persecution and turned members of families against one another. The prophecy of Our Lord was fulfilled: "Brother will deliver up brother to death, and the father his child." These family divisions were among the reasons why the Roman emperors tried to exterminate Christianity.

II. "I send you out as sheep in the midst of wolves." The world is like the grazing ground of sheep, with many rapacious wolves on the prowl — people, that is, who are consumed with selfish, materialistic desires that push them to commit all kinds of sins to acquire and abuse the goods of this world.

1) Sheep are gentle, nonaggressive creatures, attracting wolves that see them as easy prey. The Lord wants us, as Christians, to have the gentleness of sheep, but at the same time to possess the cunning of serpents and the innocence of doves, qualities which attract others to us, but which, on the other hand, will not permit others to win us over to evil ways by their wiles or deceit.

2) Isaiah describes the messianic kingdom as a place where "the wolf shall dwell with the lamb, and the leopard shall lie down with the kid, and the calf and the lion and the fatling together, and a little child shall lead them" (Is. 11:6).

3) Gentleness is a far cry from cowardice. St. Francis de Sales writes, "Nothing is so strong as gentleness, nothing as gentle as real strength." This same saintly doctor of the Church also said that when you encounter difficulties and contradictions, you should not try to break them, but bend them with gentleness and time.

4) Indian wisdom would have it expressed in another way: the smile you send out always returns to you.

III. Our Lord never promised His followers an easy road. He presented His Gospel as a challenge that demands perseverance. His Gospel will summon up the best in us. While vested in gentleness, it will not be consumed by the wolves of this world but rather attract them and win them over to Christ.

1) When England was going through intense bombing from the German Luftwaffe in World War II and seemed on the brink of surrender, Winston Churchill challenged his country's patriotism to

endure, persevere, and carry the war on to victory: "I have nothing to offer but blood, toil, tears and sweat."

2) What made our nation great was the challenge it offered to subdue and harness its vast lands and resources, a challenge that was met with enthusiastic valor and perseverance. It took at least four months to cross this land in a covered wagon from its east to its west coast. Many people disappeared in the deserts; many perished through starvation, drowning, thirst, illness, or were killed by the Indians. By dint of undaunted perseverance, they met the challenge and succeeded. We are presently enjoying the fruits of that challenge. Samuel Johnson said, "Great works are performed not by strength, but by perseverance."

IV. The Church will never grow nor win converts by peddling a soft doctrine; that only draws weaklings and is self-destructive. "If any man would come after me," said our Savior, "let him deny himself and take up his cross daily and follow me" (Lk. 9:23). We deceive ourselves if we think Christianity is anything other than a doctrine of the narrow way. Humanism tries to water down its harshness by manipulating the word "love," which is the basic commandment of Our Lord Jesus Christ, removing elements of sacrifice and endurance.

1) Indeed Our Lord tells us that we will be hated on account of Him. Yes, our faith will cost us. It will challenge us every day in one way or another, for it is designed to purify us and bring us to perfection.

2) It is worth it. "He who endures to the end will be saved" (Mt. 10:22) — from eternal death, that is. Jesus counsels us not to fear those who can harm our bodies; rather, we are to fear "him who can destroy both soul and body in hell" (Mt. 10:28). We have His assurance that we will not be left alone in the conflict, but we must persevere.

****

1) That God bestow upon us the gift of fortitude to respond to His challenge, putting our faith into practice in spite of the cost.

2) That we always remember, no matter how difficult things may be, that we never undergo trials alone and that the Lord is always with us.

3) That young people not buckle under peer pressure to indulge in drugs or illicit sex, but see the value of fortitude, chastity, loyalty to the teachings of Our Lord Jesus Christ.

4) That the Lord fill us with fortitude and zeal to bear witness to His Gospel in our daily lives.

5) That all those experiencing difficulties in their marriages not look to break their sacred bond or abandon their commitment, but that they may persevere and come to know that marriage, like Christianity itself, is a challenge designed to help partners bring out the best in each other.

Saturday of the Fourteenth Week: Mt. 10:24-33

I. President Franklin D. Roosevelt once movingly said, "There is nothing to fear but fear itself." Fear has an uncanny way of coercing us into doing things we don't want to do. It has an insidious way of crippling reason. So often reason will tell us the right thing to do, but fear prohibits us from doing it. In many cases, fear even prevents reason from functioning properly in a person. Such a person is literally pushed and pulled from one decision to another.

II. Three times in today's Gospel Jesus tells His disciples not to be afraid. Fear is an emotion that is part of all of us. Anger is also an emotion that is part of us. These two emotional forces must be curbed and placed in their proper perspective.

1) Fear, as well as anger, is designed to help us. Both are healthy defensive networks; they both alert us to danger and help us to overcome an impending or threatening evil. We all fear situations that will hurt us or endanger our lives. This is nature's way of protecting us.

2) Fear must be put into perspective; it must serve us and not enslave us. It must be proportionate to the danger facing us. We must fear God before other men or women, for it is one thing to sustain physical damage; it is an entirely different thing to suffer eternal damnation.

III. "A disciple is not above his teacher, nor a servant above his master." In other words, "What they do to me they will do to you." Jesus invites us to share in His sufferings. Just as Jesus was the butt of constant criticism by the intelligentsia of His day — the scribes, elders, and the Pharisees — we too can expect to be the objects of criticism, hatred, injustice, and persecution.

1) We must still proclaim the Gospel by being witnesses to it in our daily lives, whether people like it or not, no matter what they say to us or about us.

2) "What I tell you in the dark, utter in the light; and what you hear whispered, proclaim upon the housetops." The Lord's message will be difficult and unacceptable to worldly people. Sunlight has a way of irritating the eyes. But it must shine, for we need its light to see, painful or not. Truth of its very nature must come to the light to be seen by all.

IV. The salvation of souls is the supreme law, and truth must be told to people of good and bad will alike. Just as the Lord sends His rain upon the just and unjust, as well as permitting His sun to shine on the good and the evil, so too His Gospel must be preached to all.

1) We are our brothers' keepers, and this being the case, we must bear the torch of the Gospel message to them to light up their lives and to bring them to life in God. Your light must shine before all men and women with whom you live and work and recreate. Do not be afraid to bear the torch of the Gospel. You will only find out in eternity how many people were saved because of your being the light and salt that you were to them.

2) "He who denies me before men [that is, whoever is afraid to bear witness to me before men and women] will be denied before the angels of God" (Lk. 12:9).

3) "Courage," wrote John Courtney Murray, "is far more important than intelligence." If we don't implement what we know with certainty, we are cowards and will shrivel up, victims of our destructive fears.

4) "Blessed are you when men revile you and persecute you and utter all kinds of evil against you falsely on my account. Rejoice and be glad, for your reward is great in heaven. . ." (Mt. 5:11). Our Lord is saying through the beatitudes that if we share in His sufferings because we strive to bear witness to His Gospel and do the right thing in spite of criticism and persecution, we will share in His glory that much more.

****

1) That God may bestow a healthy fear on us — the gift of the fear of the Lord, a gift that makes us fear offending God much more than the criticism of other men and women or the pressure of our peers.

2) That the Lord give us courage and the fortitude to do the right thing in spite of criticism and scorn.

3) That we may serve as light and salt to our weaker brothers and sisters.

4) That the Lord fill us with fortitude and courage to spread His Gospel.

5) People admire strong men and women who do what they know is right; that parents and people in authority give such example to their charges.

6) That we may always remember, "No man is an island," and be conscious of our obligation to give good example.

Monday of the Fifteenth Week: Mt. 10:34-11:1

I. If we could put it in a nutshell, the essence of Christianity in the end is loyalty to Our Lord Jesus Christ. This is especially rewarding when allegiance to Him means, as a consequence, ostracism from family, relatives, and/or friends. Jesus predicted that a father would be set against a son and a mother against her daughter because of Him and His Gospel.

1) An Orthodox Jewish family would hold a mock funeral for a son or daughter who converted to Christianity.

2) Jesus said, "Do not think that I have come to bring peace on earth; I have not come to bring peace, but a sword. For I have come to set a man against his father, and a daughter against her mother, and a daughter-in-law against her mother-in-law: and a man's foes will be those of his own household."

3) Jesus's message is indeed peace for men and women of good will, but it is a sword for those who refuse to accept Him or His Gospel.

II. One of the reasons for the persecution of Christians by the Roman emperors was that Christianity was splitting many families throughout the empire.

1) It was the source of division in Roman families, where sons or daughters, brothers and sisters would convert to Christianity, while

the other members would remain pagan. Mothers and fathers did turn against a son or daughter who converted to Christianity. For many such families, Christianity was a sword of division.

2) In our own day, a Jesuit priest received a letter from a young student from overseas who had converted to Catholicism from Islamism. In the letter, the young man expressed concern about returning home to visit his parents. He had been sent to the U.S. to study. He felt that if his father learned about his conversion to Christianity, he would kill him. The young man never returned to the states. His apprehensions were correct; the priest learned that the father did kill his son because he had become a Christian.

3) It is hard to believe that those to whom we have been united by the close bonds of blood and family love would kill over the question of religion. This is what the Lord meant when He said that He had not come to spread peace but to be a cause of division, even in the inner circle of the family.

4) The price of following the Lord has been very high for many people down through the centuries. But such, at times, is the price of discipleship.

III. Loyalty to Our Lord Jesus Christ means living out His Gospel message as it is interpreted by the Magisterium of the Church. It is plain to see how this becomes a sword of division in the question of birth control by artificial contraception.

1) The term "birth control" is a misnomer, for controlling the number of children a couple brings into this world is a responsibility incumbent upon the couple, since they must provide a home and education for the children they bring into the world (cf. *Humanae Vitae*, n.16).

2) Controlling births by means of artificial contraception is what is condemned by the Magisterium of the Church. This teaching has been repeated several times by the Holy Father since the promulgation of the encyclical *Humanae Vitae*. Couples are urged to resort to natural family planning. One very effective and safe way of natural family planning is the Sympto-Thermal Method, which is gaining wide acceptance.

3) In any event, following Our Lord Jesus Christ will involve sacrifice, even the sacrifice of self-denial within marriage. Sacrifice is the sword that brings division to materialistic people.

4) Our Lord Jesus Christ wields a sharp sword that separates light from darkness, spirit from flesh, and good from evil (*The Word Among Us*).

IV. Loyalty to Jesus Christ is going to cost all of us, but in different ways.

1) There can be the slow martyrdom of being ignored or dropped by "friends" because they dislike our strict adherence to Christian moral principles.

2) There will be criticism from those who will be uncomfortable with us because we refuse to go along with them in cheating on an employer, on customers, or on their marriages.

3) There will be the perennial animadversions cast upon us for being "antiquated and hidebound" in the estimation of others, for holding on to an "outmoded moral lifestyle." All of these things are uncomfortable for us and do cause some pain, but they spring from people whose consciences are pricking them. You and I constitute reproach and a reminder to their consciences. Their attitudes and barbs are products of anger and frustration at our not going along with them. Misery loves company.

4) Loyalty to Jesus Christ means being a light to the world and salt to the earth. Light embarrasses, and salt stings. The Lord wants our light to shine before men. We will be persecuted, as the Lord warned: nevertheless, we will be participating in that beatitude which goes: "Blessed are you when men revile you and persecute you and utter all kinds of evil against you falsely on my account. Rejoice and be glad, for your reward is great in heaven, for so men persecuted the prophets who were before you." (Mt. 5:11).

****

1) Our best contribution to the world is the practice of our faith in our daily lives; that the Lord give us the courage to always do this without shame.

2) That we profess our loyalty by bearing witness to Our Lord Jesus Christ even if it means losing so-called "friends."

3) That we be light to the world and salt to our weaker brothers and sisters who look up to us for support and example.

4) That parents by their lives foster a deeper faith in their children.

5) That husbands and wives be witnesses to each other especially when great sacrifices are demanded of them.

6) That the artificial-contraception mentality be shown for what it really is — selfishness.

7) That young people have the courage to stand up to their peers and refuse drugs that are offered to them.

Tuesday of the Fifteenth Week: Mt. 11:20-24

I. God is patient, but He too has His boiling point. Opportunities are given and regiven, but alas, at the end of it all comes a day of reckoning. Jesus worked many miracles in Chorazin, Bethsaida, and Capernaum; yet these cities rejected Him. These were the hard ground on which the seed, the word of God, fell but did not take root.

II. To see marvels and miracles is one thing, but to implement the message of the Gospel is another. The Gospel of Our Lord Jesus Christ is hard and challenging. In lovers of the things of this world, it produces violent reactions. Émile Zola, the French novelist of the nineteenth century, was an atheist. He once said that he would not accept Christianity even if he saw a miracle. Standing near the grotto of Lourdes one day, he witnessed a first-class miracle, but he steadfastly refused to accept Christianity. A similar opportunity was never granted to him again.

III. A significant problem today is the noticeable number of dropouts who just drift off into indifference and cease practicing their faith, or who simply lose it through atrophy. Today, almost every Catholic family has a son or daughter, a brother or sister, a nephew or niece who has "dropped out" of the practice of the faith. George Gallop noted a few years ago that as many as twenty-six percent of all baptized Catholics in the United States are nonfunctioning. This would put the number of inactive Catholics in the U.S. at about fifteen million (A. Illig, C.S.P., Catholic Evangelization Association).

IV. How many parents claim in today's world that after they have sent a child to Catholic grammar and high schools, he or she no longer practices his/her faith.

1) The opportunity to return to the practice of the faith will be given, as is often the case, through other people whom God deigns to use as His instruments to bring about a conversion. There are many

people "out there" who are waiting for an invitation to come back home, but they need the right instrument, the right contact to start the trip home.

2) The fact that an adult who no longer practices his/her faith once attended Catholic school is still a plus, for often in crisis he/she will go back to his/her roots, returning to the practice of the faith.

V. Msgr. Liam O'Flaherty worked in the Vatican Curial offices during the Nazi occupation of Rome. He spent most of his time in helping Allied prisoners and Jews to escape the Nazis. He became an object of Nazi hatred, and he was caught and tortured to reveal the underground organization which he headed. As the Allies drew closer to Rome, the Nazi commandant who had ordered him captured and tortured sought Msgr. O'Flaherty's aid in rescuing his wife and children from the Allied forces by getting them back to Germany. He did so, and the commandant's wife and family were safely returned to Germany. After the war, the commandant was imprisoned for his war crimes. Msgr. O'Flaherty was one of the very few visitors to his cell. Touched by O'Flaherty's lack of vengeance and his charity, the commandant was won back to the faith he had abandoned in his youth.

VI. You and I may not have the heroism of a Msgr. O'Flaherty, yet our faith and our charity are a light to the blind of this world. The world does not know what marvels are wrought through prayer and the example of an upright Christian life.

1) As busy as their apostolic work may be, Mother Teresa makes her sisters spend two hours a day in prayer. It is quite evident that God has blessed and extended their great works.

2) St. Maximilian Kolbe converted many in the Auschwitz concentration camp by his warm and solicitous concern and heroic charity. He would frequently give up his food to fellow prisoners to help them fight the throes of despondency. The force of his example was all that was needed to snatch many people from despair and win them to faith and hope in Our Lord Jesus Christ.

3) Let us recall the admonition of our Blessed Lady at Fátima: "Many souls are being lost because they have no one to pray for them." We are our brothers' and sisters' keepers. Let us always be conscious of their dependence on us.

****

1) That the Lord fill us with zeal for souls.

2) We may not perform miracles, but we can be instruments in God's hands to win back those who are indifferent or who have lost their faith; that we may be very charitable and kind in our dealings with all people.

3) That we remember the importance of prayer, and that the Lord may listen especially to family members who pray unflaggingly for the conversion of a son or daughter, brother or sister.

4) "More flies are caught with a drop of honey," said St. Francis de Sales, "than with a barrel of vinegar"; that the Lord bless us with tact and warmth in our dealing with loved ones who no longer practice their faith.

Wednesday of the Fifteenth Week: Mt. 11:25-27

I. God does not hide His message from the learned and the wise of this world. He just will not permit faith to submit to reason. We must humbly ask for light and understanding. Many of the world's intellectuals simply refuse to do this; therefore, God's message remains closed to them. Our Lord Jesus Christ proclaimed the Gospel openly to all who wished to listen. The proud intellegentsia closed their ears to it; it wasn't the message that they desired and expected. Ralph Waldo Emerson said: "Nothing is more simple than greatness; indeed to be simple is to be great."

1) The lowly and childlike listen and are receptive, and God gives them the light and insight to grasp His word. The Lord does have a predilection for the poor and lowly, for humble, simple, childlike souls. Throughout history it was to such people that He revealed Himself, and he used them to do great works.

2) The prophet Amos had no preparation for prophecy. When the Lord called him, Amos's response was, "I am a herdsman, and a dresser of sycamore trees" (Amos 7:15). When the Lord called Gideon to deliver Israel from the oppression of the Midianites, Gideon responded, "Pray, Lord, how can I deliver Israel? Behold, my clan is the weakest in Manasseh, and I am the least in my family" (Jgs. 6:15).

II. What Our Lord was praising in today's Gospel were the virtues of humility and simplicity. These virtues make us childlike and pleasing to God. They dispose Him to give us an appreciation and an understanding of His truths and a firm adherence to them.

III. The characteristics of simplicity are openness, truthfulness, and sincerity. Simplicity is not afraid to manifest dependence on others, as is the case with children. A person blessed with this virtue is devoid of ulterior motives, is honest and sincere in his/her dealings with others, and shows a complete dependence on God for everything. It is interesting to note that the Bible refers to Job as "blameless [simple] and upright" (Job 1:1).

1) It is the virtue that is found in little children, and it makes their innocence shine and radiate from their countenances. It is what makes children attractive to us.

2) So too, simplicity in adults draws God to look upon them, embrace them, and fill them with faith.

3) It is these qualities that the Lord referred to when He said, "Be . . . innocent as doves" (Mt. 10:16). It was to simple people that St. Francis was most attracted. His dearest companion was Brother John, who was so beautifully endowed with this virtue. He referred to him after he died as St. John.

4) The intentions of simple people are evident and manifest. In adults, simplicity is not only a lack of guile or duplicity, it is freedom from ulterior motives. Its ever-persistent motive in all of its actions is to please God in whatever one undertakes to do.

IV. The fruits and rewards of simplicity are understanding, knowledge, and wisdom. The simple become blessed with an understanding and knowledge of divine things. God confers these gifts through infusion. Such people may not be able to put their knowledge and understanding of the truths of faith into theological formulae; yet they have a marvelous grasp of them, adherence to them, and deep appreciation of them.

V. We certainly cannot become children all over again, but we can become childlike and attractive to God through the virtue of simplicity. Simplicity restores integrity to the soul by directing all that soul's actions to God. This draws God's attention to that soul, to look upon that person with a special love.

1) St. Thérèse of the Child Jesus made a special effort at perfecting herself in this virtue. She knew that if she became childlike, God would look upon her with a special love. She was

physically unable to keep the Carmelite rule. Her philosophy was: "If I become as a little child, I will become attractive to God, and He will swoop down and snatch me up into His arms." He literally did this. He carried her off to heaven at the early age of twenty-four.

2) Simplicity and humility are brother and sister in the spiritual life. Simple people are generally devoid of pride. It is to such as these that God tends to reveal Himself and infuse into them a knowledge and wisdom of divine things. Our Lord assures us of this in today's Gospel: "I thank thee, Father, Lord of heaven and earth, that thou hast hidden these things from the wise and understanding and revealed them to babes."

****

1) That the Lord give us an appreciation of this great virtue and generously bestow it upon us.

2) That we vigorously strive to eliminate from our lives all deceit and sophistication.

3) That we may be open and straightforward in all our dealings with other people.

4) That husbands and wives may be childlike and open, manifesting their dependence on each other for their own growth.

5) That parents may be more solicitous in nourishing the faith of their children, inculcating in their minds the importance of prayer.

6) That we may be profuse in expressing our gratitude to Almighty God for the simple things in life, and especially for the great gift of faith.

Thursday of the Fifteenth Week: Mt. 11:28-30

I. The metaphor "yoke" was used to apply to the Mosaic Law with all the additions, by way of interpretations, that the scribes and Pharisees had attached to it down the centuries until by Our Lord's time it became an intolerable burden.

1) It was from this yoke and burden that Jesus came to liberate His people, especially the humble, the unlettered, and the poor who labored under its heavy legalism.

2) The sweet yoke of Jesus is the law of the Gospel, which frees one because it imparts a knowledge of God incarnated in Jesus Christ and seen in Him. Jesus placed the entire law on the solid

foundation of charity, on our relationship with God and our fellowman. Any law which would infringe upon this twofold principle of charity is invalid and ceases to bind.

II. "You will know the truth, and the truth will make you free" (Jn. 8:32). Jesus is the way, the truth, and the life. He is the Word and therefore the law of God. He is called the Word because He embodies the mind of the Father. What He preached, He received from His Father. Getting an image of Jesus means getting an image of the Father at the same time. The knowledge given in the Gospels is designed to enlighten even the simplest and most unlettered.

1) The Gospels tell us how to do the will of God, which is the sweet yoke of Jesus Christ and the liberating yoke of God the Father. What gave Jesus consummate joy was doing the will of His Father, even though it cost Him to do so. He felt thoroughly fulfilled when He carried out the will of His Father.

2) Doing the will of God, basically by keeping His commandments, literally frees us from a yoke of servitude to sin, imparting order, balance, peace, and joy to our lives. The highway to wisdom begins with keeping God's commandments.

III. All good things in life are yokes and burdens, but they are sweet and light. The different vocations to which we are called to work out our salvation in life are yokes and burdens that nevertheless impart happiness. Much, however, will depend on our attitude in fulfilling them. The motto of Father Edward Flanagan's Boys' Town is "He's not heavy, Father, he's my brother." Any sacred commitment will be like that: a heavy burden, borne with love, becomes light. It even becomes sweet.

1) Marriage is a sweet yoke designed to help two people share each other's burdens, helping make them light. If a husband and wife are motivated by unselfish love and concern for each other, they will have a bit of heaven on earth and will be able to face the hardships of life much easier together.

2) The priesthood, too, is a sweet yoke and a light burden that imparts happiness and joy to those who generously give themselves to that sacred commitment. Its work imparts a joy in striving to bring happiness and peace to others.

3) Any profession to which one is called, and for which one has the talent, will also impart happiness, a sense of fulfillment, and

satisfaction in it. A talented artist, musician, or entertainer will find a joy in his/her work together with a feeling of accomplishment in its creativity. Such people feel a sense of achievement by contributing their talent to make the world a better place to live in, so that others will benefit from their work.

IV. True freedom will always involve a yoke and a light burden. This is invariably found in knowing God and in doing his will. By striving to know, love, and serve Him, we climb the ladder which leads to the very source of freedom — God Himself.

1) No one could have carried heavier burdens than the saints; yet to the observer, it seemed that the heavier the burden the sweeter and the lighter it was to the saint.

2) The crosses we meet in carrying out our vocations are designed by Providence to drive us on to an ever closer union with God. Patiently born, they generate a mystical joy. For those blessed with the spiritual insight, the cross of Our Lord Jesus Christ can be nothing but a sweet yoke and a light burden, wrapped up with many consolations that are so many signs of a divine intimacy.

****

1) Our attitude is so important in carrying out our duties; that we may direct our attitude toward pleasing God in what we do.

2) That we not complain or grumble when we encounter obstacles in our way, but strive to change what should be changed and endure what must be endured.

3) That we express our gratitude to God for the vocation He has given us in life and strive to fulfill it well.

4) That the Lord bless us with His peace and joy.

5) That we help alleviate the burdens of others.

6) That we strive to know God's will for us, and that He give us a generous attitude in executing His will in our daily lives.

Friday of the Fifteenth Week: Mt. 12:1-8

I. Here is another example of how the scribes and Pharisees had frustrated the Mosaic Law by their ridiculous additions and interpretations.

1) They specified thirty-nine different types of work that were forbidden on the Sabbath day. Some of them were so unreasonable,

such as the prohibition against lighting a fire, going on a journey, riding a beast, or even preparing a meal on the Sabbath (W. Barclay).

2) The Pharisees charged the Apostles with violating the Sabbath because they were plucking and shelling ears of grain.

II. The Sabbath was made for man, not man for the Sabbath. Jesus here put the Sabbath in its rightful perspective. It was made for man's spiritual, psychological, emotional, and physical well-being. When it impedes man's growth, it ceases to bind.

III. In the creation story, Genesis states that God rested on the seventh day. The Hebrew word for rest is *shabbat*. It has come to be identified with the seventh day, which we call Saturday.

IV. "Remember the sabbath day, to keep it holy" (Ex. 20:8) is the third commandment of the Decalogue. God knows that we all need to take a break from our work to give the body repose. Not being worn out or distracted by our work, we can more adequately focus and direct our attention toward God on His day.

1) The Lord demands His due — that we draw apart on His day to worship Him as a community of brothers and sisters, His sons and daughters. The angels and saints worship God as a community in heaven. Please God, one day we will join them.

2) The Sabbath is Sunday for us now because the principal events of our faith took place on that first day of the week: Our Lord Jesus Christ rose from the dead on Sunday, and the Holy Spirit descended upon our Blessed Lady and the Apostles on a Sunday. We might add that the work of creation began on Sunday, the first day of the week.

V. How the Lord's day has degenerated, rapidly becoming like any other day of the week! Christians are eminently guilty of this breakdown because they participate in the commercialization of the Sabbath day by engaging in business, commerce, and unnecessary shopping on Sunday.

1) How many Christian people shop on Sunday, forcing stores that traditionally remained closed on Sunday to open lest they lose business to their competitors!

2) How many do unnecessary heavy work on Sunday, work that should be scheduled for a day other than the Lord's day! Such people make the Lord's day their day. This is pure selfishness.

3) How miserly of people who will not give the Lord one hour of

their time on His day, Sunday, to worship with their brothers and sisters, who assemble in church to co-offer the Holy Sacrifice of the Mass together as the supreme act of worship of our Heavenly Father!

4) Sunday is for the Lord and for the family. After we have given God His due, the rest of the day should be spent with the family, whether it be a day out together at the beach, a picnic, or a sporting event. How fast time goes by, and before one realizes it the children will be grown and off on their own. How much time one could spend with them if Sunday were kept as it should be, and how much closer families would be as a result of keeping the Lord's Day a family day! We are all losers in the secularization of the Sabbath.

5) Voltaire very astutely said, "If you want to kill Christianity, you must abolish Sunday." How true! How extremely secular Christians are becoming and how lax and indifferent they are, not only in not observing the Sabbath but in their general attitude toward their faith! Keeping the Lord's Day puts perspective into our hurried lives. It lets our souls catch up with our bodies in this pressurized world which has become such a commercial rat race.

6) The Sabbath is for the whole person, body and soul, and there is divine wisdom built into its observance that is so rewarding personally and for the family as a whole.

****

1) That we all have respect for and honor the Lord's Day.

2) That we all avoid unnecessary shopping on Sunday.

3) That Christians use the Sabbath to worship God and to foster family life.

4) That Sunday may become a day for more prayer, spiritual reading, and reflection.

5) That during the Holy Sacrifice of the Mass, we offer the Lord our week's work as a continuous act of homage and adoration of Him.

6) For unity among all Christians, that we might be one flock under one shepherd.

Saturday of the Fifteenth Week: Mt. 12:14-21

I. The political climate in the Israel of Our Lord's day was quite volatile. The Jewish people were yearning for freedom from the

Roman occupational forces. False messiahs would arise, around whom zealots would rally, provoking the Roman army to crush little rebellions and punish those involved with crucifixion.

II. The meekness and gentleness of Jesus would reveal the character of the true Messiah, who was establishing a spiritual and not earthly kingdom. Many people were expecting the Messiah to establish a powerful temporal kingdom in Israel.

1) Jesus' imposition of silence upon those He had cured was precisely to avoid enkindling a false enthusiasm which might stimulate the many nationalists who would seek to make Jesus their type of Messiah — a military liberator.

2) Jesus came to establish the kingdom of God, not to lead a rebellion against the Roman occupation. He would have nothing to do with demagoguery. In Him were fulfilled Isaiah's words: "He will not wrangle or cry aloud." Jesus wanted to awaken faith, not nationalism.

III. Jesus wanted nothing of triumphalism. His Kingdom would be established in the hearts of men and women by the operation of God's grace in the human soul. The kingdom of God would be announced through the Gospel, which would be offered to the people in a spirit of gentleness and meekness.

1) St. Matthew recognizes the Messiah in the "suffering servant" prophecy of Isaiah (Is. 42:1-4). More than the other Evangelists, St. Matthew portrays Jesus as the fulfillment of the Old Testament prophecies. The Jews, on the other hand, saw the suffering servant of Isaiah as the Jewish nation suffering at the hands of her oppressors like the Romans.

2) Through His meekness and gentleness, Jesus would attract sinners and the weak, urging them on to a new life in grace. These, together with the humble, the lowly, and the oppressed, are symbolized by the bruised reed and the smoldering wick. These would receive encouragement and strength. In His name the Gentiles would find hope.

3) Far from crying out or engaging in disputations and arguments with the scribes and Pharisees, as Isaiah foretold, "He will not cry or lift up his voice, or make it heard in the street" (Is. 42:2) (*Catholic Commentary on Holy Scripture*). The proclamation of His Gospel would be done with gentleness and meekness. Jesus' final

proclamation would be through the consummate act of meekness of being nailed to the cross.

4) "I, when I am lifted up from the earth, will draw all men to myself" (Jn. 12:32). He would be the Lamb led to slaughter on the cross, which would be the solemn sign of His messiahship.

IV. St. Francis de Sales said, "Nothing is so strong as gentleness, nothing so gentle as real strength." He also said, "Nothing appeases an enraged elephant as much as the sight of a little lamb," and "More flies are caught with a drop of honey than with a barrel of vinegar" (*Treatise on the Love of God*).

V. Our Lord Jesus Christ said, "Learn from me, for I am gentle and lowly of heart." We will be most convincing when our message and example are conveyed through meekness and gentleness. These two virtues are the best companions to the proclamation of any truth. Truth does not need the force of arms, nor threats of punishment to be recognized or accepted. Its most convincing garb is gentleness and mildness and meekness.

1) Even though Moses was a strong and moving leader, the Book of Numbers states: "Moses was very meek, more than all men that were on the face of the earth" (Num. 12:3), even though he had to deal with a very difficult and stiff-necked people.

2) Mahatma Gandhi won independence for India and conquered the British Army of Occupation through his patience, meekness, and gentleness.

****

1) That the Lord bless us with His virtues of gentleness and meekness.

2) That we strive to avoid anger and provoking other people.

3) That husbands and wives treat each other and their children with gentleness and meekness.

4) That we may be quick to apologize for any strong, emotional reaction, or for the irritation we might cause others.

5) That all people come to recognize Our Lord Jesus Christ as the one and only Messiah.

6) That God's kingdom may be truly established in our hearts and souls.

7) That all those in positions of authority treat their subjects with patience and gentleness.

Monday of the Sixteenth Week: Mt. 12:38-42

I. The scribes and Pharisees ask Our Lord for a sign as if to say that they are not convinced by the numerous and varied miracles Jesus had already worked. What more signs could they possibly want? The Messianic sign of Isaiah was thoroughly fulfilled in Jesus: the blind see, the deaf hear, the lame walk. . . (cf. Is. 35:5-6).

1) At a much less spectacular sign — the preaching of Jonah — the Ninevites accepted his message and did penance to stave off the punishment of God that was imminent.

2) The queen of Sheba came from the "ends of the earth" to hear the wisdom of Solomon, and she was a Gentile. She believed in his wisdom as God's special gift to him, and that it would be safe to follow his advice. The Israelites see and hear the Son of God and refuse to accept Him.

3) We see a contrast of dispositions between the Gentiles and the Jews when they are confronted with the word of God. Pride closes the minds and hardens the hearts of the scribes and Pharisees as well as their followers.

4) No sign would be given except the sign of Jonah, who spent three days in the belly of a whale. So too the Son of Man would spend three days in the bowels of the earth. If Jonah was good enough for the Ninevites, and Solomon was good enough for the queen of Sheba, how much more should the Son of God be acceptable for what He had said and done!

II. St. Thomas Aquinas has said that pride more than anything else turns a man away from God. Sacred Scripture states that the Lord resists the proud (Jas. 4:6). It is the root of all evil. Bossuet remarked that through the evil of pride we attempt to make gods of ourselves (Tanquerey, *The Spiritual Life*).

1) Pride is the most deadly of the capital sins. It is that inordinate desire for one's own excellence.

2) Pride is the mother of all vice. It was the sin of Lucifer and the fallen angels, and it was the sin of our first parents. It was the reason why hell was created.

3) Pride engenders arrogance, disobedience, obstinacy, fighting, hypocrisy, and presumption, to list but some of its children.

III. St. Augustine wrote, "Humility makes men angels, but pride makes angels devils." Pride is insidious; it deceives all of us, entering into us as a wolf in sheep's clothing.

1) Of all temptations, it is the most difficult to recognize, thanks to our self-love, and we fall victim to it because we readily believe what flatters our self-love and puffs up our egos.

2) Because of pride, we fall victims to self-deception, failing to see the truth about ourselves and about others. It closes our eyes and hardens our hearts as was the case of the scribes and Pharisees in today's Gospel narrative. God resists the proud and gives His gifts and graces to the humble.

3) Vainglory is a child of pride. "What have you that you did not receive?" writes St. Paul, "If then you received it, why do you boast as if it were not a gift?" (1 Cor. 4:7). Are we not stealing from God what really belongs to Him? Talents are His gifts; they should be recognized as such and not be used to lord it over others who are not so blessed. They are bestowed for the glory of God and for the service of our brothers and sisters in the world in which we live.

4) St. Bernard says that pride tears down the loftiest to the lowliest, while humility exalts the lowliest to the highest. How foolish it is to measure our worth by the opinions of other men and women! They praise us today and condemn us tomorrow.

5) We should always strive to see ourselves as God does, and pray for that grace to be able to really accept ourselves as He made us. We really can glorify God best the way we are, for that is the way He made us with whatever talents He has bestowed upon us. It would be sheer folly to think that we could serve God better if He made us differently or bestowed more or possibly fewer talents and gifts upon us. He made us the way we are for the best of reasons.

****

1) That the Lord give us the light to know ourselves as we truly are.

2) That the Lord bestow upon us the great gift of humility, which disposes us to grow into giants in the eyes of God.

208

3) That we have a healthy distrust of our evaluations of ourselves, and of others.

4) That we learn to profit from charitable fraternal correction and constructive criticism.

5) That we may be honest and forthright in our confessions and not excuse ourselves or rationalize our sins and faults.

6) That the Lord grant us the gifts of wisdom, knowledge, and understanding.

Tuesday of the Sixteenth Week: Mt. 12:46-50

I. When God selected Abraham, He promised to make a great nation out of him and his descendants (Gen. 12:1-2). God made a covenant with Abraham whereby his descendants would be God's people (Gen. 17:7). Moses tells his people that Yahweh would raise up from one of them a great prophet, like himself; to him all must listen (Deut. 18:15). This refers to the Messiah. God later swears to David to make one of his descendants succeed him on the throne (Ps. 132; Acts. 2:30-32).

1) From this, it was prevalent among the Jews in Jesus' day that they were a people so privileged that salvation would be theirs because they were the blood descendants of Abraham, the great patriarch and father of the Jewish nation.

2) Since only the bond of blood relationship to Abraham could make one a descendant of Abraham and member of the chosen people of God, the Jews felt that the Gentiles were shut out of the plan of salvation.

II. Our Lord Jesus Christ now makes it clear that to be a member of the kingdom of God, the type of blood we have coursing through our veins would make no difference. The new chosen people would be all those who would accept Our Lord and implement His teaching in their lives, doing the will of His Heavenly Father. Elitism based on blood would mean nothing as a requirement to salvation. Loyalty to Jesus Christ would be the only thing that would make us the chosen ones of God.

III. Unlike the Jewish belief prevalent in Jesus' day, holding that only the sons and daughters of Abraham could be saved, Jesus would say that only those who do the will of His Father would enter the kingdom of heaven. Obedience to Jesus and His message would be the necessary qualifications to enter into to the kingdom of heaven.

1) St. Teresa of Ávila wrote, "One gets closer to God more through obedience than through prayer." Obedience is a living profession of one's faith. It involves hearing the Gospel and implementing it in our lives.

2) St. Thomas Aquinas calls obedience the first of the moral virtues because the sacrifices it involves are among the greatest we can offer to God. Sometimes it will demand laying down one's life, as was the case with thousands of martyrs.

IV. Love unites us to God, and it is best expressed through obedience, carrying out God's will in our daily lives. Jesus made it clear when He said, "Not every one who says to me, 'Lord, Lord,' shall enter the kingdom of heaven, but he who does the will of my Father who is in heaven" (Mt. 7:21).

1) Jesus tells us in today's Gospel that to be part of His family we must do the will of His Heavenly Father, and that will is expressed in the Gospel message. "Whoever does the will of my Father in heaven is my brother, and sister, and mother."

2) This is the bond of grace, that grace which grafts us into the very nature of God, gives divine life — everlasting life — to us, and places us within the very family of God.

3) Obedience draws God into our souls. "If a man loves me," Jesus said, "he will keep my word, and my Father will love him, and we will come to him and make our home with him" (Jn. 14:23). The first inspiration God gives us is the desire and the grace to obey.

4) Obedience is the greatest sacrifice that God exacts of a person, and by the same token it is the greatest gift that a human being can give to God, because through obedience one gives oneself.

5) When we pray the Lord's Prayer, we ask that God's will might be done on earth as it is in heaven. What makes heaven heaven is in great part that the Lord's will is perfectly done there. What a different world we would be living in if God's will were more perfectly carried out here on earth. It would be crimeless. We would be virtually back in an earthly paradise.

6) St. Thomas asserts that obedience does not destroy liberty or freedom; rather, it perfects them. The primary object of freedom is the search for happiness. What can really give us happiness in this

valley of tears is the earnest desire and effort to do God's will in our daily lives. Love unites us to God, and obedience is love's instrument that makes that union possible.

****

1) That we all may understand the value of obedience and its power to make us free and happy and at peace.

2) That we strive to know God's will for ourselves and to earnestly carry it out in our daily lives.

3) That all people may see and appreciate the wisdom and beauty of the Ten Commandments as a perfect expression of God's will for all of His children.

4) That children reverence their parents and obey them as those who take God's place in the home.

5) That students in grammar and high schools respect the position and the person of their teachers.

Wednesday of the Sixteenth Week: Mt. 13:1-9

I. The word of God is like a seed. The seed has a tremendous potency within it for life, whether it be a plant, a bush, or a tree. An acorn, for example, can become a tremendous oak tree.

1) As powerful a potency and potential as a seed may have, its future is dependent on the ground on which it falls. Since the word of God is so intimately related to God Himself, it naturally has enormous potential, but like the seed's, its potential will not be realized unless the soil on which it falls is receptive.

2) How many people who saw Our Lord Jesus Christ and listened to Him speak had, in the words of Isaiah, "eyes that see not and ears that hear not"! They had the potential, like a seed, but they lacked the necessary receptivity and cooperation. They were like the hard ground, completely uncooperative and unreceptive.

II. The scribes and Pharisees and the intelligentsia of Israel were the hard ground referred to in the Gospel. They would not lower themselves to listen to a man who mingled with and spoke to sinners and others they considered rabble, commoners, or *canaille*.

1) The lowly, the humble, and the poor were receptive. They had been laboring under the intolerable burdens of the Mosaic Law with

211

all that the scribes and Pharisees had superimposed, whose observances they had policed.

2) Jesus offered encouragement and lightened their loads with the seed of the Gospel, which was to transform them into new men and women if it was received and nurtured.

3) With modern technology and fertilizers, farmers can get three and four times a yield of harvest from an acre of land. The harvest, however, would depend on the diligent preparation of the soil.

4) Jesus assures us of a rich harvest, but much depends upon our enthusiasm, our openness, and the preparation we take to receive His word. Just as there are redwood trees, oaks, maples, and bushes that spring from small seeds, so too in the spiritual life there are giants and dwarfs and infants, all depending upon the receptivity, the cooperation, and the enthusiasm with which the word of God is received and nurtured.

III. "Behold I stand at the door and knock; if anyone hears my voice and opens the door, I will come in to him and eat with him, and he with me" (Rev. 3:20). Let us remember that the door to our hearts can only be opened from the inside. God will never force Himself on anyone.

1) Our sanctification depends upon our collaboration and enthusiastic responsiveness. St. Augustine put it well when he said: "Without God, we cannot; without us, God will not." God will not continually waste His graces. There may well come the time when He will cease knocking at the door of our hearts.

2) If the ground of our hearts remains hard or shallow, there will be little hope for growth. God, however, will not be outdone in generosity if we generously prepare the soil of our hearts to receive His word. "If anyone thirst," says the Lord, "let him come to me and drink. . . . 'Out of his heart shall flow rivers of living water' " (Jn. 7:37-38.) God is generous to generous and cooperative souls.

IV. The mystery of our salvation hangs on our cooperation, and a close relationship with God will demand a great deal of generous cooperation. God made us without our help, but He will not save or sanctify us without our help.

1) Judas was called to divine intimacy with Christ as an Apostle. How often Our Lord tugged at his hard heart, but Judas would not respond. On the other hand, Saul of Tarsus set out to persecute the

young Christian Church, was struck with a powerful grace from heaven, and he responded wholeheartedly to become the great Apostle to the Gentiles.

2) Free will is a awesome gift which God will never force, but if it does not cooperate with the grace of God, a person will never come to possess the pearl of great price. To the will that cooperates, what God will bestow is beyond human dreams. To responsive and cooperative hearts, He will make their yield thirty-, sixty-, and one hundredfold.

****

1) That we reflect and meditate on the word of God with enthusiasm and eagerness to grow in the knowledge of God in order to love Him more fervently.

2) That we may be generous in giving time to God in prayer, so that He may speak more intimately to us, and that we strive to concentrate on His presence in our souls.

3) That the Lord give the necessary ingredients to the soil of our hearts, especially humility, openness, and a responsive generosity.

4) That we strive to eliminate the weeds of sin and the occasions of sin from the soil of our hearts.

5) That we may be eager to help one another to grow in a deeper relationship with Our Lord Jesus Christ.

6) That those afflicted with drugs, alcohol abuse, or overburdened with pressing problems may find comfort and solace in the words of sacred Scripture.

Thursday, of the Sixteenth Week: Mt. 13:10-17

I. There is nothing more frustrating than to have an enthusiastic message fall on indifferent ears. No doubt Isaiah felt this frustration with the Jewish people, even though he spoke with fiery emotion and conviction. Foreseeing the future and warning the people and their leaders of woeful consequences met with little response.

1) "His ears are open, but he does not hear" (Is. 42:20). Many of the Jewish people were bent on doing their own thing. For this reason, many of the prophets met with much resistance; yet in spite of this resistance and even in the face of rejection, the prophets felt

compelled to give the people the message the Lord gave them to announce.

2) Who could have spoken with more conviction and authority than Our Lord Jesus Christ and further authenticate Himself by miracles and still be ignored and rejected? Our Lord addressed Himself to them and said, "Truly, I say to you, many prophets and righteous men longed to see what you see, and did not see it, and to hear what you hear, and did not hear it."

II. How many Catholic parents complain that after they sent their children through Catholic schools the children no longer practice the faith! It is as if to say that they listened with their ears but heard not. Faith is a gift and a challenge. It must be nourished, or it will fade away and even be lost. Our faith will also frequently challenge us, challenge us to grow in our knowledge and love of God and into a closer involvement with Him.

1) Many young men and women heard the message but failed to take it in, failed to reflect and meditate on it, asking the Holy Spirit for light, so as to come to appreciate and understand it better so that it might become a living part of their very being. Faith is an infused virtue, a "*habitus*" (from the Latin "to have or possess") that naturally tends to become part of one's very being and flows out of us by way of our convictions, our sacrificial and charitable actions. This infused virtue of faith naturally tends to become an integral and vital part of us.

2) Faith is that precious seed given to us in baptism that craves nourishment and growth in order that it might come to maturity and produce the fruit it is designed to produce. Like an acorn seed that longs to become an oak tree, faith needs nourishment and time to grow. Faith is nourished through prayer and the practice of the virtue of charity. In our giving ourselves to serve others, God gives us a further intensification of the light of faith to help us see and appreciate more and more the revealed mysteries of God.

3) Faith is a supernatural light. When God increases this light in our souls, it is like increasing the wattage of this precious light, and thus casts light on the divine mysteries which, for all practical purposes, would otherwise remain in darkness to our natural intellects.

4) Many saints were unlettered people, yet God fed them an

infused knowledge because they were prayerful and sacrificial people.

III. Jesus used parables precisely to make it that much easier for all — down to the simplest men and women — to understand. Lack of understanding must be charged to a lack of faith, or to the poor dispositions of the listener.

1) So many are like the hard, shallow, or thorny ground upon which the seed fell and never reached maturity.

2) Depending on the response, "To him who has will more be given, and he will have abundance; but to him who has not, even what he has will be taken away." This is to say that if one fails to cultivate and nourish the little faith he/she has, even the embers of its fire will die out.

3) St. Augustine said: "*Nihil tam dives quam fides* — There is nothing so rich as faith" (*Corpus Christianorum*, Sermon XXV). We must keep telling ourselves that it is a gift which must be nourished.

4) The person who has a strong faith and nourishes it by prayer, meditative reflection, and the practice of charity — such a person will grow rich in the things of God. From our own physical natures themselves, we know from experience that if we fail to use any physical faculty, that faculty atrophies. If we fail to feed and nourish our talents, they will never mature. A person gifted in playing a musical instrument must practice and practice often; otherwise that person will never get to be an accomplished artist. It is the same with the gift of faith; it must be nourished in our daily lives by prayer, the sacraments, reflective spiritual reading, and the practice of the virtue of charity. All of these are vital nourishment for fostering a vibrant and strong faith.

****

1) That we may always be eager to hear and reflect upon the word of God.

2) That we frequently thank God for the gift of faith.

3) That we express our gratitude to Our Lord Jesus Christ often for having suffered and died to make heaven possible for us.

4) That we be conscious of the fact that we cannot stand still in the spiritual life and in our quest for union with God. We must be

constantly nourishing our faith by prayer, Holy Communion, spiritual reading and the practice of the virtues, especially charity.

5) For all those who are honestly searching for God, that they may receive the gift of faith.

6) For all men and women engaged in teaching the faith and for the success of the Confraternity of Christian Doctrine programs.

7) For all those who remain cold, indifferent, or who have lost their faith.

Friday of the Sixteenth Week: Mt. 13:18-23

I. The parable indicates that there are different ways of receiving the word of God; its fate will depend upon the listener. Of itself, the seed, the word of God, has tremendous power, but its potential will only be realized by open, receptive, and responsive hearts.

II. The hard ground represents the proud, the self-sufficient of this world, who feel that they don't need the word of God to get on or survive. Their prejudices blind them; they do not want to hear that their lifestyles are immoral because they want to continue living that way, a way that is opposed to the Gospel. These have justified their conduct and do not wish to hear a message that will censure them or their conduct.

III. The rocky ground is the shallow ground under which lies an impervious layer of stone. Here the seed quickly germinates and sends a shoot above the surface. Its roots cannot get further than a few inches below the surface of the ground before being prevented from penetrating deeper by the rocky layer of stone located so close to the surface. Growth is soon stifled, and its life is quickly cut off.

1) The shallow ground refers to shallow people who enthusiastically respond to the word of God but their attraction to sin quickly stifles it. They lack conviction, which is a quality of depth, for although they are enthused on hearing the word of God, they are quickly carried away by every new rage or fad, since the soil of their hearts is emotion rather than conviction.

2) These people bend in every direction in which the wind blows. They readily climb on the bandwagon of every new "ism" that is in vogue.

IV. The seed that fell among the briers represents many people of our own days, people with good intentions who always intend to do the right thing, but somehow the important business of the sanctification and salvation of their souls gets bumped by other things which, though good in themselves, crowd out the more important things.

1) The tempo of modern life and the speed with which it is lived just don't leave enough time for God and the things of God. One becomes so busy that there is little or no time for prayer. Prayer, meditation, and reflection are repeatedly postponed.

2) Finally Sunday Mass seems to be more and more an effort and a burden, and it, too, gets crowded out by "important" business engagements.

3) Time ticks on, and their good intentions are never realized. And so goes life. Our spiritual lives must have number-one priority. We never get a second chance to relive our lives. We must prioritize. God simply will not accede to accepting second place.

V. Finally there is the good ground that renders a fruitful yield of thirty — sixty — a hundredfold. This refers to those wise and prudent souls who strive diligently to produce and render back to God the two talents for the one received, four for the two received, or eight for the four received. These are the people who put first things first and will not let the business of their personal sanctification take a back seat to worldly affairs. They are responsive people who know how to take advantage of and cooperate with the grace of God and the inspirations of the Holy Spirit.

1) Like Our Blessed Lady, they conceive the word of God and bring it to fruition. As St. Ambrose said so well, "You are also blessed [along with Mary] who have heard and have believed, for whoever believes both conceives and bears forth the Word of God. . . . If according to the flesh Christ has but one mother, yet by faith Christ is the fruit born by all" (St. Ambrose, "Exposition of the Gospel of St. Luke," *Corpus Christianorum, Series Latina*, Vol. 13, p. 42).

VI. The word of God can be compared to the sun. It engenders life, illuminates it, and provides the warmth that is so necessary for its growth. It gives vigor and strength to all life. God's word illuminates our minds and dispels the darkness of spiritual ignorance. It imparts warmth to human coldness and gives us strength in our daily struggles against evil.

****

1) That the good Lord make us ever more receptive to His word.

2) That we be more diligent in preparing the ground — that is, our hearts and souls — to receive the word of God.

3) That we cultivate and nourish the word of God by prayer and acts of virtue.

4) That we frequently take inventory to find out what really are the priorities in our lives.

5) That priests enthusiastically prepare and preach the word of God.

6) That young people search sacred Scripture and reflect on God's word to find answers to their problems and obtain peace through reflection on His word.

Saturday of the Sixteenth Week: Mt. 13:24-30

I. The parable was very down-to-earth for the people of Palestine. They were all too familiar with the darnel weed, which in the early stages looks so much like wheat; the darnel weed has that uncanny way of intertwining its roots with the wheat. Even when the growth was such that the farmer could recognize the darnel and distinguish it from the wheat, if he pulled the darnel, up would come the wheat also. One would simply have to be patient and wait for the harvest.

II. The world is like a wheat field that is composed of both wheat and a fair mixture of weeds that manage to sprout up. Inevitably it will be so to the end of time. The world will be composed of good and evil people. Since we are victims of Original Sin, the forces of evil readily win over many weak, indifferent souls and manage to choke off the life of grace in their souls.

1) Just as it is difficult to discern the wheat from the tares or from the darnel, very often it is difficult to distinguish good people from evil people. Many evil people have a way of acting and appearing as sheep when in reality they are wolves in sheep's clothing.

2) Yet the other side of the coin is that the good example, kindness, and patience of good people will have the salutary effect of winning over evil people, converting them from darnel to wheat. For

this reason our Savior has told us that we must be light and salt in the world.

III. The parable is a salutary warning against rash judgments and an exhortation to patience. Those we may judge to be weeds may very well be wheat. We are so quick to believe in the dirt or bad things we hear about other people, and how wrong we can be, as experience has so often borne out! Only God can make guarantees, fair judgments, and we must leave all judging of other people up to Him.

IV. The Lord bids us to be good, patient husbanders, to patiently bear with the weeds until harvest time. God Himself gives us the supreme example of patience. St. Teresa said: "Patience procures all things." That includes conversion of sinners who see the light of virtue practiced by patient Christians, and helps them to see the error of their ways. God clearly wills the salvation of all souls. This is why He sent His Son into the world — to save us. He is extremely patient with sinners, giving them every opportunity to win salvation. He will never force His graces on anyone, but waits for the opportune moment. We are His instruments who serve to make that opportune moment possible. He continues to bear the injuries sinners cause Him; yet He patiently offers them more and more time and opportunities to bring about their conversion. He continually allows the sun to shine on the good and the evil; so, too, He permits the rain to fall upon the just and the unjust (Mt. 5:45). God thus patiently manifests His goodness, patience, and kindness, hoping for a response by way of repentance and conversion.

1) The supreme law must always be the salvation of souls — all souls. Evil people must be given every opportunity to change and serve God; otherwise they will be eternally lost. Some people are more prone to evil because of the poor upbringing and exposure to bad environment. These need more of the light of patient good example to move them toward a change in their behavior. They will naturally test the patience of good people. If we try to pull the weeds — that is, if we try to force these people, or in anger condemn them — we will only turn them off.

2) What we cannot change, we must endure. Impatience will only alienate people. "Patience is bitter," wrote the French philosopher Rousseau, "but its fruit is sweet."

V. The Lord tells us that we must do penance, something most of us find hard to do, or slow to get around to doing. Patiently putting up with evil people is an excellent penance which wins graces necessary to convert hard or blind hearts.

1) A woman involved in a serious accident, which required painful surgery together with a long confinement, asked her physician, "Doctor, how long will I have to remain here helpless?" "Oh," he replied, "only one day at a time." St. Teresa was such a proponent of patience that she said one day passed in patience and resignation was worth as much as forty days on bread and water.

2) It may cause us pain, yet our persistent and patient goodness and kindness will be evil people's only hope of obtaining those graces necessary to open up their hard hearts and win their conversion back to God.

VI. St. Teresa of Ávila writes in her poem "*Nada le turbe*": "Let nothing disturb thee; let noting dismay thee; all things pass. God never changes. Patience attains all that it strives for. He who has God finds he lacks nothing; God alone suffices" (E. Allison Peers, *Complete Works of St. Teresa*).

****

1) That we strive not to complain about situations we have to live in, or about the people with whom we live and work.

2) That the Lord bless us with the honey of patience, endurance, and long-suffering.

3) That we not provoke or irritate others to lose their patience.

4) That husbands and wives may be more patient and understanding with each other.

5) That parents be patient with their children in order to win over their confidence, respect, and love.

6) That we consciously and continually offer up to God, as a rewarding penance, the hard and difficult things we must endure with confidence, respect, and love.

Monday of the Seventeenth Week: Mt. 13:31-35

I. "The kingdom of heaven is like a grain of mustard seed. . . . It is the smallest of all seeds. . . ."

1) Christianity started out with a humble Galilean carpenter

declaring Himself to be the Messiah. During His short public ministry, He gathered few confirmed followers; yet within a few years after His death, Christianity spread throughout the Roman Empire. It had a very small beginning, but the power of the seed is God Himself, the Son of God made man, and there is no stopping that power.

2) The mustard tree starts out from a tiny seed, yet when fully grown it is large enough to give refuge and safety to the birds of the air which come to seek its shade and eat the little black seeds which the mustard tree produces. The birds literally find in the mustard tree a home, for it is large and ample enough to furnish the security they need to build their nests in its branches.

3) The Church, the kingdom of God on earth, is much like the mustard tree insofar as it is a haven, a refuge of security for all her children. She provides sustenance, strength, and security in her sacramental system.

II. The kingdom of heaven is like yeast which a woman took and kneaded into three measures of flour. Soon the whole mass was leavened. What is this yeast but the grace of God working in the hearts and souls of men and women, transforming them into spiritual giants, making them the Godlike beings that God's grace strives to accomplish within them by its inexorable force which Our Lord likens to yeast?

III. The divine plan of extending the kingdom of God on earth will, of its very nature, have the force and power of seed and yeast to achieve its goal. This will be so in spite of human instruments, be they helps or obstacles. God inevitably selects weak and insignificant instruments to do monumental tasks which we human beings could never hope to accomplish by ourselves.

1) The twelve Apostles were the most unlikely candidates to establish God's kingdom on earth. Yet God selected them to do this. Modern managerial administrative procedure would evaluate their selection as a pure disaster for the future of that project. By human standards, Christ would have been removed as manager.

2) After Jesus' death, the twelve Apostles turned out to be cowards and lived in mortal fear of the Jews. When the Holy Spirit entered into them on Pentecost Sunday, they were filled with the yeast of the power of God and were transformed into fearless,

dauntless Apostles who feared no threat nor torture in their efforts to establish and extend God's kingdom on earth.

IV. The parable teaches us that God continually uses the weak, the humble, and the lowly to accomplish His great works.

1) The Blessed Virgin Mary had a lowly beginning; yet God selected her to be the mother of the Messiah.

2) David, in his father Jesse's eyes, was the most delicate and fragile of his sons, who would be least likely, so Jesse thought, to be selected by Samuel to be king in Israel. Yet God moved Samuel to select David.

V. Christians, like the grace which transforms them, cannot be static beings in a world filled with forces that threaten their salvation. We must be like counteragents against evil by confronting it with the light and force of the yeast of our example. We may be weak and fragile, like the mustard seed, yet all God wants of us is our goodwill and a generous response to His graces and inspirations. Then, like the yeast within the dough, the kingdom will grow.

1) The Lord wants us to be faithful witnesses. He will use the force of our example to extend His kingdom. Seneca, the Roman philosopher-playwright of the first century, said, "It is a long journey to one's goals going by the direction of teaching and lectures; it is much shorter and easier through example."

2) Tertullian, one of the great writers of the early Church, declared that he and most of the converts of his day were won to Christ, not by books and sermons, but by observing how Christians lived and died.

3) The Star of Bethlehem led the wise men by its faithful, quiet light, not by cosmic explosions. You and I may be mere mustard seeds in this world, but let us not forget that we thrive of God's grace, an inexorable force, a yeast that can move mountains.

****

1) That we always keep in mind that the Lord does not expect us to be successful in our undertakings, but He does expect us to be loyal and faithful.

2) That we may never be daunted or uptight about our lack of talent, but that we may be generous and responsive instruments in God's hands.

3) That the Lord may give us the yeast of fortitude to be true witnesses of His Gospel.

4) That parents may be mindful of the importance of their example as an effective instrument of true leadership, formation, and inspiration for their children.

5) That we nourish ourselves daily on the light and yeast of the Gospel so that we may become a true and vigorous leaven in our work of evangelization.

6) That our example may serve as a meaningful light and support to those who are groping or searching.

Tuesday of the Seventeenth Week: Mt. 13:35-43

I. The Lord has tremendous patience, but as today's Gospel starkly informs us, even His patience does have a boiling point, and there is a day of reckoning.

1) God wills the salvation of all people; yet His mercy is tempered by His justice.

2) The Gospel is abundantly clear in the conclusion of today's parable: not everyone is going to get into the kingdom of heaven. The weeds symbolize evil people who, after many opportunities of grace, nevertheless die unrepentant deaths and consequently will be cast into hell forever.

II. The adage goes: "If you meditate enough on hell you will never go there." The horror of it all is a practical deterrent. At Fátima, the Blessed Virgin Mary showed the three children a vision of hell. Lucia described it: "We saw a vast sea of fire, into which were plunged, all blackened and burnt, demons and souls in human form, like transparent brands. Raised into the air by the flames, they fell back in all directions, like sparks of a huge fire, without weight or poise, amidst loud cries and horrible groans of pain and despair which caused us to shudder and tremble with fear. The demons were distinguished by the horrible and repellent forms of terrible and unknown animals, like brands of fire, black yet transparent. The scene lasted an instant, and we must thank our heavenly Mother who had prepared us beforehand by promising to take us to heaven with her; otherwise I believe that we should have died of fear and terror. As if looking up for help," continued Lucy, "we raised our suppliant eyes toward the Blessed Virgin, who told us kindly, but very sadly:

'You have just seen hell, where the souls of sinners go. To save them the Lord wishes to establish in the world devotion to my Immaculate Heart. If people do what I shall tell you many souls will be saved and there will be peace' '' (Da Cruz, C.S.Sp., *More About Fátima*).

III. Sin and its awful consequences are very much a part of the message of Our Lord Jesus Christ. The sad part about it all is that many people lull themselves into believing that hell doesn't exist.

1) These people have a TV mentality which subtly maintains that even though people sin, in the end God is an all-loving and understanding Father who will chide us and forgive us no matter in what condition He may find us at death. Somehow, they believe, we will all end up being received into the bosom of the Father to be happy with Him forever in heaven. This is rank presumption.

2) They believe that the love and mercy of Almighty God is so great that it couldn't permit the existence of hell and all that hell evokes.

3) Any sober meditation on the sacred Scriptures will plainly convince a person of average intelligence that indeed the Lord spoke of hell as a place of eternal punishment. The existence of hell has been defined by the Church. There are many solemn statements on it. The Fourth Lateran Council (1215), the Council of Florence (1439), and the First Vatican Council (1869-1870) made conciliar statements on hell. The First Vatican Council of 1869 stated, "Therefore, all who die in actual mortal sin are excluded from the kingdom of God and will suffer forever the torments of hell, where there is no redemption. Also, those who die with only original sin will never have the holy vision of God. The souls of those who die in the charity of God, before they have done sufficient penance for their sins of commission or omission, are purified after death with the punishment of purgatory" (Schema of the Dogmatic Constitution on the Principal Mysteries of the Faith of the First Vatican Council, 1869-1870. Cited from *The Church Teaches*, by Jesuit Fathers of St. Mary's College, Kansas, 1955).

IV. In today's Gospel, St. Matthew narrates Jesus' explanation of the parable of the wheat field in which weeds were sown. The Gospel clearly states: "The harvest is the close of the age, and the reapers are angels. Just as weeds are gathered and burned with fire, so it will be at the close of the age. The Son of Man will send his angels, and they will gather out of his kingdom all causes of sin and all evildoers, and throw them into the furnace of fire; there men will weep and gnash their teeth."

V. The reality of hell should serve all of us as a sober reminder and warning never to linger in grave sin, and it engenders a healthy fear of offending Almighty God.

****

1) That we frequently ask the Lord's pardon for our sins.

2) That the Lord give us the gift of holy fear.

3) That we may be humble, honest, and frank in our confessions.

4) That our Catholic people return to the practice of frequent confession.

5) That Christians reflect frequently on the reality of hell.

6) That we strive to sharpen our devotion to the Blessed Virgin Mary, especially in the rosary, and express our sorrow to her for having offended her divine Son.

Wednesday of the Seventeenth Week: Mt. 13:44-46

I. Palestine was the corridor linking Egypt, Syria, and Persia. It was the scene of frequent battles. As a result of this, securing one's possessions was a difficult matter indeed. Even if people could put their money into banks, these banks would not be secure enough against marauding armies on a rampage. The safest place to hide one's treasures was in the ground, for when armies moved on, one could return and dig up his/her valuables.

II. Once again Our Lord uses common imagery to narrate a parable which the people could understand without difficulty. It was not uncommon in Our Lord's day for people to find treasures in their fields which were buried years before by people who had long since died.

1) Roman law, and probably Jewish law also, granted the treasure to the one who discovered it, provided he was the owner of the land on which the treasure was found, or that it was found on public property (Prat, *Jesus Christ*). The man in this parable is obviously acting on this principle, so he sets out to purchase the field without informing the owner of his discovery.

2) Our Lord does not pass judgment on the ethics of this man.

The Lord's purpose was to show with what eagerness and enthusiasm we all should pursue the things of God.

III. The Gospel indicates that the man accidentally stumbled on the hidden treasure. He accidentally found it. He wasn't actually looking for it. It simply was there all the time just waiting to be found.

1) C.S. Lewis was a professor of English literature at Oxford University. He died in 1963. Lewis was a great spiritual writer. One of his books was instrumental in converting Charles Colson, of Watergate fame, to Christianity.

2) In his autobiography, C.S. Lewis confesses that he had lost his faith and all religious beliefs as a teenager. It was only when he passed the age of thirty that he came to believe in God again, and to accept Our Lord Jesus Christ as the Son of God. He choose the title of his autobiography, *Surprised by Joy*, precisely because it more aptly describes the discovery of something (a great treasure) which actually was there all the time, but he did not see until the Lord gave him the gift of faith, the spiritual eyes of the soul that see the treasures of God.

3) St. Augustine likewise confesses that what he had given up for Jesus Christ was nothing in comparison to the treasure he had gained. Before his conversion, he thought the price was too high to be a Christian, for he didn't see Christianity as the pearl of great value. To embrace Christianity would mean to pay too high a price. It would mean giving up his license — the freedom to live immorally, as so many of his pagan Roman friends did. Through the persistent prayers of his mother, St. Monica, Augustine received the sight of faith; then he could see Christianity as indeed the pearl of great price, worth selling everything in order to purchase it.

IV. Where your treasure is, goes the maxim, there is your heart.

1) Only faith can give us a true sense of values together with the sight to see the precious treasures of the spiritual life. These treasures can be in our midst, yet we may fail to see them or appreciate their worth as being the hidden treasures and pearls of great price which they really are, worth selling all we have for; worth making every sacrifice and effort in order to obtain and possess them. Without the discerning eye of faith, however, we will "see without seeing," and

consequently pass over these wonderful treasures without realizing it simply because we did not see what only faith could enable us to see.

2) How true it is that our vision can be dimmed as our faith, which is the eye of the spiritual life, diminishes. As our faith grows and intensifies, the keener become the eyes of the soul, and they enable us to see the pearls and treasures revealed in the Gospels. Opportunities of grace are offered to us in our daily lives. They are all so many manifestations of God's goodness and desire to enrich us with His gifts and fruits, and thus enable us to come to possess more and more of Him who is the treasure of treasures. We must nurture our faith by constant prayer and the practice of the virtue of charity.

3) Let us not take this precious gift we have received in Baptism for granted. Let us work while there is light to increase this priceless treasure of limitless value — the gift of faith.

****

1) That we frequently thank God for the gift of faith.

2) That we strive to increase and intensify our faith by frequent prayer and generous acts of charity.

3) That the Lord give us the true sense of perspective and a spirit of poverty so that we will not be deceived by wealth, prestige, or money.

4) That we take advantage of the opportunities of grace offered to us through the inspirations and promptings of the Holy Spirit.

5) That all those who "see yet do not really see" may come to see and understand and appreciate the message of the Gospel.

6) That we may be mindful to pray frequently for all those who have abandoned or lost their faith, especially members of our families, relatives, and friends.

Thursday of the Seventeenth Week: Mt. 13:47-53

I. Just as the merchant has the skilled eye to discern the value of pearls, so too fishermen know how to sort out quality fish and throw away the inferior ones.

II. God wills the salvation of all His sons and daughters, and the dragnet (which is His Church) symbolizes His willingness to take to Himself whoever flows into this dragnet. This dragnet combs the sea of the world. The Church, in her missionary effort, goes out to the entire world to bring the good news to all men and women, baptizing them and thus bringing them into the Mystical Body of Christ, which is His Church.

1) Although this dragnet picks up indiscriminately all kinds of fish, so too does the Church bring into her bosom all races of peoples. However, there comes the time when the net will be pulled up from the sea and skilled fishermen (who symbolize the angels) will sort out the good fish from the bad. The good will be retained and the bad will be thrown back into the sea as rejects.

2) So too with the Church. At the end of time the angels will sort out the good men and women from evil men and women. The good will go off to heaven, and the bad will be thrust into hell.

III. "Every scribe who has been trained for the kingdom of heaven is like a householder who brings out of his treasure what is new and what is old."

1) Anything of real value can give fresh ideas each time we meditate and reflect upon it. Good literature is an example. The works of Cervantes and Shakespeare can be reread with interest, because each time something new can be extracted and learned from them that we missed in a previous reading, perhaps when we were quite a bit younger.

2) Classics are classics precisely because of their ability to offer something fresh and valuable when they are reread. The author's genius is not exhausted in one reading of his/her work.

3) If this be the case with good literature, how much more will this be so for sacred Scripture, the living word of God! Each time we meditate on passages from the Bible, it is like entering a storeroom, from which we can pull out old and new ideas and inspirations.

IV. The Bible is the storehouse containing the food that makes us grow in our knowledge and love of God, the basic ingredients for growing in our relationship with God. Sacred Scripture is the instrument God uses to communicate His knowledge to us and inspire us.

1) Kierkegaard defined the Bible as "God's Love Letter." Love letters are cogent means for cultivating a deep love relationship between lovers. The words of Scripture are God's way of expressing His love for us.

2) The Bible is that storeroom into which we can enter and have our every need filled, both new and old needs.

3) So in love with sacred Scripture was St. John Chrysostom that he held that the cause of all evils in the world was ignorance of sacred Scripture. St. Jerome, the great Scripture Scholar of the fourth century, undertook the work of producing a clear and readable Latin Bible which was to serve the Church as its standard for more than a thousand years. He translated the Old Testament from Hebrew into Latin and the New Testament from Greek into a standard Latin Vulgate Bible. He used to say, "Familiarity with the Bible is the royal road to the knowledge and love of Christ."

4) Abraham Lincoln said that the Bible was the best gift God gave to man.

V. The Bible is the storehouse of light, comfort, support, inspiration, and consolation in times of trial and interior darkness.

1) The Bible heads the bestseller list year in and year out. This is so because it satisfies every human need.

2) Thomas Carlyle wrote, "Through its pages as through a window divinely opened, all men can see into the stillness of eternity."

3) It is the answer to restless young people and would serve them as a veritable source of solace, refuge, and support if they would take the time to reflect and meditate prayerfully on it. For from it, as from a massive storehouse, will forever come things both new and old together with endless consolations and inspirations.

****

1) The Church is that dragnet which strives to catch all men and women to help them to salvation; that all bishops and priests strive to fulfill their roles as fishers of the souls of men and women.

2) For an increase in vocations to the priesthood and religious life.

3) That the Lord may fill us with selfless zeal for souls.

4) That we all come to hunger for the Bible as our storehouse and resort to it frequently for inspiration and knowledge.

5) That we strive to spend some time each day reflecting on the word of God, but especially when we are going through a difficult period in life or a severe trial.

6) For the conversion of hardened sinners.

7) That our Catholic families do readings from the Bible as a family practice, perhaps reading a passage before the principal meal of the day.

Friday of the Seventeenth Week: Mt. 13:54-58

I. "Brother, can you spare a dime?" was a theme song during the Great Depression. The terms "brothers" and "sisters" used in today's Gospel are terms which express familiarity and endearment, and in Our Lord's day they were commonly used.

1) James is called a "brother" of the Lord, but we know that he was a son of another Mary, Mary of Cleophas or Clopas.

2) The same can be said of "sisters" of the Lord. Brothers and sisters included relatives, and in all probability it even included close friends. The Greek word employed by St. Mark is *adelphoi*. This word can be employed to refer to physical or spiritual brotherhood. The Jewish Essene community, according to Josephus, the first century Jewish historian, used the word "brothers" to refer to all the members of that community (Sena, *Weekday Homily Helps*).

3) In the New Testament, Christians are called brothers about 160 times, and Jesus Himself used the term broadly when He said that the one who does the will of His Father is His own brother (Mt. 12:50; Lk. 8:21) (McKenzie, *Dictionary of the Bible*).

II. "A prophet is not without honor except in his own country and in his own house." No matter what Jesus might say or whatever miracles He might perform, it still would count as nothing among the Jewish leaders in accepting Him as their Messiah.

1) Despite the miracles Jesus had already worked in Galilee, the people of Nazareth would not even begin to believe that Jesus was the expected Messiah. Their reaction was "Where did He get all this?" and "Where did this man get such wisdom and miraculous powers?" "Isn't this the carpenter's son?" They simply refused to let truth enter into their hearts, and they succumbed to their petty and provincial prejudices.

2) We are all so quick to judge; yet how often we fall short, becoming outright wrong! This is basically because either we refuse to allow the truth to enter into our minds on account of its consequences or our evaluation lacks sufficient information, or it is

influenced by our desires and what we would like a person, situation, or thing to be. In other words, we, too, are so much like the people of Nazareth; we allow our prejudices to influence our judgments and evaluations of persons and their actions.

3) Being thoroughly objective is very, very difficult; yet truth, justice, and charity urge us to strive toward objectivity.

III. A book cannot be judged by its elaborate bindings, nor can we evaluate the contents of a package, however fancy and decorative the wrapping paper and ribbons might be. The simple reason is that we just do not have sufficient information.

1) Prejudice is the child of pride, and it is blinding. It places so many obstacles to the light of truth that it keeps a person in the dark. The intelligentsia, the scribes, Pharisees, rabbis, and leaders of the people wanted their kind of Messiah, and Jesus did not fit into their preconceived ideas of what the Messiah would be like.

2) They wanted Israel back on the map with importance as a world power, greater than in the days of their great warrior king David. Jesus did not cut that kind of leadership image. His doctrine of love of enemies, of meekness, of humility, of turning the other cheek, was just too much for them to stomach.

3) The hearts of such people were set against hearing what Jesus was preaching. No matter how many signs and wonders He performed, He was not acceptable to them as their Messiah.

IV. The Second Vatican Council has made its objective bringing together all Christians into the one flock under the one shepherd.

1) Dialogue has become the tool and instrument used to bring about unity. Listening to where another person is coming from and exchanging information with him/her is charity's way of opening up the way for truth to enter and of breaking down the walls of prejudice.

2) It is not only in the realm of ecumenism that dialogue should be employed. The object of dialogue is to arrive at truth. Dialogue should be open, honest, and frank communication that must be insulated by charity and meekness. It should be used to resolve differences between husbands and wives, between members of a family, and between friends. Family members and friends who have been alienated, in many cases because of differences largely based

on misunderstandings, will find in sincere Christian dialogue a very effective means of reconciliation and of arriving at truth.

****

1) Tolerance is the fruit of charity; that the Lord bestow it upon us to restore peace to others.

2) That we strive to analyze our prejudices to see where we are coming from and work to honestly eliminate them.

3) That members of families not harbor grudges, but rather in the spirit of charity and honest dialogue seek reconciliation with one another.

4) That we may be honest and open in our search for truth, and that this honest search for truth may bring unity to Christendom.

5) That victims of violence be compensated for their losses by those who perpetrated them.

6) For the freedom of oppressed peoples to practice their religion.

Saturday of the Seventeenth Week: Mt. 14:1-12

I. The Herod mentioned in this passage is Herod Antipas, the son of King Herod the Great. He ruled the provinces of Galilee and Perea.

1) Herod Antipas had been educated in Rome, and it was on the occasion of a visit to Rome that he seduced his brother Philip's wife, Herodias. Herod Antipas's wife was the daughter of a King Aretas, king of a small kingdom in the Near East. She fled to her father, who later defeated Herod in a war over a border dispute.

2) The scandal that Herod caused was glaring, for not only did he not have a just reason to divorce his lawful wife but he further irritated the Jews because of the crime of incest: he married Herodias, his brother's wife.

3) John the Baptist lost no time in publicly reproaching Herod Antipas. Herod reacted by throwing John into prison.

II. Herodias was obviously a woman of loose morals. She was also highly vindictive and looked for an opportunity to vent her vengeance on John.

1) The opportunity presented itself at a banquet given on the occasion of Herod Antipas's birthday. He had invited all his friends. Salome, the daughter of Herodias, came out on to the banquet floor and proceeded to dance for Herod's audience. She performed so well

that she moved Herod to ask her what she wanted as a reward for her performance. Salome went to her mother to ask her what she, Salome, should ask of the king.

2) Herodias's moment of vengeance came, and she begged her daughter to ask for the head of John the Baptist.

3) Upon hearing of her request, Herod was taken aback; yet for fear of incurring the criticism of his guests by going back on his word, he ruefully acceded, granting the request. To incest, Herod Antipas added the crime of murder.

III. John stood up for what he knew was right regardless of the consequences. He was a man of strong character. Herod Antipas was just the opposite: he was weak and fearful, and he would buckle under the pressure of criticism from his peers.

1) To honor a foolish oath, he would even commit murder. Herod goes down in infamy, while John is recognized and remembered as a heroic prophet and martyr.

2) Weak Herod falls victim to human respect. Human respect means doing something which is wrong or failing to do the right thing out of fear of criticism from others, or simply to so act in order to please other people. It is a form of cowardice.

3) Human respect or bowing to peer pressure is what causes so many people to commit sins. Human respect chooses to offend God rather than other men or women. It is a consequence of weak faith. It sees immediate and relatively small consequences in comparison to the long-range and graver consequences which will ultimately be incurred for acting in such a cowardly and unfaithful manner.

IV. We all admire heroes because they stand up for what they believe is right. Today's Gospel narrative gives us the example of strong and weak character. John will do the right thing no matter what the consequence might bring him. Herod, on the other hand, is like a reed which bends any which way the wind blows.

1) The world we live in makes every effort to shake the true follower of Christ. It makes it very unpopular to live up to Christian morals. The new morality of convenience is in, and only the strong — that is, men and women of strong faith — will be able to live up to the teachings of Christ in spite of criticism from so-called friends or peers.

2) Our faith will cost us, and God will allow us to be tried for

His own honor and glory and for our growth and merit. The weak will take courage and grow by the example of the strong.

3) Doing what is right means placing God first regardless of the cost. We must never feel ashamed of doing the right thing. Let us be mindful of the words of Our Lord Jesus Christ: "Whoever is ashamed of me and of my words, of him will the Son of Man be ashamed when he comes in his glory and the glory of the Father and of the holy angels" (Lk. 9:26).

****

1) That God give us the grace to be of strong character.

2) That we may not offend God in order to please other men or women.

3) That the enticement of money or fame not make us compromise our Christian principles.

4) That those in positions of authority not submit to bribes or to the pressure of criticism in the execution of their duties.

5) That parents not show a double standard to their children by teaching virtue and not practicing it.

6) That the Lord generously endow us with courage and fortitude to bear generous witness to Him and His Gospel.

7) That the young overcome the fear of the criticism or pressure of their peers and not compromise their moral behavior.

Monday of the Eighteenth Week: Mt. 14:13-21

I. The compassion of Jesus literally made Him accessible and available to people in need. No doubt He felt tired after preaching, listening to and healing the spiritual, physical, and emotional afflictions of the people. Crowds pressed upon Him wherever He went. Jesus is never too tired to respond to human affliction and need.

II. In today's Gospel narrative, Jesus wanted to withdraw to a deserted place away from the crowds when He received news of the death of John the Baptist. It was time for prayer and reflection; Jesus wanted solitude for this. Getting into a boat would be the logical way to free Himself from the crowd. The Sea of Galilee is only eight miles wide, and the landing site could be seen from the opposite shore; it would be difficult for Jesus to get out of their sight. He was too much of a treasure to let go. He, more than anyone else, had done so much for them, and he was an answer to their aspirations.

III. Arriving at a deserted area on the other side of the lake, Jesus was met by a huge throng of people pressing upon Him again. They were eager to listen to Him and have Him lay His hands on their sick and afflicted loved ones. Tired as He must have been, Jesus responded with compassion.

1) So impressed were these people with Jesus that they became oblivious of the time of day, for evening was drawing on. They would need time to get provisions for their family meal.

2) Not only was Jesus compassionate with the ill and crippled among them, but His compassion now embraced the entire crowd, which was well over five thousand. He felt sorry that they had no food with them.

3) Jesus instructs His disciples to feed the crowd, knowing well that His disciples had not nearly enough provisions to feed such a crowd. Even though they had little, Jesus wanted them to share what they had. Jesus proceeded to multiply the five loaves and few fish that His disciples could muster up.

IV. The lesson is clear here: Jesus wants us to be compassionate and to share what we have with others in need. God works through the members of His Mystical Body on earth. Jesus continues to touch the afflicted and to feed the hungry through us, and much of His compassion is not felt by those in need because of stingy instruments — the members of His Mystical body.

1) Few resources generously given into God's hands will produce more than we can imagine. Like the Apostles, we too might say, "What are these among so many?" All God wants is for us to participate in His compassionate work by being compassionate and generous instruments in His hands.

2) There are immense problems in the world today, and more people live in poverty than in prosperity. If people collaborated and responded, world hunger could be abated; fears and anxieties could be vastly reduced. We all live in the same world and we are all brothers and sisters in the Lord.

3) The resources in the world abound. Compassion and charity urge us to help people get at those needed resources. The Lord does feed the birds of the air and the fish of the sea; how much more so

will He supply His sons and daughters with what they really need, but He wills to do so through us, His instruments.

V. Our compassion must extend itself beyond supplying physical needs. People are hurting in many ways. Just listening to them and offering our advice will go a long way for them and will help restore their wholeness.

1) The elderly are hurting for lack of interest in them. Our society sweeps them under the rug and forgets about them. What a visit would do for them, or even a phone call to let them know that they are thought of!

2) Compassion literally means "suffering with." It exemplifies our Savior in every page of the Gospels. It is the virtue that heals human ills, and makes us Christlike. Like St. Paul, let us strive to weep with those who weep and rejoice with those who rejoice (Rom. 12:15). Compassionating others does much toward healing our own ills as well.

****

1) That we frequently give thanks to Almighty God for the marvelous gift of the Eucharist.

2) That we strive to compassionate those in need.

3) That we try to be more understanding especially toward hurting members of our own families.

4) That we strive to help those organizations which endeavor to alleviate world hunger.

5) That we generously support the St. Vincent de Paul Society of our parish.

6) That we think more of the elderly, and that we endeavor to spend time with them as a community service project.

Tuesday of the Eighteenth Week: Mt. 14:22-36

I. Jesus sends His Apostles into the boat to go on ahead of Him to the other side of the Sea of Galilee, while He Himself seeks out solitude to be alone with His Heavenly Father in prayer.

II. It is not an uncommon phenomenon for the Sea of Galilee to pass from a tranquil, calm lake into a raging storm in the matter of minutes.

1) The lake is located some 680 feet below sea level and is

bounded by mountains on the west. When the winds blow off the Mediterranean Sea on the west, their force is increased as they are funneled through the deep gulches and ravines of the mountainside of the lake's western shore. As the wind courses its way through these ravines and gullies, it becomes compressed and increases in velocity (W. Barclay).

2) By the time these winds hit the water they accumulate such a force that they turn the lake into a raging storm capable of overturning a sizable fishing vessel. Thus it happened at three in the morning, and the boat of the Apostles was in danger of capsizing, when Jesus is seen approaching them through the storm walking upon the waters. The Apostles thought that they were seeing a ghost.

III. When Peter was assured that the figure walking on the waters was none other than Jesus, he was so caught up with enthusiasm at the marvel of this miracle over nature that he asked Jesus to bid him walk out to meet Him.

1) The Lord granted Peter's request to test his faith. Peter failed by succumbing to human fear and lack of faith. Fear and faith are incompatible companions, for deep faith casts out fear. Love and faith both have this similar quality of overcoming fear, even the fear of death. This is exemplified in the lives of so many martyrs, who at their executions seemed fearless.

2) Harry Emerson Fosdick wrote, "Fear imprisons, faith liberates; fear paralyzes, faith empowers; fear disheartens, faith encourages; fear sickens, faith heals; fear is useless, faith makes serviceable — and most of all, fear puts hopelessness at the heart of life, while faith rejoices in its God" (*Treasure Chest*).

IV. In a broad sense, the boat symbolizes the Church tossed about in the storms of persecutions which raged across the centuries from the Roman emperors to the barbaric invasions of Europe and the sacking of Rome in the fifth century, down to the French Revolution when the Cathedral of Notre Dame was changed into a temple of the goddess of reason, and on to the scourge of Communism in our own day.

V. The boat symbolizes each of us baptized Christians; we are miniature churches, whom Our Lord Jesus Christ commits Himself to be with throughout the stormy trials and problems of our individual lives.

1) Like Peter, the Lord will try our faith. During the storms of trials that befall us, will He have to say to us also for doubting, "Why do you doubt, O you of little faith?" It is precisely in the darkness of a difficult trial, as the storm fills us with fear, that we are tempted to doubt. Yet we have His word that He will be present with us even though we may not sense His presence.

2) When Pope Paul VI entered the office of his predecessor, John XXIII, for the first time as pope, he sat down at the desk to look over papers that awaited papal decisions. After a short time, he buried his head in his arm, distraught at the overwhelming problems that faced the Church. Tears came to his eyes when he realized the difficult task that was ahead of him. In the midst of his sadness and dejection, he lifted his head and his eye caught sight of a picture of Christ on the boat with His Apostles with His hands raised calming the stormy sea of Galilee. Pope Paul got the message. He knew that Christ was indeed with His Church and at His vicar's side to calm the storms that would arise.

3) St. Paul would boast of his weaknesses because of his confidence in God's help, as he put it: "I will all the more gladly boast of my weaknesses, that the power of Christ may rest upon me" (2 Cor. 12:9). The force and power of Jesus is greater than any storm. Wherever Jesus is, there the storms abate and calm is restored. What He expects of us, as He did of His Apostles, is faith and trust in Him.

****

1) That the Lord bless us with a lively faith and deep confidence in our prayers.

2) That we confidently abandon ourselves into the hands of divine providence each day of our lives.

3) In times of dark and stormy trials, that we fly to our heavenly Mother for strength and help and not displease her Son by our lack of faith.

4) That God, through the intercession of our Blessed Lady, bestow upon us a rich and vibrant faith.

5) That our love and trust in God may grow to that stature which will drive out fear and anxiety from our hearts.

6) That we take the advice of St. Francis de Sales, that during the

difficult times of trials and sadness we betake ourselves to sacred Scripture and let our eyes fall where they will on the pages of the New Testament for enlightenment and consolation.

7) For all those, especially those who are near to us, who have lost their faith.

8) For all people who are undergoing strong trials.

Wednesday of the Eighteenth Week: Mt. 15:21-28

I. Today's Gospel presents us with a Jesus who seems rather harsh and tough and even insulting. The scene of this narrative takes place in the pagan district of Tyre and Sidon, Phoenician territory just to the north of the district of Galilee. The woman was a Gentile, of the Syro-Phoenicians (traditional enemies of Israel).

II. This Gentile woman salutes Jesus with the Messianic title "Son of David." She therefore believes that Jesus is the Messiah. She knows in her heart that Jesus can cure her daughter, who, she says, "is severely possessed by a demon."

1) People in those days attributed all physical illnesses to demons. It could be that her daughter had a physical illness or affliction or that she might have indeed been possessed by a demon. The girl's mother had confidence that Jesus would cure her daughter. Jesus paid no attention to her cries for help. He was testing her faith to show the contrast between the faith of a Gentile and the faithlessness of the chosen people.

2) The woman persisted and cried out all the louder; she wanted a hearing. The disciples of Jesus were becoming embarrassed with her to the point of asking Jesus themselves to send her away to avoid further attention, for they were not in Jewish territory.

III. Jesus accedes to grant her a hearing. He calls her over and asks what it is that she wants of Him. Falling on her knees, she pleads that Jesus free her daughter of the malicious demon who was troubling her.

1) Jesus tries her faith further: "It is not fair to take the children's bread and throw it to the dogs." The Jews usually used the word "dog" in a derogatory and insulting way, especially in reference to the Gentiles. It would be shocking to think that Jesus would resort to such language.

2) Jesus uses the a diminutive, "kunaria," and not "kunes,"

which would mean common street dogs. "Kunaria" were little lap dogs, pets of the household. By using such language, Jesus is politely bringing out the importance of priority for the children (Jews, the chosen people), and thus eliminates the apparent contempt in employing the word dogs (*A Catholic Commentary on Holy Scripture*).

3) In the Near East, this is considered witty dialogue and would provoke a like response. The Gentile woman measured up to the test with her delightful and respectful reply, "Yes, Lord," she insisted, " yet even the dogs [that is, household pets] eat the crumbs that fall from their master's tables"

IV. Jesus is moved by her faith and admires her wit. He answers, "O woman, great is your faith! Be it done for you as you desire."

Even though her daughter was not there present, the Syro-Phoenician woman believed that her daughter was cured at Jesus' word, a further corroboration of her deep faith and confidence in Jesus.

V. The Gentile woman had the perfect qualities of prayer:

1) She humbled herself before the divine majesty of Jesus by first of all acknowledging His identity: "Son of David" (Messiah).

2) She asked for something beneficial for another person — her daughter.

3) She firmly believed that she would obtain her request.

4) She was sincere and in dead earnest.

5) She persevered and persisted in spite of what others might think or feel (as in this case the disciples of Jesus wanted to get rid of her for the embarrassment she was causing). Many people give up when they are not immediately heard. God works in His own good time, but He doesn't want us to give up, for this would be insulting to His goodness and generosity.

6) The Lord tried the woman's faith, and He will try ours too. Perseverance and trust is a sign of faith. The Syro-Phoenician knew in her heart that if she kept up her efforts, Jesus would respond.

VI. The Lord commanded us to pray. Such a command would be empty if He were not disposed to answer our prayers. After all, Jesus did say, "Whatever you ask in prayer, believe that you receive it, and you will" (Mk. 11:24).

****

1) That the Lord bless us with those necessary qualities for efficacious prayer.

2) That we may always be sincere and earnest in our prayer.

3) That we never be overcome by discouragement or lack of confidence.

4) That we not ramble on or be inattentive or unconscious of what we are doing or to whom we are speaking.

5) That we, like the Syro-Phoenician woman, persevere and persist in our prayer of petition.

6) That we be mindful of prefacing our petitions with a humble act of contrition.

7) For peace in the world and an end to the arms race and terrorism.

Thursday of the Eighteenth Week: Mt. 16:13-23

I. At Caesarea Philippi, Our Lord selected Peter as His successor and vicar. He entrusted him with that awesome responsibility of leading the Church, while at the same time giving him the authority and power of the Keys to bind and loosen.

II. Peter is to "feed the lambs and sheep." He is to chair or lead the original Apostolic College, the twelve Apostles, and to feed the sheep — all of the baptized.

1) Peter would be the principal teacher of the Magisterium — i.e, the teaching office of the Church.

2) The Magisterium (from the Latin *magister*, teacher) has the authority to teach in the name of Christ all the truths of the Christian faith and all that is necessary or useful for the proclamation and defense of those truths.

3) The pope as the successor of Peter would continue to enjoy this charism with a unique protection from the Holy Spirit.

4) The bishops as successors of the Apostles would also participate in the teaching office and authority of the Church.

III. As to the teaching authority of the Church, the Second Vatican Council has reiterated the declaration of the First Vatican Council, which can be summarized as follows:

1) The bishops together with the pope are successors of the College of Apostles.

2) The pope, as successor of St. Peter, is the head of the College of Bishops. The Magisterium, or teaching authority, belongs to the Holy Father in a special way. It also extends to the bishops who are in communion with the pope.

IV. The Magisterium exercises its teaching authority infallibly in a solemn way through ecumenical councils or through the teaching of the pope when, as supreme shepherd and teacher, he solemnly pronounces on truths pertaining to faith and morals.

V. Our Lord Jesus Christ gave Peter and the Apostles the guarantee of being singularly protected from error by the Holy Spirit. This guarantee would extend also to the pope and the college of bishops in union with the Holy Father.

1) This guarantee does not become the property of priests or theologians.

2) This promise of the special guidance and protection of the Holy Spirit is uniquely made to Peter, the Apostles, and their successors.

VI. God in His providence provided for the Church in the twentieth century through the declaration of papal infallibility, defined in the First Vatican Council (1869-1870).

1) This declaration served to ground the faith of people who might be tempted to follow the teaching or opinions of prominent theologians who are touted by the media. In serious matters of faith and morals we should ask, "What does Peter (the pope) say?"

2) No matter how prestigious a theologian may be, such a one's pronouncements are at best merely the personal opinions of a particular scholar.

3) The difficult and delicate work of the theologian is to help the Magisterium of the Church to explain, through the categories of human reason, and in precise and clear terms that can be understood by the ordinary faithful, the truths of faith that are proclaimed by the Magisterium. At the same time they should strive to explain the reasoning and the logic behind the teachings and position of the Church on human conduct and morality. It is not the role of the theologian to criticize or impugn the teaching of the Magisterium, but to assist it in its supremely difficult and important work of the sanctification and salvation of souls.

4) When theologians go against the reiterated teaching of the

Magisterium of the Church, it would be rash to follow their opinion. The Holy Spirit uniquely is pledged to be with and guide the Magisterium of the Church.

5) In the difficult area of contraception, it is absolutely rash to follow an opinion that opposes the reiterated statements of the Holy Father, who has consistently declared artificial contraception to be morally wrong.

VII. In his encyclical *Ecclesiam Suam* Pope Paul VI wrote, "The Christian life, as the Church is understanding and codifying it in wise instructions, will always demand fidelity, commitment, mortification, and sacrifice; it will always be marked by the 'narrow way' of which Our Lord spoke to us."

****

1) For our Holy Father, that the Lord give him the spiritual and physical strength to lead and unify the Church.

2) That the ecumenical movement may continue to move and gain momentum, so that all Christians may be united as one flock under the one shepherd.

3) That theologians carry on their great work and have a singular respect for and obedience to the Vicar of Christ.

4) That all of our Catholic people may look to the Holy Father as a father, teacher, and guide.

5) That we may all have a love for the truth and not seek to rationalize it to accommodate our personal desires.

6) For an increase in vocations to the priesthood and religious life.

7) For peace in the world and for social justice, especially in the Third World countries.

Friday of the Eighteenth Week: Mt. 16:24-28

I. Today's Gospel reiterates one of the dominant and ever-recurring themes of Christianity: the obligation to participate in the Cross of Jesus Christ. Again and again, Jesus confronts His disciples with the challenge of the cross. The words "renounce," "take up your cross," and "follow me" are all synonymous.

II. If Jesus must expect the punishment of the cross for what He was preaching, His disciples could expect a similar fate if they were to carry His message and remain loyal to Him. Martyrdom did crown their careers.

III. Cardinal John Henry Newman wrote that the cross teaches us "how to live, how to use this world, what to expect, what to desire, what to hope." "The cross," he wrote, "is the measure of all things; it is the very heart of our faith."

IV. Christ's death is our life. In Him, the very core of our suffering and death is transformed into a source of life. In His cross and sufferings, we are healed in our deepest illnesses.

V. The cross has been a stumbling block not only to nonbelievers, but even to many Christians who have absorbed so much of the humanism of the modern materialistic world.

1) The question is so often asked, "Why suffering?" "Why the cross?" "What did he or she do to deserve that?" This question can rightly be answered by posing a similar question: "Why did the Son of God become a man of suffering in our world?"

2) Suffering and death remain mysteries. Nevertheless, we do see similar phenomena in nature: seeds must die to give new plants; animals as well as human beings suffer in giving birth to their young.

VI. Christ's death makes eternal life possible for us, but to attain this, we too must pass through many trials and carry many crosses. In his letter to the Romans, St. Paul writes "Do you not know that all of us who have been baptized into Christ Jesus were baptized into His death? We were buried therefore with him by baptism into death, so that as Christ was raised from the dead by the glory of the Father, we too might walk in newness of life" (Rom. 6:3-4).

1) St. Paul speaks of transformation coming through the crucifixion of the old person in all of us in order to be freed from slavery to sin (Rom. 6:6).

2) We should accept suffering for love of Christ, basically because it transforms us into Him. In this sense, suffering should be for the fervent soul a matter of joy rather than sorrow. St. Francis of Assisi said: "More than all graces and gifts of the Holy Spirit which God gives to His friends is to deny oneself and, for the sake of Christ's love, to suffer pain, injury, disgrace, and distress" (quoted from E. Boylan's *This Tremendous Lover*).

VII. Jesus is very clear on this point of sharing His Cross in today's Gospel: "If any man would come after me, let him deny himself and take up his cross and follow me." There is no hedging here. The words are clear and emphatic. Our part and union with Christ will depend a great deal on our willingness to share in His cross.

1) Can we the members of the Body of Christ be exempted from the sufferings of its Head? Suffering configures us with Christ (Phil. 3:10). St. John of the Cross gives to the love of suffering an exceptional importance in the sanctification of one's soul.

2) Through our participation in the cross of Christ, we contribute to the sanctification and salvation of souls, a work which is incumbent on all the baptized out of sheer love for our brothers and sisters in need. St. Paul speaks of the necessity of suffering in order to make up for those sufferings that were lacking to Christ for the sake of His Body, the Church (Col. 1:24). What St. Paul means here is not that Christ's sufferings are insufficient for our salvation, but that He wills that we share in this redemptive work since we are members of His Mystical Body. If we bear our trials and suffering with love in union with Christ crucified, they become a "sweet yoke and light burden" and a powerful means of saving souls.

3) St. Philip Neri summed this up well when he said, "In this life, there is no purgatory. There is only heaven and hell, for he who bears afflictions with patience has paradise, and he who does not has hell."

4) In his encyclical *Mystici Corporis Christi*, Pope Pius XII said, "Deep mystery is this and subject of inextinguishable meditation, that the salvation of many depends on the prayers and voluntary penances which the members of the Mystical Body of Christ offer for this intention."

****

1) That we bear cheerfully whatever form of the cross may come to us, whether through illness, relationship with people with whom we live or work, or other setbacks and reverses in our lives.

2) That we strive to compassionate those who are suffering and lonely.

3) That our compassion may be effective and not stop at sighs and moans, but that we strive to positively alleviate the one suffering.

4) In all our trials and sufferings, that we make the conscious

effort to offer them up in union with Jesus Christ crucified for the motive of contributing toward the work of salvation of souls.

5) That we help others bear the cross of old age.

6) That we be generous in responding to our Blessed Lady's plea for prayers and voluntary penances to win graces for reckless souls on their way to final condemnation.

Saturday of the Eighteenth Week: Mt. 17:14-20

I. Jesus was absent when this man brought his epileptic son to His disciples in search of a cure. Jesus had sent His disciples out to preach in towns and prepare the people for His visit. He had given them power to heal and to cast out demons.

1) In the Palestine of Our Lord's day, diseases were attributed to devils who were believed to enter into people and afflict them with different maladies.

2) In this case there was present both a real physical malady, epilepsy (*Jerome Biblical Commentary*), together with a diabolic possession, because Jesus not only cures the boy but exorcises him as well.

II. What angered Jesus was the lack of faith on the part of His own disciples, like Peter; when Jesus gave him the power to walk on the waters of the Sea of Galilee, no sooner had Peter left the boat and walked on the water than he faltered and doubted the reality of what was happening.

1) The Apostles were given power to go out and heal and cast out demons, but today's Gospel narration shows that they fell short in their endeavor to cure the man's son. When they asked Jesus why they failed with the power He had given them, He responded that failure was due to their lack of faith and trust.

2) Frustrated with the Apostles, but full of faith in Jesus, the man seeks out Jesus. He complains that Jesus' Apostles were powerless to expel the demon from his son.

III. I suppose that we all at one time or another have said that if Jesus were really and physically present on this earth again the way He was in the Gospel stories, if we could get close to Him and ask a particular favor, He would indeed grant it there and then.

1) Many people feel that if they could only get to a shrine they would have a good chance of getting cured of a disease or of an

affliction of long standing. This is somewhat analogous to the thinking that if Jesus were physically present one's petition would surely be granted. One's presence at a shrine of the Blessed Virgin Mary would serve to stimulate one with fervor, and perhaps one might experience an increase in faith which would enable one to pray with deeper fervor and confidence. Such circumstances would dispose a person to be more apt to receive his/her favor.

2) The important thing to want in prayer is that God's will be done above all things, and our particular requests must be made with this in mind. It may well be to His greater glory and our sanctification that we not receive a favor for which we are praying.

3) Giovanni Battista Tomasi decided to go to Lourdes to commit suicide as a gesture of rebellion in front of the grotto where Our Lady appeared to St. Bernadette, because he had not been cured of an illness he was not willing to accept. He actually did go to the Shrine at Lourdes, positioned himself in front of the grotto, and was starting the process of suicide when the Blessed Virgin won for him a powerful interior illumination of mind and heart. God made him see the immense value of suffering. He left Lourdes full of gratitude to God for the cross he was bearing in his illness. He was so filled with zeal for this apostolate of Lourdes that he founded an association which would dedicate itself to transporting the sick and handicapped to the Shrine of Lourdes. Membership in this association is in the thousands today.

IV. No matter what sacrament of the Church we use, it will be like the Apostles facing the possessed epileptic boy, ineffective, unless we have a lively faith in God's commitment to work through that sacrament.

1) We will get out of the sacraments only what we bring to them. If we come with a deep faith in search of Jesus, we will indeed touch Him and He will touch us with His healing hand.

2) St. Teresa of Ávila spoke about the many healings she obtained from Our Lord Jesus Christ through the sacrament of the Eucharist. She writes, "Now when Our Lord was in the world, the sick were healed by merely touching His garments; how can we doubt that He will heal us when He is within us, if we but have faith? The Lord does not pay cheaply for His lodgings if we show Him true hospitality" (*Complete Works of St. Teresa*).

****

1) That we come to appreciate the sacraments that Christ left to His Church.

2) That we realize that Christ touches us, and we Him, in His sacraments, but especially in Holy Communion.

3) That the Lord increase our faith and our confidence in His readiness to help us.

4) When we receive the Eucharist, that we frequently express our desire to be united to Him and that He take more and more possession of our souls and bodies.

5) That we express our gratitude often to Our Lord Jesus Christ for the salutary helps He has left us for our own sanctification and salvation in the sacraments.

Monday of the Nineteenth Week: Mt. 17:22-27

I. The book of Exodus states, "Every one who is numbered in the census, from twenty years old and upward, shall give the LORD's offering" (Ex. 30:14). This came to be known as the "Temple tax." The tax was a half a shekel. It was employed to defray the high cost of maintaining the Temple and conducting its liturgical ceremonies.

The Temple tax was to be paid each year.

1) This tax was equivalent to a day's wage (W. Barclay). This tribute affected all male Jews both in their homeland and in the Diaspora (those living in foreign countries).

2) The Temple tax was generally collected by the Levites, descendants of the tribe of Levi, whose role was to assist the priests in those things pertaining to the Temple and its ceremonies. The imperial taxes were levied by the Roman government and were collected by publicans (Maertens-Frisque). St. Matthew, as we know, was a publican.

3) To pay the Temple tax was considered patriotic; whereas to pay the imperial tax was considered odious, because it was a constant reminder to the Jewish people of their servitude to the Romans.

4) Roman citizens did not pay imperial taxes. The expenses involved in running the Roman government were all incurred by the people who were conquered by the Romans.

II. This incident of the tax collectors questioning Peter about whether or not Jesus paid the Temple tax was most probably another trap to embarrass Jesus, for if He didn't pay the Temple tax He would be considered as failing in His obligation as a Jew, at least for those who didn't know of Jesus' dignity and rights as Messiah, which would naturally exempt Him. Priests, on the other hand, were not forced to pay the Temple tax (*Catholic Commentary on Holy Scripture*). If Jesus refused to pay, which was indeed His right, He would be reported to the Temple authorities.

III. Jesus' question to Peter obviously indicated His exemption from such a tax. "From whom do kings of the world take toll or tribute? From their sons or from others?" When Peter replied, "From others," Jesus observed: "Then the sons are free. However, not to give offense to them, go to the sea and cast a hook, and take the first fish that comes up, and when you open its mouth you will find a shekel" (worth twice the temple tax). Jesus is saying in so many words that His kingship should exempt Him.

1) Was not the Temple His Father's house? Should a son, therefore, have the obligation to pay in his father's house?

2) Jesus is declaring Himself free from the obligation of this tax. He extends this to His Apostles because of their close association with Him.

IV. It is simply to avoid scandal that Jesus pays the tax. To show that He is Lord over all creation, He sends Peter to the sea to fish and says that the first fish Peter catches will contain a coin sufficient to pay for both Him and Peter.

1) Jesus goes beyond the call of duty here in paying the tax. He does this to avoid possible scandal, lest others might think that they too were exempt from their obligation to support the Temple.

2) We too must go beyond the call of duty if another might use our example to shirk his/her obligation of doing what is clearly one's duty.

V. It is true that everything we do has either a good or bad effect on people. There will be times, as in the case of Jesus in today's narrative, that we will have to do or refrain from doing things, not because we have a duty or obligation to do or not do them, but because our doing or not doing them will occasion another to do wrong by not doing the good he/she is obliged to do.

1) Today's Gospel tells us that innocent actions can give bad

signals to others, and we are our brothers' and sisters' keepers. Conversely, exemplary actions, although not called for, can give people the inspiration they need to fulfill their duties and obligations.

2) Volunteering time, for example, to help the elderly in a nursing home should serve as an example for the nursing staff and paid employees to perform their jobs better. Going beyond the call of duty motivates others to better fulfill their own duties.

****

1) That we may be generous in supporting the Church — the House of God.

2) That we may be generous in supporting all charitable organizations that have as their direct object the caring for our indigent brothers and sisters.

3) That we may be conscious of our actions and our example lest they become an occasion of sin for others who are weaker than ourselves.

4) That the Lord give us the light to be good citizens and actively participate in civic activities, especially in the area of voting.

5) For our president, senators, and representatives, that they honestly fulfill their responsibilities as our elected officials.

Tuesday of the Nineteenth Week: Mt. 18:1-5,10,12-14

I. Hebrew tradition held children in high regard. Children were a mark of divine favor. Those marriages that produced no children were considered chastised by God, and consequently were looked down upon by the people. The birth of a child was a cause of great rejoicing, and the firstborn male was to be consecrated to the Lord.

II. What were those characteristics and qualities that Jesus saw in children which made them so pleasing to Him?

1) Children are unsophisticated, openhearted, honest, and forgiving; they do not hold grudges; they are innocent, trusting, sincere, dependent, and humble.

2) They may fantasize, but have no high opinion of themselves. They are filled with unashamed dependence. One reason why we are often reluctant in revealing our need to depend upon another human being is that we do not want to reveal our limitations; this is so unchildlike and is a consequence of pride. A child is not afraid to

reveal his/her dependence upon adults, especially upon his/her parents for just about everything he/she needs.

3) As mature adults, we, too, must recognize our dependence on others and not lose that childlike quality of unabashed trust in other good people and especially in divine providence.

III. It was in response to the personal ambition of the Apostles that Jesus placed a little child in their midst and told them that unless they became as little children they could not enter into the kingdom of heaven.

1) The first and foremost qualities we see in children are their humility and simplicity. Children are not looking for prestige. The people whom they idolize are their parents, and they are completely devoid of any desire to compete with them; on the contrary, they very much want to imitate them. Above all, they want to love and be loved by them.

2) The child's humility is expressed in a complete dependence on his/her parents for everything.

IV. Before God, we are all helpless, dependent children. We are completely dependent on Him for the very air we breathe. Our relationship with God should be like that of a child to a parent. Like children, we, too, must depend upon God openly and unabashedly for all our needs.

1) In the "Our Father," Our Lord teaches us to show this dependence on God, our Father, by begging for forgiveness for our transgressions and by asking for our daily bread.

2) As God's little ones, when we approach our Heavenly Father, let us, before asking any favors of Him, show our dependence on Him by asking Him to forgive any sins we may have committed against Him or against our brothers and sisters before we proceed to ask for any particular favors.

V. Children are pure, and we love them and are attracted to them because of their innocence. It is their innocence which gives them a singular attractiveness and beauty. Innocence makes one's soul transparent and exposes its beauty, a beauty which is sometimes called "the odor of sanctity."

1) That innocence, which when lost tarnishes the window of the soul, is restored through the sanctification and transformation of the

soul through God's grace. The gift of virginity, which is part of that innocence, when lost can never be restored.

2) Repentance is so attractive to Almighty God that it moves Him to restore that beautiful childlike quality of innocence or spiritual integrity. Sincere contrition coupled with generous penances, especially works of charity and the corporal works of mercy, restores wholeness to the soul.

VI. Children are trusting, confident in their relationship with their parents when those parents give them the security of their love. This is how we must be toward our Heavenly Father, who never ceases to shower His love upon us. He wants us to trust in His love, His goodness, and His generosity, confident that what we ask of Him, so long as it is not harmful to us, He will grant to us.

1) St. Thérèse of the Child Jesus scaled the heights of sanctity because she concentrated her efforts in cultivating and bringing to perfection in herself those childlike virtues of simplicity, humility, trust, and total dependence on God. She reasoned that if she could become like a child through the childlike virtues of simplicity and humility, God would deign to cast His eye upon her, snatch her up into His arms, and carry her off to heaven, because He cannot resist childlike souls. God did just this: He carried her off to heaven at the early age of twenty-four.

2) God calls us all to perfection, and indeed, we shall not see the Face of God until we are perfect. Concentrating on the practice of the childlike virtues is an ideal way to perfection.

****

1) That we realize that our relationship with Almighty God must be like that of a child to its parents.

2) That the Lord bestow upon us the gems of the childlike virtues: humility, simplicity, and absolute trust in Him.

3) That God fill us with a sincere repentance to restore wholeness and spiritual integrity to our souls.

4) That we go to God with confidence, trusting that He will hear our prayers, as a loving father is attentive to a devoted child.

5) That parents do everything to instill a strong faith in their children, and teach them to pray from their earliest of years.

6) That parents generate in the hearts of their children a tender devotion to their heavenly Mother.

7) That the plague of abortion cease in the world and especially in our country.

Wednesday of the Nineteenth Week: Mt. 18:15-20

I. In today's Gospel, Jesus urges us to do everything possible to be reconciled and at peace with our brothers and sisters. A breach in personal relationships between ourselves and other members of the community should never be permitted to continue. We must spare no effort to heal that wound. Jesus gives us a blueprint for the procedure we are to follow in patching up our differences.

1) First of all we are to go personally to the individual with whom we have a grievance and privately point out the fault or area of disagreement. If he/she listens, a lot of difficulty will be avoided in the future.

2) If the person doesn't listen, then Jesus instructs us to invite a third party in to referee and help arbitrate the grievance.

3) If this doesn't work, the matter should be referred to the Church, that is, to have a priest sit in and help resolve the difficulty. If this doesn't work, we have done all in our power, humanly speaking, to heal the wound. The rest must be left to God through prayer.

II. We must be careful not to allow too much time to intervene before taking the steps Jesus had outlined to be reconciled with our brother or sister. Brooding over the wrong done or the injury inflicted only intensifies the rift, and it makes reconciliation so much more difficult. The earlier we face the person in question the better. A private talk face to face can break the ice.

III. "All that is necessary for evil to triumph," said Edmund Burke, "is for good men to do nothing." Evil will not heal itself. Positive action must be taken. Positive attempts at reconciliation must be taken. Reconciliation doesn't erase our personal differences; it seeks to bring them into a workable agreement and mutual toleration. Reconciliation is always possible to humble, honest people.

IV. At the close of the Civil War, General Grant was addressing a meeting, urging reconciliation between the North and the South. A listener interrupted him and said that after the bitterness, reconciliation would be impossible. But Grant retorted, "Impossible? Why, if that is all that is wrong with it, then let us go ahead! What are Christians for but to attempt the impossible?" (*Good News Supplement*, April 28, 1985).

V. The Berlin Wall was really a double wall. Between the walls there was a "no-man's land" filled with all kinds of obstacles: spikes, barbed wire, alarms, guard dogs, and lights. There was an abandoned church standing in the middle of the double wall. Ironically, the name of that church was "The Church of Reconciliation." It stood as a powerful symbol of hope, hope for a reconciliation, a symbol of hope for the so-called impossible goal (*Sunday Sermons*, Voicings Publications).

VI. Reconciliation can be painful, for it demands humility, contrition, and courage to correct and be corrected; yet charity demands this of us. Our final judgment will depend upon our willingness to forgive together with the efforts we have made in the process of reconciliation with our brothers and sisters.

1) Talking things out tends to diffuse the hostility from the atmosphere and helps to expel needless anxieties. Nevertheless, it still takes humility and honesty to accept corrections.

2) St. Vincent de Paul once said, "A just man who abandons humility is rejected and reproved by God in spite of all his good works, and furthermore, that which appeared as virtue in him is only vice."

VII. Before approaching one who has wronged us, let us always first pray for prudence and tact. Timing, tact, tone of voice, gestures, and facial expressions, all of these are contributing factors in helping to correct a brother or sister who hurt us.

1) When offering a correction, offer it as you would want it done to you, remembering that all of us at one time or another need correction.

2) How many marriages would have been saved through honest, humble, and sincere dialogue; this does so much to make corrections easier.

VIII. When we have done all that Our Lord has recommended in the process of brotherly reconciliation, our consciences will be at peace.

****

1) That we may not harbor grudges.

2) That we beg God for the humility to seek out reconciliation with a brother or sister, especially members of our own families.

3) That husbands and wives be more open and honest with each other and not hide potential time bombs.

4) That we offer to serve as intermediaries in areas of disputes in an effort to achieve reconciliation.

5) That honesty and openness may reign in peace and disarmament talks.

Thursday of the Nineteenth Week: Mt. 18:21—19:1

I. Our Lord's notion of forgiveness went far beyond the traditional Jewish concept. During her long course of history, Israel repeatedly offended God by her frequent infidelity. After a brief chastisement, Yahweh showed His infinite compassion and forgave her.

II. It is obvious from Peter's question, as to the number of times he would be held to forgive when wronged, that there was a limit in the contemporary Jewish mentality to the number of times one would be required to forgive a brother who wronged him. Peter no doubt thought that he was exaggerating when he suggested that seven times might be a generous limit to one's obligation to forgive another. The Apostles must have been surprised when Jesus replied, "I do not say to you seven times, but seventy times seven."

III. At the root of Jesus' answer was God's nature to forgive, for He is merciful and forgiving. It is not that we are deserving of God's forgiveness; it is that God forgives because He is a forgiving God, and He expects us, who are made in His likeness, to do the same.

1) "If you forgive men their trespasses, your heavenly Father also will forgive you; but if you do not forgive men their trespasses, neither will your Father forgive your trespasses" (Mt. 6:14). Much of God's readiness to forgive us will depend upon our readiness to forgive others.

2) Jesus added a difficult dimension to the Jewish notion of forgiveness. Forgiveness must be extended to the Gentiles, and even more: it must be extended to one's enemies. He gave us the supreme

example of this when He asked His Father to forgive those who crucified and reviled Him.

3) Pope John Paul II's visit to his would-be assassin Mehmet Ali Agca in prison was a sterling example of Christlike forgiveness of enemies.

IV. The parable of the king settling accounts with his officials shows the immense generosity of God when it comes to forgiveness and the selfishness of humans when it devolves upon them to forgive a fellow human.

1) Our offenses against God are infinitely greater than the offenses other human beings have perpetrated against us. If God, who has been so outraged by our sins, is disposed to forgive those who ask Him for forgiveness, how much more should we be disposed to forgive our brothers and sisters who ask our pardon!

2) In the Lord's Prayer, which Jesus taught His Apostles, He bids us to ask God pardon for our transgressions while at the same time urging us to forgive those who have offended us.

V. How does one forgive the "unpardonable sin" or injury? In his book *The Sunflower*, Simon Wiesenthal narrates his harrowing experiences under the Nazis and how he witnessed seeing his mother being crammed into a boxcar and sent off to her death. He saw his mother-in-law shot down before his eyes. He recounted when in a concentration camp he was asked to come to a makeshift hospital and into a room containing a single bed, and lying upon that bed was a man bandaged up from head to foot and dying. The nurse left the room to leave Wiesenthal alone with the figure before him. This was done at the request of that patient. The bandaged body began to speak. The words revealed a young man of 21, a member of the dreaded and hated German SS troops. He said that he had been born and raised a Catholic, but in his teens he had joined Hitler's youth movement and abandoned his Catholic faith in favor of the new state religion whose god was Adolf Hitler.

The young man stated that while in the SS he had served on the eastern front. There he was placed in charge of a unit which was given the assignment of dealing with the Jews in a local village. Several hundred of them had been herded into an old building. The young SS officer ordered that gasoline be poured about the building and machine guns circle the building to finish off anyone who chose to escape the inferno, and so the building was set ablaze.

The incident troubled the conscience of the young officer. A short while later he was seriously wounded and taken to this makeshift hospital. He wanted a Jew be left alone with him for a few minutes in the room that he might ask for pardon. He knew that he was dying and wanted to make his peace with God. He said that he was not a born murderer and didn't want to die one. He begged Wiesenthal's forgiveness. Silence ensued: Wiesenthal got up and left the room. He could not bring himself to forgive him. He asks his readers: "What would you do if you were in my place?"

For Christians, there can only be one answer — forgive, because Christ asks it of us, for this is what God does. Our sins are far more grievous in His eyes than any offense another may commit against us; yet God forgives us.

****

1) That we bear no grudges toward anyone.

2) That we may be especially forgiving to members of our families.

3) That we use the sacrament of penance and reconciliation regularly.

4) That husbands and wives forgive and forget.

5) That nations through their representatives forgive one another, and not be vindictive toward one another.

6) The more difficult it is to forgive, the more meritorious it is; that we remember we imitate God best when we forgive one another from the heart.

Friday of the Nineteenth Week: Mt. 19:3-12

I. Here we see Jesus using His divine authority to abrogate the Mosaic divorce decree. He places marriage back firmly on the stable and permanent bond His Father had designed it to be when He created the first man and woman, Adam and Eve.

1) The whole reason for creating the two sexes, male and female, was to bring a man and a woman together to participate with God in the creation of other human beings and to establish the basic unit of society — the family, which has its likeness in the Blessed Trinity.

2) In the Blessed Trinity, there is but one mind and one love shared by the Three Divine Persons. Marriage, too, should be of one mind and an undivided love in order to be really successful and happy. Although the partners in marriage do not possess the same mind as is the case in the Blessed Trinity, this oneness comes through mutual agreement which must be a product of open and honest communication between the spouses.

II. In today's Gospel narrative, Our Lord Jesus Christ is saying that marriage is a permanent bond, and divorce is out of the question. The reference to writing out a decree of divorce refers back to concessions made by Moses in the government of his people. It was to keep peace in the community. In Jesus' day, there were two schools of thought which interpreted Moses' permission in the granting of a divorce: the Shammai school and the Hillel school.

1) The Shammai school interpreted this Mosaic permission for a decree of divorce only on the grounds of adultery. The Hillel school was far more liberal in its interpretation. It saw the Mosaic dispensation as permitting divorce for the love of another woman or for causes as trivial as inferior cooking (*Jerome Biblical Commentary*).

2) The Hillel opinion merely catered to human frailty or to the duplicity of one who was merely seeking a divorce to satisfy selfish passion. Jesus abrogated these loopholes in the Mosaic Law, and reverts back to the very beginning when God joined Adam and Eve in a permanent bond. Jesus interprets the concessions made by Moses to divorce as being due to the hardness of heart of the people; it was a deviation from the original plan of God in instituting marriage. He further solidified the marriage bond by raising it to the status of a sacrament, giving it the power to generate actual graces necessary to live married life happily.

III. The "hardness of heart" Jesus talked about refers to pure selfishness, the elemental force that destroys so many marriages. In a partnership of equals, the giving must be mutual and unselfish. Ideally, one should strive to outdo the other in generosity.

1) When St. Paul spoke about marriage, he likened it to the union between Christ and His Church, a union based on mutual sacrifice. Christ loved His spouse the Church — that is, you and me — so

much that He gave Himself up even to death that spouses might have life and have it in abundance (cf. Eph. 5:25-26).

2) The love of the spouses in marriage must be the outcome of a mutual esteem and admiration that is ultimately based on the dignity of the person. This mutual esteem will inspire a gentleness, a sympathy, and a mutual faith.

3) "No true and enduring love," wrote the philosopher Johann Fichte, "can exist without esteem: every other type draws regret after it and is unworthy of any noble human soul." Fichte could indeed be cited for such a love in his own marriage. His fiancee was an heiress in a wealthy home. Johann Fichte was a poor German student of philosophy. He determined that he would not marry her until he was able to earn enough to run a home. After a long struggle, he earned enough to ask for her hand in marriage. In one of his letters he wrote, "And so, dearest, I solemnly devote myself to you and thank you for not thinking me unworthy to be your companion on the journey of life. . . . There is no land of happiness here below — I know it now — but a land of toil, where every joy but strengthens us for greater labor. Hand in hand we traverse it, and encourage and strengthen each other, until our spirits shall rise to the eternal fountain of all peace" (*You Can Find a Way*).

IV. As in all partnerships, success in marriage depends so much on cooperation and honest, open communication. While we are human, we all have our failings. One need not be blind to the other's failings, yet it is often the imperfections of human nature rather than its perfection, that makes the strongest claims on the forbearance and sympathy of others and hence tends to produce the closest of unions.

****

1) For all young people contemplating marriage, that they realize that real love entails sacrifice and endurance.

2) That husbands and wives manifest this sacrificial love toward each other as an example and inspiration to their children.

3) That through the intercession of the Blessed Virgin Mary those couples experiencing difficulties might resolve those problems and save their marriages.

4) That husbands and wives have open and honest communication with each other in their marriages.

5) That spouses may be generous with time spent with each other.

6) That husbands and wives pray together.

Saturday of the Nineteenth Week: Mt. 19:13-15

I. In yesterday's Gospel Jesus condemned divorce, and one of the reasons for doing so was to raise the dignity of women and place them on an equal-partner basis in marriage. At that time, a woman had few or no rights in marriage. A man could divorce his wife almost at whim. Conversely, a woman could not divorce her husband at her initiation. Jesus placed marriage right back at its beginning when the Lord created man and woman equal, establishing marriage as a permanent covenant between equals modeled on the Blessed Trinity. The third reality in the divine plan for marriage is the children.

II. In today's Gospel, Jesus rebukes His disciples and affirms the dignity of children as fellow human beings with rights, entitled to His attention and care.

1) The disciples, representing the outlook of their day, scolded the children for bothering Jesus. Jesus immediately reprimanded His disciples and said, "Let the children come to me, and do not hinder them; for to such belongs the kingdom of heaven."

2) Children, as well as adults, have immortal souls equally precious in God's eyes.

3) The United Nations printed a document called "The United Nations Declaration of the Rights of the Child." It lists ten rights. The very first one is: "The right to affection, love, and understanding" (*Pulpit Resource*). This was the right that Jesus was referring to when He chastised His disciples.

III. Children, by their very existence, preach the godlike virtues of simplicity and innocence; for this reason they are so attractive in God's eyes.

1) The attractiveness of their guileless simplicity overwhelms the hardest of hearts. Their countenance bears the message of openness, unsophisticatedness, candor, and guilelessness.

2) St. Vincent de Paul said that the wise of this world hold simplicity in contempt; yet it is an amiable virtue because it leads us with singlemindedness to the kingdom of God.

3) We are all attracted to guileless people. St. Francis of Assisi

was attracted to Friar John because of his genuine simplicity. The simplicity that pleased St. Francis was that which considers everything else as of little value save that of pleasing God in all we do. This is the simplicity that glories in the fear of God. In "The Praise of Virtues," St. Francis wrote: "Hail, Queen Wisdom! The Lord save you, with your sister, pure, holy simplicity" (Celano, *St. Francis of Assisi*).

IV. Simplicity makes us speak with candor from the heart, like children, pushing us to act with a sincerity that is devoid of all pretense and double meanings. It knows nothing of double-dealing. Simplicity's "yes" means yes with no built-in "noes."

V. The object of simplicity is to please God as the first object of its intention and center of its love.

1) Simplicity spurns human respect and peer pressure, both of which choose to do or not to do things in order to please certain people, even if it means offending God in the process.

2) St. Vincent de Paul had a special admiration for this virtue. He once said that it would be better to be bound hand and foot and be thrown into a fire than to do things to please men rather than God.

3) St. Francis de Sales said, "God loves simple souls and willingly deals with them. He imparts the understanding of His truths to them because He can do with them as He pleases. Not so does He act with sophisticated, shrewd souls."

4) Children believe what they are told, especially by those who love them. So, too, does simplicity move the human heart to accept more readily the truths of faith.

5) Simplicity frees us from ulterior motives of self-interest; it places God ahead of self. In this sense it imparts freedom, the freedom of the sons and daughters of God.

****

1) That we frequently examine our motives before doing things to see if it is for pleasing God or ourselves that we undertake to do them.

2) That the Lord give us an appreciation of the virtue of simplicity, and that we asked Him for this wonderful gift.

3) That we may be open and honest in our dealings with others.

4) That our nation value its young and put an end to abortion.

5) That through the intercession of the Blessed Virgin Mary the powerful influence and attraction to drug-taking among young people may be broken.

6) For all children who have been victims of adult abuse, that they may have a successful and permanent rehabilitation.

7) That we, especially in the presence of children, strive to give good example.

Monday of the Twentieth Week: Mt. 19:16-22

I. St. John Chrysostom said, "If you remain attached to the world when heavenly things are offered to you, consider how great the insult is to the One who is offering them." When all is said and done, the tragedy of the rich young man was that he loved things more than his fellowmen, and if this is so, we may conclude that he loved himself more than his brothers and sisters in the world. The opportunity to serve them with total dedication was offered him because he kept the commandments. He did what was required of him, no more, no less. Perfection demands heroic sacrifices. It was offered to him, but he did not rise to the occasion to meet that divine challenge.

II. Christ gave the rich young man a vocation to the inner circle of the disciples. We can only imagine what would have become of his life had he accepted. No doubt his name would have been written on the pages of the New Testament, and history would be honoring him among the disciples who went out to evangelize a certain sector of the world, one whom people would be honoring today as a saint, whose feast day would be repeated each year with veneration.

1) That opportunity was offered once and was never to be repeated. How many young men and women receive the call to follow Christ as a priest or religious, to give themselves in full dedication to God's people, and, like the young man of today's Gospel, find the challenge too much, for their hearts are attached to things, other careers, wealth, or the intimate circle of certain people, be it family or friends.

2) St. Francis de Sales noted that a bird cannot fly if it is tied by a cord, a string, or even by a thin thread. The challenge to perfection means to free yourself of all attachments that prevent you from flying to union with God. Perfection will always demand a

detachment that is the spirit of poverty — the poverty in spirit spoken of in the beatitudes.

3) The Danish theologian Søren Kierkegaard wrote about a wealthy woman who felt that God was calling her to the religious life. She felt that she would be able to give up everything in order to do this — everything, that is, with one exception. She had a garden which was very important to her. It was a place for her to be alone, to be at peace, and to renew herself. Yet she was unable to give up this key to her secret garden (Colaianni, *The Giant Book of Sunday Sermons*). We all have keys to possessions which tie us down when God calls us to closer union with Him; these are stumbling blocks on our road to perfection and union with God. God's grace is constantly challenging us; yet our attachments are our obstacles to His grace.

4) When wealth and possessions shackle us to the point that we spend more time in striving to preserve and increase them than we do in using them to serve God and our brothers and sisters in the world, then we have became enslaved to things, and will not acquire the true freedom of true sons and daughters of God, which is the reward of poverty in spirit. Poverty in spirit is a beatitude, and its fruit and reward are peace and wisdom.

III. Jesus challenged the rich young man to perfect detachment from things and utter dependence on God. This was for him the road to perfection that Jesus offered him. The challenge was too much. The young man chose the lesser instead of the greater gifts, an inferior to a superior life. Jesus offered him a unique vocation, that of being a disciple, but the price was perfect detachment from his material possessions. He could not bring himself to rise to the challenge.

1) The young man went away sad. He was not free; he was shackled to his possessions. Detachment gives freedom and happiness. This wealth he would not know, nor possess, because he was so tied down to material possessions.

2) We all have our attachments that impede or shackle us, be they money, friends, hobbies, or work projects. If we are not disposed to use these things in the service of God or fellow humans, we are not growing in our relationship with God.

3) May God give us a proper sense of values. In the last analysis, it can be said that what we will possess in eternity is what we give

away here on earth to those in need, because in so doing we are giving to God, who will not be outdone in generosity.

****

1) That we may be generous toward those in need.

2) That we may never become enslaved to things, wealth, prestige, or people.

3) Whether a bird be held by a cord, a string, or a thread, it is still shackled and cannot fly; that God free us from those things that impede us from flying up to Him.

4) That God give us the gift of wisdom so that we might see things in their proper perspective.

5) That we may be satisfied with the simple and basic things in life and be delivered from all forms of jealousy and envy.

Tuesday of the Twentieth Week: Mt. 19:23-30

I. It was a popular belief among the Jewish people that God rewarded just people in this life with material wealth. Conversely it was thought that poverty was a chastisement for one's sins. Job is criticized by his friends and is said to have lost his great wealth due to his personal hidden sins (cf. Job 22:4-11).

1) Jesus challenges this prevalent notion by saying that it is easier for a camel to pass through a needle's eye than for a rich man to enter into the kingdom of God.

2) Jerusalem was a walled city, as many cities were in those days. It had several entrances which were called gates, and each gate was given a name. Among these gates was the "needle's eye" gate. It was designed to prevent large animals, like camels, from passing through. There was only room enough for a single person to pass through at a time.

3) Some commentators believe that Jesus was referring to this "needle's eye" gate in Jerusalem, which was used by people to enter and leave the city at night when the larger gates were closed. The symbolism, however, is clear: the impossibility of a camel's ever passing through the needle's eye is directed at wealth's making it impossible for a human being to attain to the heavenly Jerusalem.

4) Jesus is saying that riches are dangerous and can easily occasion the loss of one's immortal soul. There are some fifteen

passages in the Gospels where Jesus warns us that wealth and material possessions can destroy us.

II. Our relationship to God is one of a child to a father; it is one of complete dependence. Riches tend to "independicize" from God, that is, free us from our dependence on God.

1) Since money can buy so much of this world's goods, a wealthy person doesn't feel the need to approach God in prayer for such necessities as employment, education for one's children, a home, an automobile, or sufficient money to support one's family.

2) Wealth "frees" one from such dependence which normally would cause a person to have recourse to God in prayer. Consequently wealth can readily fill one with self-sufficiency and pride. Pride is the source of much evil and leaves one wide open to be manipulated by the devil.

III. Wealth enslaves more than it frees people. It engenders a false sense of security and consequently blinds the one who possesses it. Instead of satisfying people, it makes them greedier.

1) When asked by a reporter when he thought that he had enough money, John D. Rockefeller replied when you feel you just want a little bit more.

2) Wealth shackles people to it. They spend so much time in seeking ways to secure it and increase it. Losing it or even part of it becomes a preoccupation and worry. Howard Hughes is a typical example of what wealth can and does do to many. Trying to conserve it, he died miserable and of malnutrition.

3) Roger Bacon put it well when he said, "Money is like fertilizer; it is used best when it is spread around." Benjamin Franklin said that money is a good servant but a dangerous master.

4) An English newspaper held a contest for schoolchildren wherein the children were asked to write a definition of the word "money." The young girl who won wrote, "Money is something that will buy you anything but happiness; it will pay your fare to any place except heaven."

IV. Wealth tends to blind us and cause us to have misguided priorities. Because of wealth our priorities tend to become placed more on the things of this world than on those of eternity.

1) We should always ask ourselves, "Do my possessions control me, or do I control them?" Our possessions must be our servants and

not our masters. For all too many they prove to be their masters. This was evident in the stock market crash on Wall Street in 1929. Many people committed suicide because they lost what proved to be most important to them — their material possessions.

2) When Dr. Karl Menninger, the famous American psychiatrist, was asked what advice he would give to a person who felt a nervous breakdown coming on, he replied by saying, "I would tell them, 'Lock up your house, go across the railway tracks, find someone in need, and invest yourself in helping that person' " (Pulpit Resource). In other words, forget yourself and your possessions, and concentrate on what God sent you into the world to do — to help your brothers and sisters who are struggling. In this way you will find the wealth of wisdom and peace.

3) Let us remember that we leave all our possession behind us when we die. The only possessions we take with us are what we have given away to others in this life.

****

1) That the Lord bless us with the gift of poverty of spirit.

2) That we may always be generous and compassionate to those in need.

3) Almsgiving is a salutary penance which makes up for the temporal punishment due to our sins; may the Lord make us aware of its value in our spiritual lives.

4) For all those who are searching for gainful employment.

5) For all who are suffering from hunger.

6) For an end to abortion in our country and in the world.

7) That we be sensitive and compassionate to our brothers and sisters in need, knowing that our best lasting investment is our charity toward the poor.

Wednesday of the Twentieth Week: Mt. 20:1-16

I. Heaven is the ultimate reward of all the elect who die in the grace of God. It is the reward of the person who never lost his/her baptismal innocence as well as it is the reward for the hardened sinner who repents on his/her deathbed.

II. The parable in today's Gospel brings out the generosity and mercy of God, who is good to both the just and the unjust. It does not fault the justice of God, but it does show that in Him justice and mercy embrace and kiss.

1) The Lord is just and will mete out rewards according to individual merit; nevertheless, He is merciful and generous and wills the salvation of all men and women at whatever point in time they may turn to Him for forgiveness.

2) Our Lord Jesus Christ did say, "In My Father's house there are many rooms; if it were not so, would I have told you that I go to prepare a place for you?" (Jn. 14:2). In heaven the elect will differ like star from star in glory depending on the reward or amount of glory God deigns in His justice to bestow on His elect.

III. The basic complaint of the laborers against the owner of the vineyard (God) is his lack of justice. This had also been the complaint of the elder brother in the parable of the Prodigal Son. (Lk. 15:29-30). Jonah, too, complained when God forgave rather than punished the Ninevites (Maertens-Frisque).

1) The complaint seems just — that is, to human eyes. Yet the perfection of justice, justice come full turn, is mercy, and justice and mercy in God embrace and kiss. Jesus is affirming the unbounded goodness, mercy, and love of Almighty God.

2) The owner of the vineyard is just, after a human fashion, with the group of workers whom he hired first and with whom he reached an agreement to work for a stipulated wage.

3) The apparent "injustice" comes into play with those workers who were hired merely with the promise of being paid with, as the owner said, "whatever is right." Finally what appears to be an abuse of justice arises from the case of those men who were hired last, and who worked but one hour in contrast to those who had borne the heat of the sun during the long workday.

4) Jesus is emphasizing the mercy of God, which transcends the narrow limits of human justice in human relations and bilateral contracts and agreements (Maertens-Frisque).

IV. The parable may well also refer to the Jews who were the first called to God's kingdom (vineyard) in the early hours of the day. It shows God's mercy in extending an invitation into the vineyard to the Gentiles, those invited to work in the vineyard at the noon, afternoon, and evening hours of the day.

1) Jesus sums up the parable by saying, "So the last shall be first,

and the first last." The masses of the Gentiles will flock into the kingdom ahead of the Jews who were called first.

2) "Many are called, but few are chosen" (Mt. 22:14). The whole Jewish race has been called to the Kingdom, but the Jewish people did not respond en masse. Only those have deserved to be chosen to belong to it — the "remnant" spoken of by Isaiah when he said, "If the LORD of hosts had not left us a few survivors, we should have been like Sodom, and become like Gomorrah" (Is. 1:9) (*Catholic Commentary on Holy Scripture*).

V. A practical lesson to be drawn from today's Gospel is that God will not reward us strictly according to the works we have performed or accomplished. He looks rather to the motives behind them and the quality of our works as expressions of our love for Him and our neighbor. In the final analysis, salvation will be meted out to us by divine justice through the gift of faith rather than mere works. Our works, then, must be so many expressions of our faith. This is quality over quantity. Thus the person who does a little work with a pure love of pleasing God will gain more merit than a great deal of work done begrudgingly or out of a sense of obligation. St. Thérèse of the Child Jesus capitalized on this: doing ordinary and little things out of pure love of God. She thus scaled the heights of sanctity in a short time.

1) As for the workers in the vineyard, their reward was not for the quantity of the work turned in; it was a reward for their willingness to go to work in the vineyard. This willingness was an expression of their faith — belief in a reward based on the goodness and the mercy of God.

2) It is a warning against idleness. The master asked the last group, "Why do you stand here idle all day?" Our faith cannot be idle or static; it must produce works, works of charity. Idleness is the devil's workshop; it make us targets for the devil and temptation. Faith will always move us to do works in the vineyard of the Lord. If we don't produce, the depth of our faith is very much in question. On this point we should frequently examine our conscience.

****

1) That we frequently express our gratitude to Almighty God for making us His sons and daughters and heirs to His kingdom.

2) That we strive to know what our talents are and bring them to maturity in order to better serve God and our brothers and sisters.

3) That we use our leisure time well both in wholesome recreation and in corporal works of mercy.

4) That we always find laziness what it really is — abhorrent.

5) For all those searching for the type of work that best suits them, that providence may lead them to it.

6) That we strive to offer up all our work to God as a continuation of our prayer, as worship and praise of Him and also as an expression of our love for Him.

7) That working men and women take pride in their work and perform it well, doing it with the motive of pleasing God and serving their brothers and sisters.

8) That labor and management treat each other respectfully and honestly.

Thursday of the Twentieth Week: Mt. 22:1-14

I. Jesus refers to the kingdom or reign of God many times in the Gospels. In today's narrative, he compares it to a wedding feast. The feast was prepared for special guests (the Jews as God's chosen people). These, by and large, refuse as a group to come to the banquet. The outraged king then extends the invitation to all who can be found on the byroads; this symbolizes the Gentiles.

II. The kingdom described in today's narrative involves the kingdom on earth — the Church — and the kingdom of heaven. All indeed are invited to be members of both kingdoms. The kingdom on earth, the Church, is an imperfect one, since it is composed of the baptized who are both good and evil. Its members are either in God's grace or out of it. The wedding garments symbolize the members who possess sanctifying grace. To pass on to the eschatological banquet or the kingdom of heaven, however, one must have the proper wedding banquet attire on, namely, sanctifying grace. There is simply no possibility of participating in that banquet without being in God's grace at the moment of death. Living members of the Church still have time to ready themselves by returning to sanctifying grace through repentance and the sacraments.

III. In this parable we see a parallel with the parable likening the kingdom to a field of wheat in which someone had sown weeds, yet

269

the owner of the field would not allow his workers to pull out the weeds; rather he bade them to wait patiently until harvest time. Then there would be a definitive separation of the wheat from the weeds (Mt. 13:24-30).

1) In both of these parables, it is clear that the Lord wills the salvation of all men and women. To this end, He gives everyone every opportunity possible to achieve it. If they fail to enter into the kingdom of heaven, they will have no one to blame but themselves.

2) The universality of the call to the kingdom of God is also evident from the parable of the dragnet cast into the sea which gathers in every kind of fish (Mt. 13:47-50). The parable of the "Lost Sheep" clearly manifests how God will go out of His way to bring everybody safely into His kingdom.

IV. In spite of the universality of the invitation to the eternal banquet of heaven, today's Gospel brings out the clear lesson of misguided priorities and spiritual blindness. We must set our sights on the kingdom of heaven and do it as a top priority in our lives. Our Lord clearly tells us that if we seek first the kingdom of heaven all secondary good and necessary material things will be added for us (Lk. 12:27-31).

1) It is possible that the excuses offered for not attending the wedding banquet were plausible ones; perhaps the one man had a serious matter to attend to on his farm, and the other man had a weighty business matter to resolve. Nevertheless, first things must come first. The things of time can never displace those of eternity.

2) Grace-filled opportunities may seldom be repeated. Secondary things should never crowd out primary ones. Such shortsightedness will make one miss golden opportunities. The Lord will not throw His graces to the wind. If they do not find a responsive heart, they will cease to come one's way. Such divine and delicate invitations may not return if one has no room in his/her heart to graciously receive them.

3) We must learn to seize the moment. Opportunities to grow spiritually must be taken advantage of. We simply cannot take for granted that such opportunities will keep knocking on our door.

V. Today's parable has a clear built-in warning not to be presumptuous. This is indicated by the man who dared to enter the banquet hall without the proper attire. Judgment was quick and executed with dispatch.

1) God is merciful, generous, and patient, but when His invitation is abused or rejected, there comes a day of reckoning. The kingdom of God on earth is His Church, and in it there are "dead members" walking around in grave sin, and in their blindness they feel that in the end all will be well, that they will make heaven after all. This is presumption and sheer folly.

2) Hell is paved with good intentions, intentions which were never fulfilled. Many, alas, are overcome by death who are not clothed in their "wedding garments." The Lord cautions us to be vigilant (Lk. 12:42-48).

****

1) That we frequently express our gratitude for the gift of faith.

2) That through prayer we may become familiar with and responsive to the inspirations of the Holy Spirit, who continually works within us, urging us on to perfection through the practice of the virtue of charity.

3) That we become more conscious of and sympathetic to those in need and respond by offering our help in the form of time, presence, or resources.

4) That we frequently fix our eyes on our heavenly destiny and thank God for sending Our Lord Jesus Christ into this world to make it possible for us one day to enter into the banquet hall of heaven.

5) That we cultivate and sharpen our devotion to the Blessed Virgin Mary and ask her to help us grow in our relationship with her Son.

6) For all those who have lost their faith.

7) That the Lord deliver us from all presumption and touch the hearts of hardened sinners perhaps members of our own families or possibly some of our friends.

Friday of the Twentieth Week: Mt. 22:34-40

I. In responding to the lawyer's question as to which was the greatest commandment of the law, Jesus first cited Deuteronomy 6:5, which states, "You shall love the LORD your God with all your heart, and with all your soul, and with all your might." He cited this as the first and the greatest of the commandments. Jesus then cited the book of Leviticus, ch. 19:18, which states, "You shall not take vengeance, or bear any grudge against the sons of your own people. You shall love your neighbor as yourself. I am the LORD."

II. Jesus' response then contains the two commandments of the law of love: the love of God directly as number one, and the second, which flows as a consequence of this, is the love of one's neighbor as oneself.

1) The whole of religion, the whole of our relationships with God and with our brothers and sisters is summed up in these two fundamental commandments which are so intimately tied up with each other. So St. John could rightly conclude, "If any one says, 'I love God,' and hates his brother, he is a liar" (1 Jn. 4:20). The beloved disciple used to repeat frequently to his disciples the need to love one another. He repeated this so often that his own disciples became annoyed and asked why he kept pounding this lesson home to them. He replied that by loving one another they fulfilled the whole law.

2) They are so intimately tied up with each other that they can be considered as one, for whatever we do to each other we do to God, as Our Lord Himself said, "As you did it to one of these my brethren, you did it to me" (Mt. 25:40).

3) These two commandments state in so many words that we are all members of God's family, and when one of the members is hurt, God, the Father of us all, feels it. St. Augustine said it so well when he said, "How can you love and kiss the Head and trample on the members?"

III. God's weakness is our love for Him. How marvelous God responds to our love for Him. It is, after all, the reason why He created us: that we might love Him and share in His love and experience His great love for us. The greatest testimony of the Father's love for us is as St. John stated: "God so loved the world that He sent His only Son into the world" (Jn. 3:16).

1) St. Teresa of Ávila wrote, "Lord, if I could hide myself from You as You hide from me, You couldn't bear it." To St. Margaret Mary, Jesus complained: "Behold the Heart that loves men so much and is so little loved in return." God craves our love.

2) St. Francis of Assisi once said, "Love is not loved enough."

So precious in God's eyes is our love for Him that it makes recompense for our sins. The Church has always recognized the priority of the contemplative vocation over the active life because of its concentration on a more perfect love of God. Yet we can safely say that our love for our brothers and sisters is a thermometer of our love for God. The more love we give away, the more enriched and the more intense becomes our love of God.

3) Love of neighbor must be understood not as a parallel to our love of God, but rather as a consequence and fruit of our love of God. St. John of the Cross, the great Spanish mystic and doctor of the Church, said, "There is no better or more necessary work than love. We were created for love, and God is nothing but love. . . . In the eventide of life we shall be judged by our love" (Peers, *The Complete Works of St. John of the Cross*).

IV. The love of God literally transforms us. Bishop Diadochus of Photice in his book *On Spiritual Perfection* wrote: "Anyone who loves God in the depth of his heart has already been loved by God. In fact, the measure of a man's love for God depends upon how deeply aware he is of God's love for him. When this awareness is keen it makes whoever possesses it long to be enlightened by the divine light, and this longing is so intense that it seems to penetrate his very bones. He loses all consciousness of himself and is entirely transformed by the love of God. Such a man lives in this life and at the same time does not live in it, for although he still inhabits his body, he is constantly leaving it in spirit because of the love of God that draws him toward God. Once the love of God had released him from self-love, the flame of divine love never ceases to burn in his heart and he remains united to God by an irresistible longing" (Matins, Friday's second reading of Second Week in Ordinary Time).

V. In the end we will be judged by love; not so much on what we did, as on how much love we put into to what we did.

****

1) That we truly strive to love God with all our minds, all our hearts, and all our souls.

2) That we lift up our hearts frequently by ejaculatory prayer to briefly express our love and gratitude to Almighty God.

3) That we strive to express our love for God in our treatment of our brothers and sisters with whom we live and work and recreate.

4) That we remember that we are all members of God's family, and that Christ is most apt to reveal Himself through our brothers and sisters.

5) That we make a conscious effort to improve the quality of our work and offer up all our work to Almighty God as our expression of love for Him.

6) For peace in the world and an end to terrorism and violence, especially among our Christian people.

Saturday of the Twentieth Week: Mt. 23:1-12

I. Jesus detested hypocrisy more than any other vice He ever encountered in people. Hypocrites are people who do not practice what they preach, and in many cases they don't even believe what they preach. A hypocrite is a person who pretends to be better than he/she really is and even better than those around him/her. In the end, hypocrites generally give themselves away by trying too hard to convince others of their virtue, their talent, and their wisdom. They usually wind up fooling no one but themselves.

II. The whole of religion for the Pharisees consisted in outward observances of religion and its ceremonials. They dressed and acted in such a manner as to draw attention to themselves. Jesus criticized them for their vain display.

1) Phylacteries were little leather boxes worn on the wrist and on the forehead which contained the written texts from the book of Exodus and Deuteronomy which served as reminders to keep the Law. Many of the Pharisees used larger phylacteries to appear more religious.

2) Tassels were worn by the Pharisees on the corner of their garments as a reminder to keep God's commandments. This was mandated by the book of Deuteronomy in chapter 22:12: "You shall make yourself tassels on the four corners of your cloak with which you cover yourself." As usual, the Pharisees overdid this too. They made the tassels extra large to make people believe they were extra conscious of God's commandments. Jesus saved His most scathing "woes" for them because of their hypocrisy, making religion a

manifestation of external observances and trappings while their hearts were bent on evil.

III. The Pharisees literally wore their religion on their sleeves. Jesus didn't condemn the use of phylacteries or tassels as such; what He condemned was the ostentatious piety of these men who strove to draw the attention and admiration of the people by their sanctimonious actions. They were not being true to themselves, and were at the same time lying to the public by confessing a life they were in fact not leading.

1) Just as Jesus did not condemn the use of tassels and phylacteries, He did not actually forbid the use of the title "rabbi." What He condemned was teachers' use of that title to further their own selfish ends or to gain and enjoy the prestige of the office of rabbi while not living up to its high moral standards.

2) All authority ultimately comes from God; consequently, human titles like father, rabbi, teacher, etc., have their honor and authority from God, and as such should be directed back to Him, and not arrogated to oneself to bask in such honor independent of God, from whom it comes. What Jesus was attacking was the pride of the Pharisees in arrogating to themselves and reveling in the honor and prestige that comes from the use of such titles to blow up their own egos. Instead of using the offices these titles represent, especially religious ones, to bring people closer to God, they employed them to bring people to venerate and serve them. Thus they usurped what rightly belongs to God under the guise of those titles.

IV. Jesus also criticizes the scribes and Pharisees for the excessive burdens they imposed upon the people. Instead of making religion attractive to these people, they made it distasteful, with the result that they drove people away from God.

1) When religion becomes an intolerable burden, something is wrong. God never meant it to be so. He wants it to be attractive, yet demanding, a body of convincing truths that motivate one to acts of virtue, especially charity, and not a superficial external manifestation of sanctimonious piety through the wearing of religious symbols.

2) Our Lord Jesus Christ summed the whole of religion in the one principle and commandment of love: genuine love of God and love of neighbor. This love does make demands on us, but certainly

they are healthy demands that bring happiness and peace, not intolerable burdens.

3) When one feels that the practice of his/her faith causes depression or sadness, something is being misinterpreted. For such a person, counsel should be sought out. True religion must be positive, not negative; it should generate peace, not turmoil. When our faith doesn't bring us happiness, we must stop to ask ourselves why, seeking out guidance from a wise spiritual director.

4) True religion really is, and always must be, the "sweet yoke and light burden" our Savior preached.

****

1) That we not do things out of the motive of being seen by others for the purpose of gaining their esteem or praise.

2) That we not try to falsely impress others.

3) That we may be simple and yet sincere in our religious practices.

4) That we strive to help those who are overburdened.

5) That we consciously try to cheer up other people and strive to create an atmosphere of cheerfulness by doing our work cheerfully and enthusiastically.

6) For those searching for peace, that they may find it through prayer and reflection on the word of God.

7) For all of those who have been alienated from the practice of their faith by the harshness or imprudence of priests, rabbis, and ministers.

8) That we make an effort to take the last place, and to sacrifice ourselves to serve those who are even distasteful and repugnant to us.